ARCO

"or anyone seeking a place in the sports world, David Fischer's
he 50 Coolest Jobs in Sports should be required reading."

Sy Berger, VP, The Topps Company

he 50

Coolest
Jobs in
Sports

**What They Are, Who's Got Them,
and How You Can Get One Too!**

the

50

cooLest jOBs in sPortS

who's got them,
what they do,
and how you can get one!

the

50

cooLest
jOBs in
sPortS

who's got them,
what they do,
and how you can get one!

daviD fIscHeR

MACMILLAN ·USA

Macmillan Reference USA
A Simon & Schuster Macmillan Company
1633 Broadway
New York, NY 10019

An ARCO Book

ARCO is a registered trademark of Simon & Schuster, Inc.
MACMILLAN is a registered trademark of Macmillan, Inc.

Library of Congress Cataloging in Publication Data: 97-071477

ISBN: 0-02-861872-6

Manufactured in the United States of America
99 98 97 10 9 8 7 6 5 4 3 2 1

TABLE OF CONTENTS

Preface

Introduction

And Now...A Few Words From
Our Author

CHAPTER 1: Careers Related to
the Playing Field

Manager/Coach	3
Video Coordinator	10
Sports Agent	14
Players Association	22
Personal Business Manager	28
Basketball Referee	33
Football Official	36
Baseball Umpire	40
Hockey Official	45
Sports Turf Specialist	47

CHAPTER 2: Careers in Team Adminstration

Team President	54
General Manager	58
Director of Community Relations	67
Ticket Operations Manager	72
Equipment Manager	78
Traveling Secretary	83

CHAPTER 3: Careers in Stadium Operations

Executive Director	90
Stadium Manager	98
Events Coordinator	104
Scoreboard Operator	108
Game Production Manager	112
Public Address Announcer	115

CHAPTER 4: Careers in Sports Marketing and Public Relations

Director of Promotions	120
Director of Public Relations	128
College Sports Information Director	130
Sports Publicist	135
Director of Corporate Sports Marketing	142
Sports Marketing Manager	152
Special Events Manager	156
Marketing Director of Licensed Merchandise	161

CHAPTER 5: Careers in the League Office

Commissioner 173
Director of Operations 178
Director of Communications 182
Properties 187
Design Director 193
Director of Publications 201

CHAPTER 6: Careers in the Sports Media

Sports Announcer 208
Sports News Broadcaster 217
Television Director 223
Television Production Assistant 227
Radio Talk Show Host 231
Radio Producer—Talk Show 237
Sportswriter 243
Photographer 251
Picture Editor 258

CHAPTER 7: Careers in Sports Medicine

Athletic Trainer 270
Nutritionist 275
Strength and Conditioning Coach 281
Sports Psychologist 285
Sports Performance Management 293
Specialist

P<small>re</small>F<small>ACE</small>

On the surface, *The 50 Coolest Jobs in Sports* is about jobs; some 200 positions that comprise possible career paths in the world of sports. But read between the lines, and you'll meet over 100 people currently working in the sports industry. These are eclectic individuals with interests in areas as diverse as marketing and public relations, team administration, stadium operations, the media, and sports medicine, to name a few.

All the people we spoke with exposed a fundamental truth: You first need to become a professional in your chosen field and then translate those skills to the sports world. A deep, abiding love for sports is not a qualification to get an interview; the sports industry is much too competitive for that. If you wish to enter the area of sports marketing, for instance, you'd better prove yourself capable of marketing toothpaste or cereal before approaching a sports team.

Bearing this in mind, *The 50 Coolest Jobs in Sports* was written to be much more than an occupational reference guide. To be sure, the book's primary function is to explain job duties, educational requirements, employment opportunities, prospects for career advancement, skills and personality traits, as well as a broad range of earnings possibilities. However, the book is also designed to impart practical experience, real-life advice, and biographical background of individuals who have succeeded in the sports industry. In short, who are these people who have the jobs you so covet?

As you read this book, notice several common threads. Everyone quoted is unanimous in their belief that an internship is most imperative to achieving future goals. An unpaid internship prepares an individual for life in the business world and provides a reference point as to the skills one needs to acquire in order to be successful.

It's also the key to creating a network of contacts that will serve as a home-made employment agency for the rest of your professional life. Later, when seeking a full-time position, an internship will demonstrate to a prospective employer your commitment and dedication to obtaining a job in the sports industry. In addition, an unpaid internship is preparation for the meager wages you'll probably earn in an entry-level position.

Another signature characteristic of the sports industry is money—or lack of it. Since so many people are eager to work in sports, starting salaries generally are low. The experts we spoke with urge aspiring candidates not to be concerned with money until a career is well established. Take heart: it's not where you start, it's where you finish. Individuals in top-level jobs are well paid. Similarly, don't bother worrying about job titles. A person determines the scope of a job; not vice versa. And don't be alarmed if an Ivy League education is being squandered while you answer telephones and perform menial word processing tasks. Think about it: If a supervisor can't trust a new hire to make copies, the odds of earning a promotion are nil. Rather, perform entry-level duties with a smile and set your sights on the subsequent job, and the one after that.

The professionals who participated in this book all claim to be lucky. Indeed, serendipity can play a leading role in a successful career. More to the point, however, these humble individuals were able to seize the day because opportunity knocked when they were in a position to take full advantage. Our panel of experts advise job applicants to map a creative job-search strategy, be persistent, and remain patient. As Brooklyn Dodger general manager Branch Rickey once said, "Luck is the residue of design."

introDuctioN

The sports industry is one of the most exciting and fastest growing industries in the nation. It's also one of the most difficult businesses to break into. You rarely, if ever, find a job listed in the newspaper's classified advertising section. The number of opportunities in sports is limited, even to those who are well connected. But during this decade, the job scenario is undergoing a transformation. Back in 1987, the "gross national sports product" was calculated at $50.2 billion. Based on that figure, sports were larger than the auto industry and were responsible for slightly over one percent of the total U.S. gross national product.

Today, sports is the 22nd largest industry in the United States. The sports GNP is estimated at well over $80 billion and growing at an unprecedented rate in the business community. And explosive growth means opportunity for you. The sports field now generates some 4.5 million jobs. Employment prospects will continue to increase for two major reasons: league expansion on the national and international level and corporate America's reliance on sports to market its products and services. Understand that the dynamic growth of sports translates into more leagues, more teams, more stadiums, more media outlets, and more opportunities to work in a field that we all love.

Because the best qualified people are the most likely to be hired, it's vital that applicants obtain a solid education. Thumb through a college catalogue and you may be surprised to find a program in sports management (sometimes called athletic administration). Today, over 200 colleges and universities offer a bachelor's degree in sports management. Two professional organizations—the National Association for Sport and Physical Education and the North American Society for Sport Management

— have established national standards for the content of the courses, and publish a directory listing the schools with approved programs.

ADDRESS BOOK

National Association for Sport and Physical Education
1900 Association Drive
Reston, VA 22091
703/476-3410

North American Society for Sport Management
196 Main Street
Houlton, ME 04730
506/453-4576

Finding Employment Is a Full-Time Job

Individuals who aspire to a career in sports must gain grass roots experience in their chosen field. But how to break through the barriers? By getting some professional assistance. Two companies—Sports Careers and E.J. Krause & Associates, Inc.—follow the changing world of global sports business and help expand your expertise and improve your chances of building a career in the sports industry.

Sports Careers bills itself as the premier career management firm in the sports industry. Based in Phoenix, Arizona, the ten-year-old company provides a wide range of career-driven programs, conferences, seminars, educational products, and publications, designed to "expose you to the hidden job market." For an annual fee of under $300, members will receive career development tools and information services on how to package yourself to prospective employers.

The game plan includes a twice-monthly subscription to the "Career Connections Newsletter"; a computerized 15-page career enhancement profile that defines your career objectives; a resume-writing kit to help you get an interview; access to a computer data base that puts your resume into a system used by over 2,000 sports companies; an audio cassette series of past conferences; and Sports Market Place, a listing of over 24,000 sports business contacts.

J. Krause & Associates, Inc. is a global leader in exhibition and conference management. Headquartered in Bethesda, Maryland, with offices in eight foreign cities, the company organizes events in twelve different industries. Their sports event, established in 1973, is called "The International Sport Summit," which is the longest running and most established conference and exhibition in the business of sports.

The International Sport Summit emphasizes the total business of sports events and sports facilities. The summit attracts only the upper echelons of management. Because event sites change annually, the costs vary accordingly. The International Sport Summit also publishes *The Sports Business Directory*, the official who's who of over 18,000 sports executives and more than 7,500 companies related to the sports industry. The directory costs $149.

ADDRESS BOOK

E.J. Krause & Associates, Inc.
7315 Wisconsin Avenue
Bethesda, MD 20814
310/986-7800

Sports Careers
2400 East Arizona Biltmore Circle
P.O. Box 10129
Phoenix, AZ 85064
602/954-8106

aND nOW...
A fEw woRdS
FROm
OUr AUtHOr

Terry Bradshaw, the former Pittsburgh Steelers quarterback and Hall of Famer, commented on the demands the banquet circuit and his television announcer's job have made on him since retiring from the National Football League: "When you're unemployed, you have to work all the time."

As a freelance sports journalist, I often reflect on Bradshaw's statement. I haven't had a steady job in three years, yet I've worked consistently during that span. I don't claim to be an expert in career guidance, or even a novice, but I do believe my experiences mirror the advice so regularly conveyed by the professionals quoted in the forthcoming pages.

Early in the research process, before a single word had been typed, it became evident that the very skills needed to obtain a job were necessary to write a book about the topic. I contacted a network of friends working in the sports industry who, in turn, led me to other people, and then they gave me another name, and so on, and so on. Not everyone returned my phone calls. Usually, I found a way to reach these people; it's called persistence.

Networking cannot be underestimated, nor can it begin too soon. When I was the junior high school sports editor, I conducted an interview for the school newspaper with Dave Anderson, *The New York Times* columnist, who lived in my hometown. He treated me as a professional, like a peer, and I am forever grateful. In high school I was also sports editor, in addition to covering the school basketball team in the local newspaper. I received seven dollars an article (the team won just one game all year). At Ithaca College, I served as sports editor my junior year and editor-in-chief as a senior. Dave Anderson would receive an occasional column of mine in the mail.

By the time I'd reached college, I was determined to become a sportswriter. My first day in Ithaca I joined the newspaper and soon got the baseball beat. During my sophomore year, I vowed not to accept a summer job like the past ones in the dry cleaner or as a school janitor scrapping off chewing gum from underneath desks. Since I was male and could type 75 words per minute, I opined that I might stand apart from the usual suspects. I bounced around employment agencies until I found one that placed temporary secretaries at television and radio stations. I was assigned to the operations director at NBC Sports in New York. Yes!

While at NBC I made my first foray into the sports world. I befriended a production assistant who suggested I apply to become a weekend logger. In this job, I was paid to watch sporting events and assist in the compilation of highlights packages. Even at this low level, I was stunned by the intense pressure of live television. Preproduction, now that's more my style.

The next summer I easily secured an internship at NBC Sports assisting the statistician for baseball's *Game of the Week*. My first day on the job I inadvertently insulted New York Mets' public relations director Jay Horwitz, who gave me a viscious tongue-lashing. I'd earned my stripes, and a valuable lesson in respect. The highlight of the summer occured at Yankee Stadium on Old Timer's Day, sitting in the booth with announcers Vin Scully and Joe Garagiola. The Yankees were playing against the Texas Rangers, and I was concentrating so hard that to this day, I can almost remember every pitch.

During that summer of 1983, I was also preparing to take over as editor-in-chief of *The Ithacan,* the college's weekly newspaper. The business manager was a workaholic named Mark Alpert, who called me at home one day in hopes of discussing the upcoming budget (there was none). Of course, I wasn't home and my mother asked for the caller's name in order to take a message. Moments later, my NBC telephone rang and what I heard was my mother's voice informing me that Marv Albert had just called—he needed to talk to me right away!

Well, I was supremely confident the job I'd been doing at NBC was exemplary. True, I'd been in the position only a few weeks, yet extraordinary talent cannot be kept under wraps. I guess a big-time network like the National Broadcasting Company recruits young talent every day and locks them up with long-term contracts. I dropped what I was doing, sashayed down the hall at Rockefeller Center, and walked smack into the middle of Marv Albert's office.

"Hi, Mr. Albert, I'm Dave Fischer. You wanted to see me?"

I extended my right palm. Marv, probably too flabbergasted to react any differently, shook my hand. He claimed not to know me—and swore that he hadn't called me.

"You spoke to my mother," I corrected him. "My mommy said to come see you." At this point my voice cracked. "I'm the new statistician from Ithaca College." I was grasping for something to hold onto. Then Marv must've realized my embarassment, because he saved me. "If I wanted to see you," he said, "it was to ask how you're doing."

My first job out of college was at an on-line sports statistical service. The company went out of business nine months later, but it was the single most important job I ever had. Eventually, the majority of my colleagues found new jobs within the sports industry; many high-powered friends appear within these pages. It was there that I learned to operate a computer tennis program that kept match statistics. I was working the U.S. Open quarterfinal match between John McEnroe and Ivan Lendl, with the national media watching this epic battle, which Lendl won in straight sets. After the match I was discussing the events with Frank Deford, who was covering it for *Sports Illustrated*. I informed Deford that Lendl had completely dominated McEnroe from the service line. A server who wins close to 50 percent of his service points will usually win the match, I explained, and Lendl had won an amazing 75 percent. Deford made use of this statistic to illustrate a point in his story.

Though the database was bankrupt, I continued to show up at the office for work. There was no work to be done, of course, but I could utilize the telephones, computers, and fax machines to find another job. I'd had good luck with an employment agency once, so I thought, "Why not try again." My friend gave me the business card of an agent he'd recently met who specialized in computers, but I had nothing to lose. It turned out this agent had just come from a luncheon attended by human resources professionals, where he'd met the director of personnel for *Sports Illustrated*. He gave me the name and address.

It took approximately five hours to compose a cover letter to this man at *SI*. I spent another five hours deciding which sports columns from the college paper to include in the portfolio. A few weeks later, he telephoned me (I took the call directly this time) and I was invited to come in for an interview. He said the magazine had no openings at the moment, but I was confident the interview had been a success. Several days later I received another call that a position was available reading letters to the editor. I got the job, ecstatic to be at a station higher than the mail room (the office was on the fourteenth floor).

I did my job, but all I could think about was the next one. I called every department head at the magazine and requested a meeting. I hoped to learn how the magazine ran, who ran it, and if any of my fundamental skills could translate to that area. Surprisingly, all but one person was glad to speak with me. One day I was eating lunch with my boss in the cafeteria when Frank Deford walked to our table to say hello. He remembered me! My boss treated me differently from then on.

Meanwhile, my friend's computer tennis statistical service got off the ground, and he secured contracts to provide stats at the U.S. Open, Wimbledon, and the Australian Open. I took vacation time from *SI* to travel and work the Grand Slam events. The magazine featured me in the "From the Publisher" column accompanying the 1987 U.S. Open coverage. During the 1988 Aussie Open, ESPN tennis commentator Mary Carillo credited me—by name—on the air after I provided her with a particularly timely statistic regarding Boris Becker's unspectacular cross-court backhand. My career prospects seemed fantastic.

In 1990, after five years with *Sports Illustrated*, the company downsized me. I was stunned. This was the magazine I'd grown up reading. I was a loyal employee. But Frank Deford was starting the *National Sports Daily*, and some former *SI* cronies hired me there. Less than a year later, *Sports Illustrated* recruited me to return to help develop a version of the magazine on Prodigy, the home computer service. Three months later, *The National* folded. Six months after that, the *SI*-Prodigy project was cancelled. I was out of a job again. *SI* rescued me by agreeing to keep me on for 1992 as a researcher and publicist, helping out for the Olympics. Ironically, my research supervisor was that lone person who couldn't make time for me when I wanted to learn about the company. That's another lesson: Never burn bridges.

After the Olympic year of '92 I had no job again. Looking back, I'd worked for two companies that had each gone out of business, and I'd been hired twice by *SI*—and downsized twice. Desperate, I called the New York Yankees for a job, any job. I spoke with the editor of *Yankees Magazine*, who gave me the opportunity to write for his publication. The pay was terrible, but I needed the work.

To supplement my income I started getting fact-checking assignments from *SI* and *SI for Kids*. A friend at *SI* in the legal department hooked me up with another freelance writer who needed research assistance and help with data entry. I worked at the writer's apartment, and one day the writer's agent called with a children's book deal. My friend recommended me for the job. I wrote three kids books; two were never published, but I had an agent.

Suddenly, I was a hot commodity. I became a contributing writer in the *SI for Kids* books division, helping to co-author several projects. The *SI* books editor is friendly with an editor at major league baseball, and I was recommended to audition as a writer for the official magazine to be sold at stadiums during the baseball playoffs. Thankfully, I had written several published articles for *Yankees Magazine,* which became the basis for securing the job. While *Yankees Magazine* paid little, major league baseball more than made up the difference.

So you see, nobody is an expert in career guidance. There's no one way to go about landing that dream job. To be sure, it takes dedication, persistence, experience, maturity, luck, networking, and lots of hard work. To paraphrase Terry Bradshaw, getting a job is a full-time job.

Careers Related to the Playing Field

In 1989 the sports world was shocked when the Minnesota Twins, considered a small market baseball team, made Kirby Puckett the first $3 million player. Three years later, Puckett's contract was dwarfed by the San Francisco Giants, who signed Barry Bonds to a free-agent contract worth over $7 million per season.

In fact, just prior to the 1997 season, Bonds signed a two-year extension that will pay him $11.45 million in 1999 and 2000.

In 1930, as Babe Ruth was trying to negotiate an $80,000 contract, reporters asked him if he wasn't embarrassed to be seeking more than the $75,000 that President Herbert Hoover earned.

"I had a better year," the Babe answered. Now Shaquille O'Neal has signed a $17-million-a-year contract with the Los Angeles Lakers, meaning he'll make every five days what Mr. Clinton makes annually. But did Shaq have a better year?

What makes a player worth such extravagance? By and large, there are four factors that determine a player's salary: the overall quality of the player's performance, the player's contribution to the team's performance, the experience of the player, and the popularity or recognition factor of the player.

No book can teach you how to hit a round ball with a round bat squarely. Reading about the heroics of others cannot create the exhiliration that comes from sinking a game-winning jump shot as the buzzer sounds. Mere words cannot explain the thunderous feeling caused by a teeth-rattling tackle.

This book is not designed to provide naturally talented athletes with the secret to making it as a professional ballplayer. The purpose of a career reference guide is to inform potential pro prospects of the educational requirements and employment opportunties available to young athletes.

STAY IN SCHOOL

The educational expectations for college athletes is cut and dry. The National Collegiate Athletic Association's Proposition 48 requires that in order to qualify for an athletic scholarship, incoming student/athletes must have a cumulative grade point average of 2.0 (a C average) in eleven core curriculum classes.

In addition to maintaining a C average, students also need to receive a minimum score of 700 on the Standarized Achievement Test (SAT), or 15 on the American College Testing (ACT) exam. To put the test scores in perspective, a 700 on the SAT requires that only 25 percent of the questions be answered correctly. And individuals who place their name on the application form are automatically awarded 200 points.

Professional athletes are dedicated people who, after years of perserverance, have beaten the odds. Right now, there are approximately 300,000 high school basketball players; less than 3,000—under one percent—are on college scholarship at the Division I level. Each year the National Basketball Association drafts just 54 players. Of those 54, only 25 will become NBA rookies. Seventy-five percent of all active NBA players were drafted in the first round. Concerned? Thinking of practicing those foul shots? Consider this dismal statistic: The average NBA career lasts just four years. On the bright side, sports-minded individuals should know that there is life after athletics. Once your playing career has ended, the opportunities open to you are numerous. Take advantage of them. Colleges use athletes to generate revenue and provide the pro ranks with a psuedo–minor league system. Turnabout is fair play; athletes should use colleges to further their education and advance their careers.

To examine the success of the student/athlete, we turn our attention to startling statistics of a different sort. In March 1991, *The Chronicle of Higher Education*, a weekly journal that reports on the nation's colleges, made public the athlete graduation rates of Division I schools. Of the 295 Division I members, 262 responded to the *Chronicle's* poll.

Between 1984 and 1989, the years that were surveyed, 56 percent of all athletes graduated within five years, compared to 48 percent of the student body as a whole. This didn't surprise most educators because athletes generally have advantages over regular students. They have few financial worries and don't have to hold part-time jobs if they are on full scholarship. They have special counselors, tutors, and on-campus dormitories, and their routine mandates study time, albeit between practice sessions.

The disturbing part of the findings involved basketball players. Fewer than 39 percent of the basketball players graduated within five years (athletes in golf, tennis, and baseball brought the overall average up). By comparison, the grad rate for football players, student/athletes involved with the other main revenue sport, was 47 percent).

Interestingly, a month after the report was released, the two schools with the best and worst basketball graduation rates (Duke, 100 percent, and Nevada-Las Vegas, 0 percent) played in the NCAA semi-final. The game was won by Duke, 79-77.

Athletes who prepare wisely for real life will be better equipped to handle the transition after their playing career is over. To be sure, former athletes enjoy a huge advantage when seeking employment within the sports world. Individuals may find opportunities in careers that relate to the playing field. These job prospects include positions in coaching, player representation, and as game officials. Other posts filled by former athletes include roles in team administration, stadium operations, marketing and public relations, the league office, the media, and sports medicine, as well as other miscellaneous careers in the sports industry.

MANAGER/COACH

The manager or coach is responsible for preparing a team to compete on the playing field at the highest possible level of performance. To accomplish this goal the individual must be equal parts teacher, tactician, and motivator. While specific duties vary depending on whether the coach works for a professional sports organization or with a college athletic program, the pressure to win at all costs is common to this job.

Coaches working at the collegiate level will be expected to recruit student-athletes. This entails scouting talented high school players and wooing them with the offer of a scholarship to select your school. In an effort to protect young student-athletes, the National Collegiate Athletic Association—the governing body of college sports—closely monitors the conduct of coaches during this annual feeding frenzy.

Once the players have satisfactorily reached the school's admission requirements, the coach begins to hold practices. Because there's not a moment to waste, each practice session is designed much like a teacher's lesson plan. The few hours alloted to practice time are chock-full of conditioning exercises and drills to formulate a winning strategy.

While college coaches ideally build character through sport and hope to turn young boys and girls into men and women, professional coaches are in the business of winning. If success wasn't equated with winning, they wouldn't keep score. Therefore, pro coaches have only to answer to the team owner who, by nature, will have perennially lofty standards. It's often said that coaches are hired to be fired. But a coach who can consistently put a winning club on the field will have a job—somewhere—for a long, long time.

Jerry Glanville, former Atlanta Falcons and Houston Oilers coach, on the hazards of his profession: "If you're a pro coach, NFL stands for 'Not For Long.'"

IT'S MORE THAN X's AND O's

The successful coach is a patient teacher, an innovative tactician, and a master motivator. As a teacher, the coach's main function is to instruct athletes on the basic skills needed to play a particular position. College coaches obviously need to concentrate on the specific fundamentals more than their professional counterparts because a pro athlete has already exhibited the requisite talent. But coaches at all levels preach teamwork and strive to develop this elusive intangible. Teaching a group of athletes to play together as a unit is key to becoming a successful coach.

As a tactician, the coach must devise strategy. He or she may call upon a scouting report to learn the opposing team's tendencies and study videotape to discover weaknesses to be exploited. During the game, the coach is expected to assess the productivity of said strategy and then determine what changes, if any, are to be implemented. A change in game plan may mean a shift in strategy or the replacement of a player to create a favorable matchup for your team. To this end, the coach must know his or her personnel extremely well.

As a motivator, the coach is ultimately responsible for the team's mind-set. The coach may give a pre-game pep talk or a rousing halftime speech, but psyching-up players requires a delicate balancing act. Athletes should perform intensely, but never while tense. When tailoring motivational techniques to an individual, the coach needs to remember that some people respond better to coddling while others need a swift kick in the rear.

All coaches strive to create team chemistry. Like the chicken-or-the-egg conundrum, people ask: "Does team chemistry breed winning, or does winning breed team chemistry?" It's an age-old question, as is the dilemna that asks if players need to like their coach. The answer is probably no, that coaches need only to be respected by their players.

Casey Stengel, who managed the New York Yankees to ten pennants and seven World Series titles in 12 years from 1949 to 1960, seemed to have mastered the difficult task of maintaining a high level of team morale. "Ten guys are going to love the manager no matter what," he said, "and ten guys are going to hate him. My job is to keep the five guys who are undecided away from those other ten."

PUT ME IN COACH!

Some coaches invariably get appointed to the job after their playing career has ended. Retired athletes are eminently qualified for the job—history indicates that a mediocre player fares better than a superstar, the explanation being that naturally gifted athletes tend to be less of a student of the game—but for our purposes here we will focus attention only on coaches who never played the game.

The opportunities to break into coaching are most plentiful at the high school level. Individuals can train on-the-job and learn what works and what doesn't. He or she may then get promoted to assistant college coach, followed by head coach at a junior college, before taking control of a small Division I program, and eventually making it all the way to a major university.

Successful college coaches are most attractive to the professional ranks. Some go directly from a bucolic campus setting to the frying pan as head coach. Others prefer to gain seasoning as the head coach in the minor leagues or in the pros as an assistant coach learning under a respected manager. Like players, coaches must prove themselves at low levels and then climb the corporate ladder.

The majority of coaches have planned for a lifetime and trained extensively for their chosen profession. Most have a college degree in one discipline or another. Many have majored in education and have a teaching degree, while others have studied physical education, recreation, or sports sciences.

IF THE SHOE FITS

Head coaches and managers earn more than assistant coaches. For the most part, professional coaches earn more than their collegiate counterparts.

The variables related to salaries are dependent on such factors as the individual's level of responsibility, experience, qualifications, and past history of success. Other areas that influence earnings potential relate to the team, such as it's popularity, prestige, and, in the case of colleges, its emphasis on a winning athletic program.

Pro coaches can make an annual salary that ranges from $25,000 to $1.5 million. Individuals at the minor league level earn wages on the lower end of the scale, while major league coaches, who are perceived as having drawing power, will earn top dollar.

The majority of college coaches receive far less for their efforts. At small schools where coaches also teach classes, the coaching position may pay a mere stipend. Some coaches earn additional money by taking over the helm of more than one sport. Full-time college coaches generally earn between $18,000 and $35,000 a year. A few of the big-name coaches at big-time universities do command the million-dollar contracts, but they are the exception rather than the rule.

To be sure, college coaches at major Division I programs can also supplement earnings—sometimes at an astounding rate of $250,000 a year—simply by signing an athletic shoe endorsement contract. The sneaker company pays the coach to have his players wear its brand of sneaker. The Duke University Blue Devils basketball team wears Nike sneakers; Duke coach Mike Krzyzewski earns $6.5 million over 15 years.

PLAYING THE GAME

The ability to communicate with players is paramount for any coach. Players must know their roles within the structure of the team concept and fully understand what is expected of them. The coach also needs to verbalize a formal set of rules for off the field behavior. That may be in the form of instituting a dress code for traveling on road trips, imposing a curfew for the athletic dormitory, or levying fines and suspensions should a player not behave in a proper and appropriate manner.

Communication skills are also handy when dealing with the press. While college coaches are expected to make themselves available to the press, much of a pro coach's time is spent dealing with the media. This requires tact. The media often tries to stir up controversy by second-guessing the coach's decisions. If the coach can calmly and effectively explain his or her reasoning, attention can then turn to the upcoming game. And the next game is yet another opportunity to prove you can coach in this league.

TIPSHEET

- ⓦ Start out by getting a job as a counselor at a summer camp, preferably one devoted to sports, to see if you enjoy working with large groups.

- ⓦ Volunteer to coach local youth teams, such as Little League baseball or Pop Warner football, to hone your organizational skills and develop basic strategies to teach young athletes.

- ⓦ Enroll at a college that offers a comprehensive education program or sports management degree. Bear in mind that a school with a powerhouse athletic program is more likely to offer a course load related to coaching.

- ⓦ Subscribe to (and read) *Scholastic Coach* to learn about the coaching industry and stay abreast of current trends.

- ⓦ Coaches, like athletes, must begin at the lower levels and prove themselves in order to get promoted. Obtain a high school coaching job and start your career climb up the coaching ladder.

REAL-LIFE ADVICE

Carmen Cozza,
head football coach, Yale University

After 32 seasons at Yale, 1996 was Carm Cozza's last. Entering his final campaign, his teams had won 177 of 293 games and ten Ivy League titles. A native of Parma, Ohio, Cozza had never traveled east of Pittsburgh before coming to Yale as an assistant coach in 1962 from his alma mater, Miami of Ohio.

"You have to be yourself. I played under two coaches, Woody

personality sketch

Knowledge of sports; detail-oriented; supervisory; skillful communicator and motivator; ability to work well under pressure, deal with stress, and remain calm in a crisis.

Hayes and Ara Parseghian, who had two different personalities. I admired them both so much. But I know if I tried to be Woody, they'd probably have to put me in a straitjacket. I churn inside a lot. After we lose, I don't want sympathy. I want to be left alone. I go home and watch television, another football game. My wife, Jean, doesn't understand this.

"Sometimes a good look in a kid's eyes is worth a hundred words. I have always felt if you lose your poise, the kids are going to lose theirs. The first way to get beat is to lose your control. I've picked my spots to raise my voice. I've always felt if you scream all the time it's not to your advantage.

"There's a key to [dealing with alumni]. I got out and met them and told them the way it is, what it's all about. I was willing to answer their questions and I answered every letter I got—except from the ones who didn't sign their name. So for a number of years I was out a couple of nights a week talking to alumni. I admitted I didn't have all the answers.

"Then I recruited Brian Dowling and Calvin Hill, and they end up winning 16 in a row, and everybody got on the bandwagon. Easiest coaching I ever did. I wasn't so sure I wanted to come here at first. It turned out to be the best thing I ever did.

"There were times I thought wouldn't it be nice to play in the Rose Bowl, things like that. But I saw friends go on to what they thought were greener pastures and soon were out of a job. I said to myself, I couldn't have more challenges here in recruiting, in trying to mold people from all parts of the country into a unit.

"People at Yale were good to me. I had some rough years, but no one ever came to me and said, 'Hey coach, you better be looking.' Yale gave me a contract and I felt I had to honor it.

"You hear about how coaches touch their players' lives. What you don't hear about is how players touch their coaches' lives. I'm going to miss them. I'm going to go over the highlight films, the programs, and see if I can memorize all the names. There's close to 2,000, and it gets pretty hard. Seven have had sons who played for me. That's nice. It lets you know you've been in this business a long time."

SPOTLIGHT

Frank Keaney,
basketball coach, Rhode Island State

The first basketball coach to use the fast break was Frank Keaney, coach of Rhode Island State from 1921 to 1947. It was a strategy born of desperation, for Keaney's teams had no size. But they were quick and could shoot, and the 1936 Rhode Island State team (the Firehouse Gang or the

Runnin' Rams, as they were known) averaged 51 points when the center jump after each basket was eliminated.

Although that doesn't sound like much today, the point-a-minute pace was breathlessly reported in the press. Keaney's players charged down court after every rebound or made basket, hauling in long passes to the amazement of fans. His teams also were the first to use the full-court press on defense.

Keaney was a master psychologist. Wanting to prepare the team to run in smoke-filled Madison Square Garden in 1945-46 season, when Rhode Island State was in the National Invitational Tournament (the equivalent of today's NCAA tournament), Keaney had students collect cigarette and cigar butts for weeks. He then burned them in a barrel during practice, thoroughly acclimating the players.

SUCCESS STORY

Mike Holmgren,
head coach, Green Bay Packers

Making Packer history has become an annual habit for Mike Holmgren, who took over as Green Bay's head coach in 1992. In directing the Packers to the NFC Championship Game in 1995, he became the first Green Bay head coach to lead the Packers to four consecutive winning seasons and three consecutive playoff berths since the fabled Vince Lombardi. Now, following a victory in Super Bowl XXXI, Holmgren has secured a place in Packers' history.

Before coming to the Pack, Holmgren was quarterbacks coach and later offensive coordinator for the San Francisco 49ers. Prior to joining the professional ranks he had been the quarterbacks coach for four years at Brigham Young University.

Holmgren earned a bachelor of science degree in 1970 from the University of Southern California, where he played quarterback on the football team. He then returned to his alma mater, Lincoln High School in San Francisco, to begin his coaching career in 1971. A year later, he moved to Sacred Heart High as a teacher and assistant coach, struggling to a three-season record of 4-24 at a school that had no practice facility. From 1975 to 1980 he coached at Oak Grove High, where he led the school to a sectional title. Holmgren entered the college ranks as quarterbacks coach and offensive coordinator at San Francisco State in 1981, preceding his move to BYU in 1982.

ADDRESS BOOK

National Association of
Basketball Coaches
9300 West 110th Street
Overland Park, KS 66210
913/469-1001

National Collegiate
Athletic Association
6201 College Boulevard
Overland Park, KS 66211
913/339-1906

National Federation of
Interscholastic Coaches
Association
11724 Plaza Circle
Kansas City, MO 64195
816/464-5400

Scholastic Coach
555 Broadway
New York, NY 10012
212/343-6100

VIDEO COORDINATOR

Most basketball coaches are strong believers in scouting. If Team A's point guard dribbles to his right the majority of the time in clutch situations, the coach wants to know. If Team B's center loves to shoot from a certain spot on the floor and gets distracted by trash-talk, the coach wants to know. Coaches all over America are hungry for every scrap of information they can get on opponents' patterns, defenses, and if possible, personalities.

Usually there are a number of flaws that a sharp scout can see and a sharp coach can exploit. Do most of Team A's plays start with the guard passing to a forward to the right at the top of the key? Team B can try to influence the guard to his left as he dribbles upcourt. Are Team A's guards poor ballhandlers? Team B can work on a full-court press.

Most of the time the head coach is too busy to do much scouting, so the chore falls to a scouting specialist. This expert, called the video coordinator, is so often in the video room that he seldom gets to see his own team play. But some coaches like to have their own teams scouted, just as if the reports were for opponents.

With video playing an ever-increasing role in modern coaching and preparation, the video coordinator is a key member of any coaching staff. The individual in this position will prepare videotape analyses of the team and its opponents, as well as scouting tapes on college prospects.

The video coordinator is responsible for overseeing a digital-editing system that is capable of breaking down a game by any desired specification. Using basketball as the example, if a coach wishes to scrutinize how his team defended against the fast break, the coordinator can prepare a two-minute videotape of precisely those plays for review.

TECHNO HOOPS

Prior to playing an NBA opponent, coordinators prepare a videotape of the upcoming team's last eight games. The coordinator creates a tape on every opposing player, as well as a tape on every formation that team operates out of. The players and coaches can then search for a player's tendencies or a team's weaknesses.

In addition to preparing videotape analyses of the team and its opponents, the video coordinator is also responsible for preparing scouting tapes on college prospects. With hundreds of talented college players each year eligible for the NBA draft, it's impossible for the scouting department to be knowledgable about all of them. The utilization of this advanced technology, however, makes the job easier. Whereas it once required watching some 15 games to acquire a feel for a player's skills, because of the work done by the video coordinator, scouts can now watch those 15 games condensed into a one-hour highlight tape.

All this collected videotape needs to be stored and catalogued for easy retrieval. The coordinator will be expected to implement an extensive library system for archival purposes. The job of video coordinator is growing in stature. In the high-pressure world of the NBA, even the slightest edge is a big advantage.

The majority of video coordinators aspire to become a bench coach. Employment opportunies are extremely bleak, but positions are available in all sports. Teams normally employ just one full-time video coordinator and three part-timers. The salary for a video coordinator can range from $30,000 to $70,000 per year, depending on the coordinator's reputation and level of experience. The part-timers earn a minimum hourly wage.

A college degree in computing is helpful but not required. In terms of education, a keen understanding of the sport is most essential to becoming a video coordinator. A candiate for this position can always be taught to operate the computer system—he or she cannot cram a lifetime of sports learning into one or two training sessions. According to the coordinators we talked to, the basic computer knowledge needed to operate the equipment can be acquired in just two or three days.

MAJOR BASKETBALL JONES

The video coordinator is also responsible for organizing a schedule for videotaping games from the satellite feeds. "We tape over 1,000 games," says Bob Peterson, video coordinator for the Milwaukee Bucks, "and we watch more basketball than a human body can tolerate."

Peterson's career path is common to the majority of NBA video coordinators. He's been with the Bucks for ten years, having served for nine of those seasons as assistant video editor. He started his coaching career at the CYO level while earning his education degree in 1970 from the University of Wisconsin-Milwaukee.

He then taught and coached in elementary school and high school for ten years before taking the job of head basketball coach at the Milwaukee School of Engineering. He eventually became the school's athletic director and during that time he pulled double-duty by working for the Bucks.

"I was at a coaching clinic and heard [then-Bucks head coach] Del Harris speak. Afterwards, I wrote him a letter volunteering to do anything to help the team. He called me and asked if I'd be interested in learning about their brand new video system."

NUTS AND BOLTS

The system, designed by Avid Technologies, is comprised of a videotape machine and a computer. Here's how it works. Each key on the computer keyboard represents a pre-programmed function. Specific functions vary depending on the particular software program. There are keys to represent offensive and defensive plays; keys to signify highlighted strategies, such as the screen and roll, pick and roll, transition breaks, and low post efforts.

While the videotape machine records the game in progress, the computer stores in memory each keystroke initiated by the operator. This creates what is known as a logging string. When a specific type of play is requested, the computer searches its logging string and easily replays the selected edit. Because the computer has immediate recall, a coach is capable of making adjustments in an emphasized area during halftime and time-outs.

SPOTLIGHT

Bob Salmi,
assistant coach/video coordinator, Dallas Mavericks

When Bob Salmi joined the Dallas Mavericks staff prior to the 1996-97 season, he became the franchise's first-ever video coordinator. Salmi, who spent the past seven seasons working in a similar position for the New York Knicks, is responsible for helping the Mavericks assemble the most cutting-edge digital video-editing system available.

Salmi, 36, specializes in state-of-the-art video editing, statistical analysis, and player development programs. He will be stationed behind the Mavs' bench at all games, home and away. He will play a key role in the staff's pre-game and halftime scouting reports.

"We feel Bob is the right person to lead us to the next level in the high-tech areas of our basketball operations," says Mavericks vice president of basketball operations Keith Grant. "With the Knicks, he earned a reputation as one of the best computer and video coaches in the NBA. We feel Bob is a key addition."

Prior to his work with the Knicks, Salmi spent five years with the Philadelphia 76ers. There his duties included advance scouting, college scouting, video operations, shooting instruction, and directing the Sixers summer basketball camps.

"It's a competitive edge when your players can see, not only from a scouting report standpoint but from a videotape standpoint, their opponents and study their plays," says Salmi.

Salmi played basketball at Florida Southern, where he helped lead the team to the 1982 NCAA Division II championship game. He began his coaching career as an assistant at Kings College in 1984 and then spent one season as an assistant at Muhlenberg College.

SUCCESS STORY

Tom Sterner,
assistant coach, Orlando Magic

Prior to his promotion as assistant coach three years ago, Tom Sterner served as the team's video scout for four seasons. He developed the Magic's current computerized video scouting format as well as the computerized evaluation of NBA and college players.

Sterner earned his undergraduate degree in elementary education from Millersville (Pa.) State College and his master's degree in sports administration and computers from Temple University. He was the head coach at Lancaster (Pa.) Catholic High School for six years before landing a position at Franklin & Marshall College, where he served as assistant coach from 1987 to 1990.

During the summer of 1992, Sterner served as assistant coach and director of player personnel for the Tampa Bay Sun Blasters of the United States Basketball League. His responsibilities included drafting and signing players as well as coaching.

Sterner serves as co-chairman of the NBA Technology Committee. He has been instrumental in the development of the Coaches Tools software currently being used by NBA teams for scouting preparation. Sterner and IBM have recently worked on the Advance Scout software package, and he also consults with Avid Technologies on the development of team digital editing systems used for preparing for NBA opponents and scouting players for the college draft.

SPORTS AGENT

Sports agents represent professional athletes by overseeing all aspects of the player's career. The individual is responsible for advising clients on all business decisions in an attempt to guide the athlete to prosperity. Sports agents are mainly responsible for contract negotiations, as well as seeking out and securing endorsement deals for their clients.

Individuals in this job may represent more than one athlete, and, to be sure, successful agents boast an impressive roster of elite athletes. After the agent and athlete reach agreement on the terms of their working relationship, a personal management contract will be signed. The contract signed between the agent and player will usually run for a specific number of years, but a termination clause may be included should one party become disenchanted with the other.

Sports agents spend the majority of their time guiding their clients. The two parties will speak on a regular basis to set career goals and to discuss strategy. Sports agents also spend long hours dealing with others on their client's behalf by developing new projects and methods of advancing the athlete's career and public image.

An agent is directly responsible to his or her client. Sometimes the athlete will heed the advice of the agent and at other times will not. But a career as a sports agent can be extremely rewarding, especially when an agent discovers a talented young player and makes that athlete financially secure for a lifetime.

NO SECRET AGENTS

Almost anyone can become a sports agent by obtaining the proper licensing. This is accomplished by gaining certification through the particular sports' players association.

The National Basketball Players Association has certified over 200 agents who pay annual dues of $1,500. The Major League Baseball Players Association has also certified over 200 agents, but no registration fee or annual dues are required. In the National Football League, some 800 agents have paid to the Players Association a $400 application fee and an annual membership fee of $300, most of which covers the cost of the annual seminar all agents are required to attend. The National Hockey League does not certify agents, but about 100 agents have voluntarily registered with the Players Association at an annual fee of $900.

Prospective agents must also be aware of state requirements. To date, some 20 state legislatures have taken action to control unethical agents and thus protect the student-athletes and universities in their state. Individuals who wish to become agents in these states must register with the state. Fees differ greatly, from $1,000 annually in Oklahoma and Texas, to just a $100 annual fee in Arkansas and Louisiana.

While anyone can become an agent, not everyone can be successful at it. The sports agents who thrive are individuals who attract the big-name stars.

David Falk is without peer in the business of NBA player agenting. His firm, Falk Associates Management Enterprises (F.A.M.E.), represents more NBA first-round draft selections, lottery picks, Rookies of the Year, and All-Stars than anyone else in the athlete management business. Falk, 46, has conducted contract negotiations and endorsement marketing on behalf of top clients such as NBA stars Michael Jordan, Patrick Ewing, John Stockton, Dikembe Mutombo, and Alonzo Mourning. At one time or another, Falk has had 12 lottery picks as clients, including four who were the number one overall choices in their respective drafts.

Despite his recognized status as a high-powered sports agent, Falk must still seek out new athletes to expand his client base. This he does the old fashioned way: by schmoozing people. Indeed, Falk spends so much time on the telephone that his associates jokingly claim that a phone is surgically attached to his ear. "I've been in this business for almost 25 years," he says. "I represent some of the best-known basketball players in the game, and I never get a call. You have to work at it."

SOLDIER OF FORTUNE

It is difficult to determine the potential total income for sports agents due to the nature of the job. Factors that affect earnings include the number of clients that an agent advises, as well as the prestige and success of each client.

Sports agents receive their fee by taking a percentage of their clients' earnings. While this percentage varies with each client, and should be negotiated before a contract is signed, a commision of 10 to 20 percent is the norm. Falk has fashioned complicated, big-money, multi-year contracts, such as Ewing's six-year, $36 million inflation-proof deal with the New York Knicks, and Danny Ferry's 10-year, $37.5 million deal with the Cleveland Cavaliers, to cite two well-publicized examples.

Falk has also carved out lucrative endorsement deals for his clients with the likes of McDonald's and Wendy's, Kellogg's and Wheaties, Nike and Reebok, and Gatorade and Minute Maid. The standard commission for negotiating a sports-marketing agreement is 20 percent, which is what Falk earned at ProServ during his first few years representing Jordan. (He now gets 15 percent.) Agents who represent successful clients will themselves become financially successful and, therefore, influential. Falk has been called the second-most powerful man in professional basketball, behind NBA commissioner David Stern.

CREATING A SENSATION

There are a number of ways to advance as a sports agent. One method is to locate and sign a client or clients who have already achieved stardom. In order to do this, however, the agent must have already established a proven track record. Another way to advance is for the agent to coddle a relatively unknown client or up-and-coming athlete and guide his or her career to a higher level of success.

"One of the first things we do for a client," Falk says, "is put him or her in a public service spot for free to gain awareness and let companies know they are personable and articulate. Then we marry public service spots to a company that donates money if a player scores a touchdown or blocks a shot. It starts off very, very slowly. We don't think there will be another Michael Jordan. That's a historical fluke.

"The public is very perceptive when you're exercising ultimate spin control," Falk adds. "You have to promote the natural personality." No relationship between an athlete and a company is as perfectly natural as is the Nike-Jordan match.

In August 1984, Falk and two key men from Nike (a marketing guru and a design artist) sat down in the offices of ProServ, in Washington, DC. Their goal was to come up with a slogan around which to build a campaign for a rookie named Michael Jordan, whose talent and personality were expected to help sell a few pairs of basketball shoes. They had discussed the name Prime Time, but that soon lost its luster. At the time, Nike had a shoe on the market called Air Force, and Falk began to fiddle around with variations on that name. Falk finally blurted out the magic words: "How about Air Jordan?"

That brainstorm placed Falk right in the middle of a Jordan money machine that earns between $40 and $50 million a year in endorsements—above and beyond the $25 million the Bulls paid him for the 1996-97 season. "If I could redo Michael's first Nike deal," Falk says now, "and if I had any glimmer of how successful it would be, I would have asked for one dollar a year and 50 percent of the profits."

THE REP'S REP

While there is no educational requirement to becoming a sports agent, a college degree in business and finance is useful, as is a knowledge of contract law. Courses in communications, marketing, and public relations are also helpful.

Falk's face sours whenever he hears himself referred to as "Jordan's agent," and is quick to remind everyone that he is a lawyer and a good one. "I want to be known as an artist," he says, "rather than a mere mechanic; someone who did deals creatively and didn't sign a bunch of players just to sign them."

After graduating with honors from Syracuse University with a B.A. in Economics in 1972, Falk set his sights on the burgeoning field of sports representation. His career was launched in 1974, when he joined a Washington, D.C., sports law firm as an unpaid law clerk. At the time he was still completing his law degree at the National Law Center of George Washington University. Falk honed in on the law firm's promotional arm, ProServ. When he completed his J.D. with honors in 1975, he was hired full time at a starting salary of $13,000. By the end of that first year, he had become a ProServ executive, and in 1977, as the director of the company's activities in team sports, he represented the firm's first NFL player (Mike Butler, for you trivia fans). Falk joined ProServ's Board of Directors as a senior vice president in 1983 and was named vice chairman in 1990. He left ProServ in January 1992 to launch F.A.M.E..

A fine resume notwithstanding, a twelve-year relationship with Michael Jordan has given Falk a power base that few agents could ever hope to achieve. On his way to the top, Jordan has become the league's only one-man Fortune 500 conglomerate. Falk has landed him major endorsement contracts with Nike and Wheaties, among others. Says Falk, "If you were to create a media athlete and star of the 90s—spectacular talent, midsized, well-spoken, attractive, accessible, old-time values, wholesome, clean, natural, not too goody-two-shoes, with a little bit of deviltry in him—you'd invent Michael."

Falk has a talent, by no means unique among agents in the industry, of exaggerating his client's value, particularly when he's holding the leverage—such as when the team on the other side of the table clearly needs his client's skills. Falk rarely raises his voice during negotiations, and he apparently hates to be hollered at. Says one general manager: "He starts out tough and sometimes obnoxious, and stays that way."

"My job," Falk says, "is to get a great contract for the player. I do not have loyalty to the team; I have loyalty to the player." Falk strongly believes that a player, even in a team sport, absolutely owns the rights to his name and likeness. In a meeting in 1984 with Rod Thorn, then the general manager of the Chicago Bulls, Falk recalls the discussion turning to Jordan's initial relationship with Nike.

"The sneaker company had just introduced a red and black shoe which violated team color rules," said Falk. "Thorn asked, incredulously, if we were trying to turn Michael into a tennis player. I told him that was exactly what we were trying to do."

THE ULTIMATE SPIN DOCTOR

Experience in any facet of the sports industry is valuable to becoming an agent. Sports agents who begin with one client often learn as they go. Others obtain experience by assisting an established agent and learning the business from that person.

It is also necessary for an agent to be able to tap into a reliable network of contacts within the industry. If individuals do not have these contacts, they must have the ability to cultivate them. A sports agent should possess strong communication skills and be an aggressive negotiator. The ability to recruit and develop new talent is essential to success in this field.

Virtually everything being done today in the field of sports agenting, sports management and corporate sponsorship of athletic events, in merchandise licensing and in made-for-television sports events started with Mark McCormack. He launched a business that would become a billion-dollar industry and forever change the landscape of professional sports.

McCormack was a young lawyer from Cleveland who loved golf. In 1960, he signed his first client, Arnold Palmer, and from there he quickly became the original sports superagent. McCormack, now 65, founded his company, the International Management Group (IMG), on the simple idea that corporations would pay a lot of money to have their company names associated with great athletes. McCormack convinced the business world that sports—with their high visibility, positive image, and international appeal—were an ideal marketing vehicle.

McCormack is also a globally strategic thinker. He signed the best athlete in each country, then used that athlete to open corporate doors in his or her homeland. McCormack locked up golfers Gary Player of South Africa and Tony Jacklin of Great Britain, auto racer Jackie Stewart of Scotland, skiier Jean-Claude Killy of France, and tennis player Bjorn Borg of Sweden, among other notables. And it was IMG that proposed the idea of stretching the Olympic Games over 17 days and three weekends, which translated into bigger TV audiences and rights fees. By 1994, IMG had grown hugely profitable: 64 offices in 25 countries, amassing annual revenue of $1 billion.

McCormack has perfected the notion of controlling every aspect of a sporting event. For example, in 1995 IMG helped set up the IBM-ATP Tour World Championship in Frankfurt, Germany—a tennis match that happened to be won by IMG client Pete Sampras. McCormack has long tapped into the events his athletes played in. Wimbledon became an IMG client in 1968, allowing McCormack to handle its TV and video rights, as well as create licensing deals. He also created merchandising logos for golf's U.S. and British Opens, then licensed the logos around the world. Golf's Ryder Cup; tennis' Italian, Australian, and U.S. Open; and the European PGA Tour are all IMG clients. Explaining the expansion into event management, McCormack once said, "Bjorn Borg can break a leg. Wimbledon cannot."

REAL-LIFE ADVICE

Jack Mills,
director, Sports Lawyers Association

Mr. Mills began his career as the assistant athletic director at the University of Colorado, then went into private law practice in 1966. As an attorney and sports agent, he has represented 32 first-round NFL draft choices. He also represents golfer Hale Irwin.

"The number one requirement to get into this business is to have a client that wants to let you represent him. That's the biggest hurdle when you're first starting out. Don't try to make a living solely on representing athletes right away. Keep something else going, whether it's a law practice or a CPA practice, so that you have the ability to sustain yourself financially while you're learning this business and while you're developing the experience you need to attract clients.

"The hard part is getting clients and then keeping those clients. Always maintain communication with your clients. The biggest complaint you hear from athletes is, 'My agent doesn't pay attention to me.' Keep in constant touch with your clients. It's not glamourous taking care of someone else's little personal details. But it's important to your client that you are there when they need you. If you're doing your job properly, you will become a close friend of your client. You may be the one guy in the world that he really trusts."

SPOTLIGHT

Steven Kauffman,
principal, Kauffman Sports Management Group

Twenty-five years ago, Steve Kauffman was working as a tax attorney and certified public accountant. Today, he's one of the most powerful and well-respected sports agents in the business. With clients that include NBA players Dominique Wilkins and Rony Seikaly—to name just two—Kauffman has built a full-service, multi-million dollar sports agency.

His landmark achievement occured prior to the 1989-90 NBA season, when he orchestrated a free-agent bidding war between the Atlanta Hawks and Detroit Pistons for client Jon Koncak, the seven-foot, back-up center for the Hawks. At the time, Koncak was earning $600,000 a season. When Kauffman was finished negotiating, Koncak had become the fifth-highest paid player in the league with a six-year, $13.2 million pact, earning him the nickname "Jon Contract."

Although Koncak had averaged only six points and six rebounds a game for four years, he'd always played behind Tree Rollins and Moses Malone. The Hawks' original offer for Koncak was five years at about $1 million a year. Kauffman told the team he would buy disability insurance and wait it out. He knew that the Detroit Pistons had lost forward Rick Mahorn in the expansion draft, and needed a replacement. Sure enough, Detroit offered Koncak $2.5 million for one year. Kauffman convinced Atlanta to commit to a long-term contract, and it was a done deal.

"There are agents that seriously underestimate how important it is to understand the game," says Kauffman, 48. "It's crucial to be successful in the long run. Knowledge is power; it gives you an edge during negotiations, and the respect of players and management."

Kauffman graduated from Temple University in 1970 with a degree in accounting, and then matriculated at the University of Pennsylvania Law School. While the majority of his clients are basketball players, Kauffman's Ivy League connection was useful in recruiting New York Mets pitcher Ron Darling, a Yale alum, as the firm's first baseball client.

In preparation for Darling's 1987 contract arbitration hearing, Kauffman took a unique approach. He produced a five-minute videotape devoted to Darling's on-field talents as well as his marquee value to the team. Near the end, Tim McCarver, the Mets' television broadcaster, came on-screen to espouse Darling's virtues.

"McCarver said, 'I have never seen a pitcher with worse luck than Ron Darling,'" says Kauffman. "He went on about how good Ronnie was. When we turned off the tape, the Mets brass had their mouths hanging open. Their own employee was making our case."

To become a competent agent, says Kauffman, you don't necessarily have to be a lawyer. His firm employs fourteen people in three cities, yet only three lawyers. But he stresses that an agent should be affiliated with a law firm to ensure proper supervision. "I've seen major screw-ups occur because agents who were not lawyers did not bring in outside people," he says.

Kauffman advises aspiring agents to be creative in breaking into the business. Securing that first client in a legal, ethical manner is almost impossible, he says with regret. Sometimes it's a stroke of luck: The kid is a family friend, or maybe you grew up with him, and he wants to give you a break. But more often than not, the player you know well still isn't going to sign on with you.

Says Kauffman, "He'll be told by enough people, 'If you were having brain surgery, would you go to a general practitioner? No, you better have an expert, someone with experience.' But a smart young agent can use that potential lucky break to his advantage. Instead of taking a chance on that player, and maybe blowing it, he can come to me and offer up that athlete as a bargaining chip to getting a job."

ADDRESS BOOK

Advantage International
1025 Thomas Jefferson
Street N.W.
Washington, DC 20007
202/333-3838

F.A.M.E.
5335 Wisconsin Avenue N.W.
Washington, DC 20015
202/686-2000

*International Management
Group*
One Erieview Plaza
Cleveland, Ohio 44114
216/522-1200

*Kauffman Sports
Management Group*
29350 Pacific Coast Highway
Malibu, CA 90265
310/589-5790

*Major League Baseball
Players Association*
12 East 49th Street
New York, New York 10017
212/826-0808

*National Football League
Players Association*
2021 L Street N.W.
Washington, DC 20036
202/463-2200

*National Basketball
Players Association*
1775 Broadway
New York, NY 10019
212/333-7510

*National Hockey League
Players Association*
One Dunas Street West
Tonorto, Ontario, Canada
M5G 1Z3
416/408-4040

ProServ
1101 Wilson Boulevard
Arlington, Virginia 22209
703/276-3030

Sports Lawyers Association
2017 Lathrop Avenue
Racine, WI 53405
414/632-4040

PLAYERS ASSOCIATION

Like any union, the players' associations were organized in an effort to improve the working conditions of their member athletes. The associations address such union-wide issues as pension plans and health insurance. The organization operates for the benefit of the group of athletes as a whole.

The players' associations working for the four major sports list among their objectives the desire to enhance, protect, and defend the individual rights of their member athletes. When a player is fined or suspended, most of us hear from a representative of the players' association. Athletes traditionally appeal the league's disciplinary action and have a right to request a hearing regarding the suspected transgression.

An additional goal of the players' associations is to prevent, attack, and eliminate any and all limitations or restrictions on a player's ability to market his skills and services. Free agency for his players will be the legacy left in pro football by Gene Upshaw, the executive director of the NFL Players Association. Upshaw, who went through strikes in 1982 and 1987, decertified his own union for five years to help boost his players' chances to win free agency in court.

The struggle was lengthy, but through a series of court battles and testy negotiations, Upshaw and the NFL team owners finally came to terms on an agreement in 1993. The NFL was the last of the major sports to adopt it. "In many situations," Upshaw recalled, "I was the only black in the room—and I'm in there talking about freedom issues."

The continuance of group licensing efforts, post-career preparation, and the enhancement of players' incomes off the field are among other primary objectives of the associations. Said Charles Grantham, who served from 1990 to 1995 as the executive director of the National Basketball Players Association, "I'm not as concerned with how much our players make, I'm more concerned about how much they keep."

SHARK-INFESTED WATERS

Employment prospects are fair for individuals who aspire to enter the inner sanctum of the players' associations of the four major sports leagues. The most publicly recognized aspect of the players' associations involves labor lawyers. But attorneys are just a small fraction of the people who work there. The NFL Players' Association, for instance, has a staff of about 60 people. In addition to the legal hotshots that form the basis of the executive committee, these people are divided into areas such as accounting, player benefits, licensing, merchandising, membership drives, fund-raising, public relations, and research. And the number of employment opportunities is sure to grow. The NFLPA has recently developed Players Inc. as a source of new revenue for the association, and the company owns all licensing rights to the players as groups and in much of their sports merchandise.

The surest way into the players' association is by first earning a law degree and then serving a labor union. Doug Allen, the president of

Players, Inc., was a Buffalo Bills linebacker for two seasons before moving on in 1976 to work for the American Federation of Labor and Congress of Industrial Organizations, better known as the AFL-CIO. Six years later, he joined the NFLPA as an assistant to the executive director. Since then, Allen's climb up the ladder has been a steady one.

But for regular folks like us, entry into a players' association is best accomplished at an entry-level rung. At this level—where an individual operates as a support staffer, handling many of the day-to-day functions of the office—he or she will gain knowledge as to the intricaces of professional sports and be exposed to the important people behind the scenes.

A four year college eduaction is usually required for entry into this field, and an advanced degree in a specific area of expertise will be helpful for advancement. Good choices for majors include business administration, marketing, public relations, finance, and accounting.

Salaries will be commensurate with experience. Generally, the pay scale is condidered to be below average for the majority of the employees within the players' association. Members of the executive committee are well compensated.

CORPORATE RAIDER

Qualified applicants with no legal expertise and no labor union experience are advised to focus thier energies on the other job areas within the players' association. There was heavy criticism leveled at Upshaw from the start because, as the skeptics argued, a former football player without a law degree had no business leading such an organization. But Upshaw has risen above the criticism. In a rocky climate for sports labor bosses, Upshaw has not only survived, he has flourished.

He has proven that a firm management style, coupled with astute business administration skills, are more important than passing a bar examination. When Upshaw assumed his post in 1983, the players association was $4 million in debt. It used to rent its offices. Now, according to Upshaw, it's $62 million in the black and owns the eight-story building on L Street, just a forward pass away from the White House.

"My first year, in '83, my salary was $85,000," says Upshaw. "I used to take my checks and stick them in the desk drawer because I couldn't cash them. We didn't have the money."

A HISTORY LESSON

The NFLPA was formed in 1956 after members of the Green Bay Packers became upset with the dirty condition of their uniforms. When team management refused to address this minor complaint, the players rallied together and organized a formal meeting to discuss the matter.

The first player rep meeting was called to order in November of 1956. On the agenda were the following proposals: a request for clean jerseys and equipment, a minimum salary of $5,000, per diem pay for players, a rule requiring clubs to provide players' equipment, and the inclusion of an injury clause in the standard player contract that would provide for continued salary to an injured player.

The NFL refused to recognize the association until 1959. At that time, the NFL Players' Association president Billy Howton threatened to sue the league for violating antitrust laws unless the league would bargain with the union. Thirty-five years (and numerous lawsuits) later, the NFLPA now has 1,800 active members and a retired membership of nearly 3,000 football players.

REAL-LIFE ADVICE

Gene Upshaw,
executive director, NFL Players Association

Before being appointed to his current position in 1983, Gene Upshaw was a member of two Super Bowl championship teams during his 16-year Hall of Fame career as an Oakland Raider offensive lineman. Upshaw is a guard on the NFL's all-time 75th anniversary team. He was inducted into the Hall of Fame in 1987.

"It's easy to be a leader in easy times. You've got to lead all the time. We've got nearly 1,800 active players, nearly 3,000 retired players, and all football agents, as many as 900, are certified through us. When I joined the Raiders in 1967, the veterans told me: 'Here's a card, rookie. Sign it and pay your dues.' Being a part of the union was expected of you, but I always wanted more than that. I wanted to be in the process. I jumped right in from the start.

"I am always aware that I represent what the players want, what the majority wants and needs. They don't need a blabbermouth. They don't need a screamer. They don't need a lamb. They need vision and for you to listen, listen, listen. It's owners, fans, and players. It's a delicate balance. It's what's in the best interest for the league. We don't need winners and losers. That's what the game is. 'How can we represent these players and this league? How can we execute this game plan?' That's what I ask. And I know who I work for.

"NFL players are so proud and have such big egos. When they turn to you, it might be the only time they do, to anyone. So when they do, if you don't answer, later it might be too late. No matter what has been said or how they have acted, at some point, I know they will call. I know that phone will ring. And regardless, we will answer. That's the thing about our group. Whether you play for the Super Bowl champion or you're the 30th team in the league, whether you are All-Pro or reserve, we are there for everyone.

"I'm proud of the deal we have with the league, but it expires in 2002 and I want us ready to bargain the next one. I won't get stuck. Every day is a learning experience. Every day you've got to grow some. It's perspective. It's understanding. I actually don't believe I've worked a day in my life in the way that most people think of work."

SPOTLIGHT

Donald Fehr,
executive director, Major League Baseball Players Association.

Donald Fehr, 47, is the head of the most visible and, arguably, most successful labor union in the country. Since being drafted into the role of executive director of the MLBPA in 1983, when he was 35, he has reaped rewards for the players. Fehr has negotiated agreements with baseball-card companies that have resulted in a licensing bonanza for the MLBPA, with revenues soaring from $2 million a year in 1981 to $70 million in 1992. Under Fehr's leadership, baseball players continue to enjoy a liberal free-agency system and an average salary that topped $1 million in 1992 (thanks in part to contracts like that of Barry Bonds).

Fehr (pronounced "fear") grew up in Prairie Village, Kansas, and accepted a college scholarship to Indiana. In 1972, while at Missouri-Kansas City law school, he worked for the George McGovern campaign. "One thing I learned then," he says, "was a healthy degree of respect for the individual, and the skepticism over the nature of big business and monopolies." Fehr's first job out of law school was as a clerk for a U.S. district court judge in Kansas City. He then joined Jolley, Moran, Walsh, Hager, and Gordon, a Kansas City firm that specialized in labor law.

In 1976 the Andy Messersmith free-agency case landed on his desk. Messersmith, at the time a pitcher for the Los Angeles Dodgers, had played the 1975 season without a contract to challenge the reserve clause in the standard baseball contract. An arbitrator had ruled in Messersmith's favor, rendering him a free agent and prompting an appeal by the owners. As local counsel, Fehr successfully represented the MLBPA in the appeal, and baseball hasn't been the same since.

Impressed with Fehr's handling of the case, Marvin Miller—a former labor lawyer who had gained expertise in collective bargaining with the

United Steelworkers of America, and who organized the MLBPA in 1966 and ran it until he stepped down in 1982—asked Fehr to join the MLBPA in 1977 as general counsel. Fehr took over six years later. With a salary of about $550,000, Fehr is well paid, but in baseball terms, he is underpaid. In collective bargaining agreements, Fehr's negotiations have given the players a huge payoff: In 1984 the players received 40 percent of base-ball's $600 million in revenues; in 1992 they got more than half of the estimated $1.6 billion in revenues.

Despite his 55- to 70-hour workweeks, Fehr says, "I don't do any work anymore. I go to meetings, talk on the telephone, and conduct interviews. That's the nature of being an executive in America. You have to rely on other people to do something you used to do yourself."

He conducts a large part of his business on the telephone—keeping the players informed, talking to agents, being interviewed. He answers reporters' questions with a single purpose: To inform, even persuade, the interviewer of the union's way of thinking.

"You always tell the truth—always. You don't make up things. You don't chisel with the press. If you can't tell the press something, you say that. As regards the press, sometimes you have to tell it what it should be asking if it doesn't understand the issues.

"It does get tiring talking about the same issues with the same people month after month, year after year," he concedes. "You get the feeling you've done it all before, which you have, of course."

SUCCESS STORY

Bob Goodenow,
executive director, NHL Players' Association

A 1974 graduate from Harvard with a degree in economics and gov-ernment, Goodenow also captained the Crimson hockey team to a Final Four appearance as a senior. He then tried out for, and was cut by, the NHL's Washington Capitals.

He attended law school while playing in the International Hockey League with the Flint Generals. In 1979, Goodenow passed the Michi-gan bar and practiced labor and tax law in Dearborn, Michigan. He represented many hockey players, including Kelly Miller of Washing-ton, Joel Otto of Calgary, and Brett Hull of St. Louis. In 1990, Goodenow made a name for himself by negotiating on Hull's behalf a landmark four-year, $7.1-million contract. He spent just over a year as the union's deputy director, then replaced Alan Eagleson as executive director in 1992.

SUCCESS STORY

Simon Gourdine,
executive director, NBA Players Association

The New York native is a graduate of Fordham Law School. He served as deputy commissioner of the NBA from 1974 to 1981. Gourdine then left the league to become commissioner of the New York City Department of Consumer Affairs and, later, director of labor relations for the Metropolitan Transportation Authority. In 1990 he returned to basketball as the NBA's general counsel. Gourdine became the top man in the union when Charles Grantham resigned in 1995.

ADDRESS BOOK

Major League Baseball
Players Association
12 East 49th Street
New York, NY 10017
212/826-0808

National Basketball
Players Association
1775 Broadway
New York, NY 10019
212/333-7510

National Football League
Players Association
2021 L Street N.W.
Washington, DC 20036
202/463-2200

National Hockey League
Players Association
One Dundas Street West
Tonorto, Ontario, Canada
M5G 1Z3
416/408-4040

PERSONAL BUSINESS MANAGER

Uninformed athletes spend their money as if it were going to last forever. It won't. The average professional football career lasts just five years, and some National Football League contracts can be voided by the team if a player is injured. Football players particularly don't learn until it's too late that a career in the NFL, and the pay that comes with it, can be short-lived.

The rising salaries being paid to professional athletes has created an important niche: the personal business manager. The main function is to oversee the athlete's financial affairs and optimize the individual's earnings power.

Business managers often act as financial advisors and counsel their clients on investment choices, tax issues, and legal matters. He or she is also expected to summarize a client's investments, properties, business dealings, and financial status, and to provide financial statements to the client.

personality sketch

Knowledge of business management, finance, and accounting; experience in tax laws and investment; ability to comprehend client's goals as well as communicate to client the risk vs. reward scenario.

Business managers must keep track of all personal expenses and business-related expenditures incurred by the athlete, checking each bill for accuracy, and then remitting payment. The manager may also be expected to ensure that the athlete is paid on time and as contracted.

In the case of mega-athletes like Joe Montana and Wayne Gretzky, who are themselves a pseduo-company, the business manager may have other duties. The individual may then be responsible for setting up a payroll system and paying personnel employed by the athlete, including attorney, accountant, press agent, and secretary.

MINDING YOUR OWN BUSINESS

Business managers charge clients a fee. Individuals may charge the client a flat fee on a retainer basis, an hourly fee, or a percentage of a client's total gross income. If the manager's earnings are dependent on a percentage of a client's gross income, the more money a client makes, the more the business manager can earn.

Personal business managers can service more than one client. They may also advise people in other fields outside of sports. Advancement for business managers in the sports industry is indicated by a larger and more prestigious client list. The number of clients represented will play an important factor in determining earnings potential.

There is no single clear-cut way to enter this field. Some business managers started out as accountants, stockbrokers, or financial advisors. Others worked as business managers with clients in fields that were not sports-oriented. Some individuals were involved in the business end of the sports industry in some other capacity.

All successful business managers possess an innate business sense. While there is no formal educational requirement to become a business manager, a minimum of a four-year college degree is recommended with majors in accounting, finance, and business administration. A graduate degree in one of these fields will be helpful in honing skills.

Individuals must also stay on top of an ever-changing financial world. Continuing education in the form of seminars, workshops, and classes in tax laws, tax shelters, and investments will be useful. Seminars in all aspects of the sports world will also help a business manager to be aware of the specific business needs of athletes, as well as assist in building a network of contacts.

YOUNG MILLIONAIRE

Ki-Jana Carter of the Cincinnati Bengals suffered a season-ending knee injury in his first preseason game of 1995. Carter, 23, the top draft pick in the NFL in 1995, has a $19.2 million, seven-year deal that included a $7.125-million signing bonus, the richest to date for a rookie. The contract also called for an extra $100,000 for scoring 12 or more touchdowns in a season, and a clause that could make the running back a free agent after four years.

"I came out of college and felt invicible," said Carter. "After the injury happened it was like, "Wow, I may not be making any more money." Carter now views his career and his pay on a year-to-year basis. "In the beginning I counted on the four years of the contract. Now I just look at the money I have."

Relatively speaking, Carter does not spend a lot. And the running back is an excellent saver, even though he receives his annual salary in 17 tempting weekly checks during the football season. Carter's 1995 income was $7.875 million—$7.125-million signing bonus and the $750,000 first-year salary.

The New York Times' Larry Dignan reports that, of the 1995 income, 42 percent was saved, 42 percent went to pay taxes, and 16 percent was spent. Excluding big expenses—the agent's fee for Leigh Steinberg, and the average annual premium of $50,000 he pays Lloyd's of London for a $3-million disability policy—Carter's 1995 expenditures equaled only 10 percent.

Carter's knee injury reinforced an already cautious nature. He had already put all his signing bonus money into low-risk, fixed-income investments, mostly municipal bonds from Florida, where he is building a house. This type of conservatism is unusual; most young people with money to invest are advised to put it primarily into stocks.

"I knew what was safe," said Carter, who majored in business marketing at Penn State. "I got a $7 million bonus, so there was no need to gamble. I wanted to be safe and then branch out."

THE SELECTION PROCESS

When Carter set out to find a financial planner, he interviewed 14 candidates by telephone. He narrowed the pool to seven, all of whom paid to fly themselves to interviews with Carter. Nearly all the planners were "fee only," charging a set amount regardless of the investments their clients made. But some planners receive commissions on certain investments; many experts, believing that such advisers may give self-interested advice, discourage investors from using people with these pay arrangements.

In the end, Carter chose Mark Griege, a fee-only planner who is paid a percentage of the assets he manages. Griege is a principal at Robertson, Griege & Thoele, a financial planning firm in Dallas that also works with Troy Aikman, the Dallas Cowboys quarterback, and other prominent NFL players.

The clincher in Griege's selection was his commitment to personal service. Griege flies around the country to meet with Carter. He boils down information about each investment to a one-page summary that addresses tax issues, risk, and asset allocations, with graphics showing how the funds perform in relation to one another.

And because young, wealthy people can unwittingly be conned when it comes to financial matters, Griege also teaches Carter about investing. Griege is teaching Carter how to use Quicken, financial planning software, and he has explained to Carter how to read the reports put out by Morningstar, the fund research company. "Many tell you that you should do this or that," says Carter. "Mark tells you the reason why you should."

RISK VS. REWARD

Griege acknowledged that Carter's conservatism is not ideal for someone in the running back's position, but he says it is important that Carter's intitial investments match his risk tolerance and his knowledge of investing. "Rule Number One," says Griege, "is never invest in something you don't understand."

After an extensive portfolio review, according to Dignan, the planner and the player eventually decided to allot 45 percent to municipal bonds and 40 percent to equity mutual funds (15 percent in small-cap funds, 15 percent in large-cap funds and 10 percent in international funds). There is also a 5 percent weighting each in real estate, oil and gas, and cash.

Putting 45 percent of a 23-year-old's portfolio into tax-free funds may still seem like an overly prudent attitude. But according to some experts, the riches bestowed on today's young athletes make such a strategy worthwhile. After all, an athlete has a lucrative but relatively brief working life in which to achieve their financial goals.

"Players are making so much money, there's no need for a lot of risk," says Bernard Wolfe, who runs a financial planning firm in Rockville, Maryland. He tends to use municipals for 45 to 55 percent of the assets of his clients, many of whom are professional hockey players.

If there is a danger in being prudent, according to Griege, it's inflation. Griege admits that Carter's portfolio needs more equities to insure that his money will whip inflation. "Inflation is a significant threat for athletes," says Griege. "Ki-Jana is looking at 50-plus years of inflation. The time he has can work for him or against him."

Griege expects Carter's portfolio to evolve, and the planner wants to increase the overall equity portion of his client's portfolio. Griege is planning to introduce Carter to individual stocks in fields he knows, like Nike, the shoe manufacturer, and Planet Hollywood, the restaurant chain with a celebrity theme.

"I don't expect Ki-Jana to understand all of the terminology in a stock prospectus, but he knows why he has to diversify," says Griege. "For the moment, playing football is Ki-Jana's best investment. Pro athletes who focus too much on business in their first contract often don't get a second."

Griege wants his clients to understand investing from a commonsense perspective. He and Ki-Jana Carter often discuss the risky ventures that other athletes jump into. Some young players plow money into starting sports bars, which Griege says "saps money from the core of a portfolio and should only be done toward the end of a career."

Other players simply spend like it's going out of style.

Carter is determined to be different. "Some guys go out and spend just to show they have a lot of money," he says. "That's good now, but I'm trying to live like this when I'm 50 years old."

TIPSHEET

① Accumulate as many qualifications and as much experience as possible. Break into the business by taking any job within the industry.

① Try to find an internship or a part-time position with a business management company. This will be helpful in learning the ropes and making contacts.

- Enroll in financial seminars on investment strategy, tax shelters; obtain a college degree in business management, finance, or accounting.

- It's often easier to break into the business management end of the sports industry on the local level. You may also need to volunteer your services at the beginning in order to earn a reputation and start building a client list by word-of-mouth.

BASKETBALL REFEREE

A basketball referee's job is one of the least enviable in the world. He can't please everyone and seldom pleases anyone. The game is ten large men moving quickly in a confined space. While the crowd, the coaches, and sometimes the players scream at him, the referee has to make difficult instant judgments: Was it charging or blocking? Was the man hacked just as he shot or a half-second after?

Three referees work as a unit, and their decisions inevitably effect the game's outcome. Refer-ees call fouls; fouls lead to free-throw points and player disqualifications. The crew's senior referee is in charge of making sure that the court is playable, the backboard is secure, and the basket is ten feet from the floor—and he get to toss the ball up to start the game!

In running the game, the referee is helped by a scorer, timer, and a man who operates the 24-, 35-, or 30-second shot clock (24 in the NBA, 35 for college men, 30 for college women). The scorer records the names and numbers of all players and keeps track of field goals, free throws, fouls, and time-outs.

The college timer keeps track of two 20-minute halves and the 15-minute half time, starting and stopping the scoreboard clock at the refer-ee's signal and on all violations. He keeps a spare clock and/or stopwatch at the table in case something goes haywire with the scoreboard. The pros have four 12-minute quarters, with 90 seconds between quarters and a 15-minute half time. The greatest pressure on a timer comes at the end of a close game. The team behind wants the clock to crawl; the team ahead wants it to sprint. The timer cannot please both and, of course, shouldn't try to please either. He should sound the buzzer when time has elapsed regardless of who is leading or trailing or who is about to take a shot.

The operator of the shot clock starts it when a team gets possession of the ball. If the offensive team does not attempt a shot that hits the rim within the time limit, it loses possession.

THE ACTION IS FANTASTIC

Basketball officials are needed wherever the sport is played; in high school, college, and professional leagues throughout the world. Individuals can climb the career ladder by being awarded a spot in a more prestigious league.

Candidates must work high school basketball games, college games, and games in lesser professional leagues like the Continental Basketball Association and/or the United States Basketball League. Individuals must then win the esteem of the National Basketball Referees Association, which is composed of NBA refs. The association then passes on the names of qualified people to the NBA's Rod Thorn, vice president of operations, who makes the final judgment.

Basketball referees need drive, determination, talent, luck, and an encyclopedic knowledge of basketball rules and regulations to advance their careers. Individuals must also be in exceptional physical condition in order to run up and down the court for an entire game. While the players are given an occasional breather, the refs are not.

IT PAYS TO BE A WHISTLE-BLOWER

The major college conferences pay each of the three basketball referees an average of $400 per game. They also usually pay an alternate ref who lives near the site of the game an average of $400 merely to stand by at home in case one of the assigned refs fails to show up. The fees for the assigned refs are in addition to all travel expenses (airfare, hotel, and meals).

Referees are free to work games in more than one conference. They're not employed by a particular conference, but rather furnish their services in the manner of an independent contractor. That's why you may have seen high-profile refs such as Ed Hightower, Jody Silvestri, and Larry Lembo work a Big Ten game on Saturday and a Big East game on Sunday.

The majority of refs have away-from-the-court jobs, so the number of games they can work depends on how flexible their hours are. Although you don't get rich on referee wages alone, the job can provide up to and around $20,000–$24,000 a year—not a bad part-time job. It's not unheard of for refs like Hightower to officiate 50 or 60 games a season.

In the National Basketball Association, rookie refs start at $67,000 and receive advances over the years. After 20 years of service, refs can earn $200,000.

SPOTLIGHT

Earl Strom,
former NBA official

Not just a whistle-blowing relic of the 1950s, Earl Strom was still at the top of his game when he retired from the NBA after the 1989-90 season. He was a basketball referee for all times, all ages, all players. He blew the whistle on Bill Russell, Julius Erving, and Michael Jordan.

So much of Strom's refereeing history was woven into the history of the NBA. Strom officiated Game 7 in five (1966, '69, '78, '84, and '88) of his era's nine NBA Finals that went the distance.

He railed against the modern-day refs, believing they depersonalized the art of officiating by discouraging interaction with the players and the fans. The human aspect of refereeing was always what interested Strom. That, combined with sound judgment, compassion, and a love for the game, made him the best basketball referee who ever lived.

ADDRESS BOOK

National Basketball Referees Association
P.O. Box 3522
Santa Monica, California 90408
310/393-3522

REAL-LIFE ADVICE

Gene Monje,
NCAA official

After completing his education at Ithaca (N.Y.) College, Gene Monje moved to North Carolina to pursue a master's degree at East Carolina. While there, a friend encouraged him to answer an ad for a high school official.

"I knew from the start it was going to be something I liked," says Monje.

He began officiating hardwood high school games in 1965 and by 1972 was working on the collegiate level in upstate New York. He was promoted from Division III to Division I in 1980. Monje's primary conference at the Division I level is the Big East. He worked the 1991 Big East tournament title game, as well as the 1992 conference title games in the Metro Atlantic and Patriot League.

Monje has officiated numerous postseason NCAA and National Invitational Tournament contests, but the top moment in his career came in March 1996, when he was selected to call the Arkansas-North Carolina semifinal game at the NCAA Division I tourney.

"It is without question the highlight of my officiating career. To be in the Final Four environment was something special that I will never forget."

For 30 years Monje has worked as a physical education teacher at Rush-Henrietta High School in Rochester, New York. He encounters few problems in juggling his full schedule.

"On an average week, I'll work about four games. I have to travel by plane a lot because I work in the Atlantic 10, Big East, Big Ten, Southeast, Patriot, and Metro Atlantic conferences, and that takes me to eastern and central portions of the United States. I have to be at games about an hour and a half before the tip-off to go over things with the guys that will be calling the game with me."

As for the stress of officiating college basketball games, Monje says, "You have to hear out players and coaches, but you don't have to listen to them. If a play happens so quickly that I kick a call, I'll admit it, but you can only do that so many times before you start to lose your credibility."

FOOTBALL OFFICIAL

In all, seven officials work a game, each with his own job. The referee, who stands about 10 yards behind the quarterback, is the final authority on the rules and gives signals on penalties.

The umpire, positioned five yards behind the defensive line, is responsible for watching for scrimmage line violations.

The head linesman stands on the sideline at one end of the scrimmage line. He marks where the ball is to be placed after each play and keeps track of the downs and the yards needed for a first down.

The line judge stands opposite the head linesman and is the official timekeeper. The back judge, side judge, and field judge all stand downfield watching for penalties on pass plays.

FLAGMEN WORKING

If a football player breaks the rules, a penalty is called by an official. The official signals this by throwing a flag made of yellow cloth into the air. Teams that commit penalties are punished with a loss of yardage and, in some cases, the loss of a down.

Most penalties occur during a play. When the play ends, the official announces what the penalty is and gives the team that has not committed the violation the choice of accepting or declining the penalty. If the penalty yardage is more than the yards gained on the play, the team will usually accept.

Some common penalty calls are *holding, offsides, pass interference,* and *clipping.* Holding is called against a blocker who uses his hands to grab an opponent. It results in a 10-yard loss from the spot of the infraction. Offsides is called when a player crosses the line of scrimmage before the ball is snapped. It is a 5-yard penalty, and the offensive team gets to repeat the down. If a pass receiver is bumped, pushed, or tackled while attempting to catch the ball, pass interference is called. This is a costly penalty because the offense gets the ball and a first down at the spot of the foul. Clipping is a 15-yard penalty for an illegal, below the waist block from behind.

MOONLIGHTING

The National Football League is unique in that it does not employ full-time officials. Each of the 112 officials employed by the NFL hold regular jobs during the week, ranging from high school teachers to research scientists and from service center owners to CEOs. These men are professionals both on and off the football field.

There are several factors that weigh against hiring full-time officials. The officials would only be working 16 to 20 days a year. What would they do on their 345 days off? Also, the NFL has 112 officials—would football team owners want to pay the $75,000 to $200,000 that major league baseball umpires make?

The NFL goes to great lengths to ensure the quality of their officials. A job candidate must have 10 years of experience, including at least five years in intercollegiate football. But don't bother sending unsolicited applications. "If somebody is worthy of working for us, we'll go after him," says Jerry Seeman, the league's director of officiating and himself a former NFL ref with 16 years on-field experience.

The NFL has 50 scouts who scour the college ranks, the World League of American Football, the Canadian Football League, and the Arena

Football League looking to recruit the best officials. Each fall the scouts keep close tabs on about 150 candidates. That number is whittled to 15 in the off-season. The recruits are then interviewed by a committee, subjected to a series of psychological tests, and drilled on the rules of the game.

From the group of 15 candidates, the league usually hires six new whistle-blowers each year to replace retiring officials and the few who are fired. The pay is generous. In the regular season zebras earn $1,325 to $4,000 per game, depending on experience. Playoff games pay $9,800 and the Super Bowl, $11,900. The weekly travel benefits include first-class airfare, classy hotels and a per diem of $205. Upon retirement officials receive a pension of $150 a month for each year of service, provided that they have worked at least 10 years.

Veteran officials must take two extensive written exams every year and are given weekly quizzes during the season. Also, each game is videotaped and reviewed by the NFL officiating department. This department consists of the NFL's director of officiating, Jerry Seeman (a former official) and his nine assistants. The department then sends back to the officials edited tapes with voiceovers describing their good calls and bad calls. It is these evaluations that determine how long you will survive in the NFL.

NFL officials have their own off-season clinics and visit football training camps to work on mechanics and techniques.

TIMES CHANGE

In big-time college football, the pressure to win has outlasted the personal integrity of officials. Consider the following two examples which occured 50 years apart.

In November 1940, Dartmouth played host to Cornell. With less than two minutes to go and Dartmouth ahead 3-0, Cornell had the ball at the Dartmouth six-yard line. The Indians held for three straight downs, and Cornell inadvertantly committed a delay of game penalty. Walter Scholl of the Big Red then failed to connect on a pass into the end zone, and with six seconds left, Dartmouth fans began celebrating. Referee Red Friesell, however, signaled that one more down remained. Scholl then completed another end-zone pass for a touchdown and the win.

After reviewing game films, Friesell, who had gotten confused by the penalty, recognized his gaffe and formally apologized to Dartmouth. His admission of error, though, did not alter the score. Only when Cornell's president, athletic director, and coach agreed that such a victory was not worth keeping did the score go down in the record books as a 3-0 win for Dartmouth.

A similar mixup occurred in October 1990 when national co-champion-to-be Colorado used a fifth down against Missouri to score a touchdown for a come-from-behind victory with two seconds left. The Big 8 Conference, however, refused to reverse the game's outcome, and Colorado declined to relinquish the victory.

REAL-LIFE ADVICE

Duke Carroll,
NFL official

"I began officiating on the high school and small-fry level about 18 years ago," Carroll says. "I had thought about it for a while, and then a friend who officiated encouraged me to start. I fell in love with it from the beginning."

Carroll spent his first six years as an official in the Elmira, New York area. After five seasons of Division II and III games, he moved to the Division I-AA scene, which includes schools in the Ivy and Patriot Leagues.

From there he applied to the World Football League in 1990, but as luck would have it the league folded that same year he sent his resume to the head office. On the positive side, the WFL forwarded his application to the NFL.

After five years of waiting, a full psychological evaluation, an extensive background check, and a rejection for the 1994 season after making the final cut, Carroll received a phone call that let him know he would be entering the NFL ranks.

"Officiating takes me out of the office less than I thought it would," says Caroll, the president of MacNamara-Carroll Insurance Company, which has upstate New York offices in Elmira and Corning. "For a Sunday game, the NFL requires the officials to be in the city in which the game is being played by noon on Saturday. So in most cases I would work in Elmira from Monday morning until Friday afternoon and then leave for my destination on either Friday evening or Saturday morning.

"The hardest thing about being an NFL official is that we're under a lot of pressure. There are 8 to 15 cameras on the game at all times, so you know that at least one of those cameras is on you. If a play is in your area, you'd better be ready to make the correct call.

"Players and coaches also get in your ear about calls that you make. Obviously, I'm going to make someone very happy and someone very upset with every call I make. If someone has a gripe, at the next dead-ball situation, I will go over to that person and give him an answer. It might not be the answer he wants, but at least I communicated with him and that's basically what they want."

ADDRESS BOOK

National Association of Sports Officials
2017 Lathrop Avenue
Racine, WI 53405
414/632-8855

National Federation of Interscholastic Officials Association
11724 Plaza Circle
Kansas City, MO 64195
816/464-5400

BASEBALL UMPIRE

"They expect an umpire to be perfect on opening day and to improve as the season goes on."—Nestor Chylak, former American League umpire.

Despite the wearisome travel and often abusive treatment from fans and players, umpiring is a respectable and desirable vocation. But the odds against becoming a major leaguer are far greater for umpires than for players. Competition is keen, as normally only one or two positions are available each year. There's very little turnover because umpires love their job, they're well paid, and they've put in too much time and effort to quit.

Like the players themselves, umpires must pay their dues in the minor leagues. However, just reaching the minors can be an arduous task. To begin your career, interested individuals must apply to the Major League Umpire Development Program. In addition to good eyesight and communication skills, candidates are required to possess a high school diploma in order to apply. If accepted, you'll then undergo a five-week program at an umpire training school.

The three schools that are accredited by baseball's Umpire Development Program are the Brinkman-Froemming Umpire School, the Harry Wendelstedt School for Umpires, and Jim Evans' Academy of Professional Umpiring. Each school offers a five-week course beginning in January. Tuition costs around $1,500, but the actual price is more like $3,000 with additional expenses such as room and board, meals, taxes, and insurance.

After graduation, the best of the lot are chosen to attend the Umpire Development Program, which evaluates their ability and further prepares them for the long trip ahead. The lucky few then proceed to Class A minor league rookie ball, where their work is carefully monitored, scrutinized, and rated against one another. Top umpiring candidates are then promoted to Double A and Triple A leagues. Excellent young umpires may remain in the minors for at least 10 years before being considered major league material.

DIAMOND NOTES

A minor league umpire starts his career earning $1,700 a month and that pay scale rises to $3,100 a month at the Triple A level. In the big leagues, the range increases significantly, from $75,000 in an umpire's first year to $225,000 after 30 years. In addition, major league umpires earn extra money by working prestigious events. An umpire nets an extra $5,000 for working an All-Star Game, $12,500 for a wild-card playoff series, $15,000 for a league championship series, and $17,500 for the World Series.

There are only 64 major league baseball umpires in the world, 32 in each league. Due to the exclusivity of their number and the nature of their job, they live lives that bear little resemblance to our own. The pressure on an umpire to be perfect is enormous. "We have to not let the pressure ruin our lives," says Harry Wendelstedt, who, with 30 years of service through 1995, is the dean of all active major league umps. "We do that by preparing well. We have to have a knowledge of the rules and we have to learn how to perform."

An umpiring crew consists of four umpires, led by the senior member who is called the crew chief. During a regular season game, one umpire works behind home plate calling balls and strikes, and one umpire is stationed at each of the three bases to decide if runners are safe or out. During the All-Star Game and all postseason games, two extra umpires are needed: one to work the right-field foul line and one to work the left-field foul line.

The four men work and travel together as a unit throughout the season, and some crews may stay intact for years. These umpiring crews evolve into a small family. The ballplayers enjoy home games, but an umpire is always on the road. Umpires are constantly on the move from city to city between games.

And unlike the players, umpires are completely on their own. They book their own flights. They reserve their own hotel rooms. They carry their own equipment. As Marty Springstead, a former American League umpire and now the league's executive director of umpiring, explains, "It's a very strenuous life. You move every three days. You go from series to series with very little time off."

While all umpires face great pressures, to be sure, the home plate umpire realizes stress on every pitch. There may be 300 pitches made during an average game. That's 300 split-second decisions that the home plate umpire must make regarding a ball that's speeding toward his face at 90 miles per hour. To limit the stress, umpires rotate their assignments for each game. The home plate umpire moves to third base, the third base ump to second, second to first, and first to home.

Prior to each game, the umpire scheduled to work behind home plate prepares 60 baseballs with, of all things, mud. This process helps take some of the shine off a new ball, and it also provides pitchers with a slightly better grip. The umpire rubs the balls with Lena Blackburne Baseball Rubbing Mud, which is found only at a secret location on the Delaware River in New Jersey. This particular goo apparently doesn't dirty the ball as much as other types of mud.

GIVE 'EM THE THUMB

"When I'm right, no one remembers. When I'm wrong, no one forgets," says Doug Harvey, former National League umpire

An umpire has done his job well if nobody notices him. These self-assured individuals must be thick-skinned and able to walk away from confrontation. Fans come to the ballpark to watch the players perform; not to see an umpire defend his reputation. Recent criticism leveled at the men in blue concern their lack of tolerance. Arguments between frustrated players and umpires—and managers and umpires—are as old as the game itself. But where should an umpire draw the line?

Major league baseball's umpire development program recommends instant ejection in three cases: arguing balls and strikes, getting personal in an argument, and physical contact.

Former American League umpire Ron Luciano made the following observations about the subjective nature of ejections in his book *Strike Two*:

"The object is to throw out the right people at the right time, and that is not as easy as it sounds. Ejecting that first player is very traumatic because you feel you've lost control, but the 40th man is simple—by that point you don't care. Throwing people out of a game is like learning to ride a bike—once you get the hang of it, it can be a lot of fun.

"Eventually, most umpires draw a line in their mind, and any player or manager who goes over the line gets ejected. It can be a curse word, a motion, an offensive nickname. The important thing is to establish that line, let the managers and players know what it is, and be consistent.

"For example, anyone who mentioned my weight was gone. 'Fatso' was the key word, but it got so that any word starting with 'fa' was close enough."

LADY IN BLUE

Clearly, the deck is stacked against female umpires. They are subjected to far more abuse from fans, players, and managers than their male counterparts, whose daily routine isn't exactly a day at the beach in the first place.

Pam Postema, who had hoped to become the major leagues' first female umpire, was released in 1989 after seven years of umpiring in Triple A. "I still think I can do the job as well as anybody," Postema said after her release. "I don't want to brag, but if I couldn't make it, I don't see how any woman can." At last knowledge, Postema was driving a truck for United Parcel Service.

Theresa Cox made her debut in 1989 in the Arizona Rookie League and is baseball's only remaining female umpire. "I was pulling for Pam, but I guess that won't be. But if and when I make it [to the majors], I'll know it's been easier because of her."

SPOTLIGHT

Bill Klem,
former major leage umpire

Hall of Fame arbiter Bill Klem umpired in the National League for a record 36 years (1905-40) and for 16 of those seasons worked every game behind the plate (instead of rotating with base umpires). He popularized emphatic hand signals to indicate strikes and fair and foul balls, as well as the use of the inside chest protector, and the posture of calling pitches from just behind the catcher's shoulder. He drew a line in the dirt when players argued with him; one step over meant automatic ejection.

To him, baseball was nothing less than a religion, and he worshipped at its altar. It was Klem who uttered the immortal words, "It ain't nothin' until I call it," and who summed up his dedication to the art of umpiring when he said, "I never missed a call in my heart."

SPOTLIGHT

Harry Wendelstedt,
major league umpire

Harry Wendelstedt has been umpiring major league baseball games for almost half his life. The 59-year-old Florida resident has been settling disputes for 31 seasons, making him the most senior umpire in baseball, and one of the game's most respected mediators.

After attending Essex Community College and the University of Maryland (where he played baseball), Wendelstedt decided on a career as an umpire. He began his decade-long journey through the ranks of the Georgia-Florida, Northwest, Texas, and International Leagues. In 1966, he became a regular member of the National League umpiring crew.

Now a crew chief, Wendelstedt has worked four All-Star Games, eight League Championship Series, and four World Series. He also served four terms as President of the Major League Umpire Association. During the off-season, he is the owner-operator of an umpire school in Florida that bears his name.

ADDRESS BOOK

Umpire Development Office
201 Bayshore Drive S.E.
St. Petersburg, Florida 33731
813/823-1286

Brinkman-Froemming
Umpire School
1021 Indian River Drive
Cocoa, FL 32922
407/639-1515

Harry Wendelstedt School
for Umpiring
88 South St. Andrews Drive
Ormond Beach, FL 32174
904/672-4879

Jim Evans' Academy of
Professional Umpiring
12885 Research Boulevard
Austin, TX 78750
512/335-5959
(Course conducted in
Kissimmee, Florida)

STRANGE BUT TRUE

Umpires began using hand signals for "strike," "out," "safe," and other calls in the 1890s. The signals were created for outfielder William "Dummy" Hoy, who was deaf and unable to hear an umpire's call.

HOCKEY OFFICIAL

Most ice hockey rinks are 200 feet long. If you can skate the length of the ice 400 times a game, while eluding a hard rubber puck traveling 80 miles per hour, have we got a job for you. But your skin had better be as thick as the puck is hard.

As stated before, the best officiated games in any sport are the ones in which the referees go unnoticed. National Hockey League officials are about as inconspicuous as the Goodyear blimp.

Just in case an irate fan doesn't know whom he's screaming at, the league, until recently, put the names of the officials on the backs of their jerseys, contrary to the practice in all other sports, which identify them by means of numbers. However, this practice was stopped a couple of seasons ago.

"We used to have numbers," says Scotty Morrison, the NHL's chief of officiating from 1965 to 1986, "but it was always assumed that the referee with the lowest number was our top guy, and the one with number 35 was a rookie. So we decided to identify them [by name], and the response was immediately favorable." Indeed, in no other sport are spectators so conscious of the officials and their respective reputations.

Play is watched by two linesmen and a referee. The two linesmen call illegal passes and offsides, while the referee rules on goals and calls penalties. In no other sport are referees charged so much with the responsiblity of who wins and loses.

All players who receive penalties must leave the ice and sit in the penalty box. A player serving a minor penalty, such as tripping or slashing, can return immediately if the opposing team scores a goal. Five-minute major penalties are given to players who try to injure an opponent. These penalties include unnecessary roughness and fighting. All five minutes must be served no matter how many goals the opponent scores.

The National Hockey League officiating department scours the amateur ranks and selects prospects it wishes to train. These amateurs are moved into the professional minor leagues and are closely monitored. The best minor league officials are given temporary NHL assignments, where they are evaluated and, hopefully, signed to a pro contract. The process may take five to ten years.

Hockey Officials Skate by Nicely

The 43 referees and linesmen employed by the NHL work close to 70 regular-season games. The sliding pay scale for NHL officials ranges from $50,000 to $80,000 during the first four years of service, and from $80,000 to $125,000 after 10 years. The most senior referees can earn an annual salary of $175,000.

Longevity, and consequently experience, is a concern. "I'd love to have guys on our staff with 25 years' experience," says Morrison. "But in hockey the demands are so strenuous that our officials are retiring at about 45 years old. Beyond that they just can't keep up with the play."

Even if you never learned to ice skate, take heart, there are jobs available. An off-ice official is stationed in each of two penalty boxes to release a penalized player from jail at the appropriate time. You can also become one of the two goal judges who activates a red light when a puck crosses over the goal line.

SUCCESS STORY

Ian "Scotty" Morrison,
chairman, Hockey Hall of Fame

A native of Montreal, Quebec, Morrison played junior hockey in the Montreal Canadiens organization during the days of Dickie Moore, Jean Beliveau, and Boom Boom Geoffrion. After his playing career ended, he turned to officiating in the Quebec Senior League.

In 1952 he was signed by the Western Hockey League, and two years later, NHL referee-in-chief Carl Voss signed him to an NHL contract. At 24, Morrison became the youngest referee in league history. He replaced Voss as referee-in-chief in 1965 and retained that title until 1981, when he was appointed an officer of the league and named vice president of officiating.

In 1986, NHL president John Ziegler promoted Morrison to the position of vice president, project development, and president of hockey's Hall of Fame. In this new post, Morrison was responsible for securing a future site for the new Hall of Fame in Toronto, which opened in 1993. Two years before its doors opened to the public, Morris was named to his current post as chairman.

SPORTS TURF SPECIALIST

What's the difference between a sports turf specialist and a groundskeeper? A sports turf specialist owns a college degree and is employed by a fancy country club. A groundskeeper borrows a rake and labors in the school yard. The difference is your perspective because both love their job.

The groundskeeper is responsible for the condition of the playing field. The job starts long before the game begins and ends long after the spectactors have gone home. In some instances, the grounds crew may be requested to redesign the field overnight for another sporting event to take place the next day.

The field is the players' stage. Without a proper stage, the players cannot perform. Similarly, the field is the groundskeepers' canvas. The artistry of the field can be elaborate or simple, depending on the sport.

When preparing for a football game, the groundskeepers paint the yard lines and hash marks on the field, as well as stencil the team and conference logos in the end zone. Prior to a baseball game, the groundskeepers smooth the infield dirt, water the base paths, and mark the baselines and batter's box. At the game's midpoint, the crew drags the infield dirt and replaces the used bases with new ones.

Individuals work under the supervision of the head groundskeeper. This person is expected to make sure that the design of the field conforms to league specifications and is completed on time and within the budget set by the team owner.

Once a field is readied for play and the game begins, the grounds crew must remain poised to respond to inclement weather. Only the head official can signal for a delay of the game. Should this be the case, the groundskeepers will unroll a plastic tarpolin atop the field to protect it. When the weather clears up, the grounds crew will be given the okay to remove the tarpolin by rolling it back up. The crew then begins to once again prepare the field for play. This may involve pouring and raking fresh dirt, or squeegying water off artificial turf.

In addition to keeping the field lush during the season, groundskeepers may also be required to spruce up the stadium during the off-season. During this time, it's not uncommon for the grounds crew to act as maintainence workers: painting the bleacher seats, polishing the bulbs on the scoreboard, or fixing a speaker in the public address system.

Talented groundskeepers can transform a gridiron or diamond into a field of dreams. George Toma, 67, is the National Football League's groundskeeper extraordinaire. As the NFL's turf supervisor, he has been in charge of the playing fields for all 31 Super Bowls and every Pro Bowl game.

A groundskeeper, Toma insists, isn't just someone who cuts grass. "I'm a doctor. When the grass gets sick, I'm a pharmacist preparing chemicals; I'm a dietician, prescribing the right food, adding minerals like iron and zinc; I'm a weatherman—I've got to know when to water and when not to water."

THE EMPLOYMENT LANDSCAPE

Groundskeepers will find employment opportunities all around the country. Wherever sports take place, there are playing fields. And all playing fields require the services of a groundskeeper.

A sports turf specialist, however, must know the difference between Kentucky bluegrass and Adelphi. Interested individuals should pursue their agricultural studies at a college with an agronomy department. Basic courses include soil science, plant pathology, entomology, and inorganic chemistry. The Sports Turf Managers Association is an excellent source for seeking a scholarship.

While a degree in agriculture will not guarantee a job as a groundskeeper, it is recommended. "We have more job offers than graduates," says professor Tom Watschke, head of Penn State's turf management program. Individuals participating in these programs will develop contacts and obtain training and hands-on experience.

Toma first developed his enviable green thumb while still attending Edwardsville (Pa.) High School. By pulling the drag around the infield after school and on weekends, Toma found himself in the right place at the right time. When Bill Veeck bought the Cleveland Indians in 1946, he traveled to Pennsylvania to reorganize the Wilkes-Barre Barons, a Cleveland farm club in the Class A Eastern League. Veeck promoted the head groundskeeper to team trainer and put the inexperienced 17-year-old Toma in charge."I didn't know bluegrass from rye grass," Toma admits.

For more than a decade, Toma was a minor league groundskeeper, kicking around in the Cleveland and Detroit organizations, tending fields in Buffalo, New York and Charleston, West Virginia. It wasn't glamorous work.

"When you're a groundskeeper in the minors," he says, "you're almost alone." Toma had to clear litter from under the bleachers, clean the dugouts and dust the press box. For some clubs he ran the ball and strike lights on the scoreboard, and in Wilkes-Barre he even pitched batting practice to young prospects.

In 1957 Toma was offered the job in Kansas City's Municipal Stadium. He cut the Bermuda to half an inch and dragged the infield with obsessive care. The results were beautiful. The field looked like an oasis in the desert. "I don't think we had a bad hop all year," Toma says with pride. "We had a pool table outfield and a pool table infield."

Dedication is the key ingredient to promotion. At Toma's first head job, his crews at Municipal Stadium were younsters who grew up in the shadow of the ball park. With a big game coming up and rain in the forecast, Toma's kids would sleep at the park, ready to cover the field with a tarp when thundershowers hit. "I don't think you'll find that [kind of dedication] anymore," Toma says.

GROWTH PROSPECTS

Groundskeepers who are talented, creative, determined, and lucky can advance their careers in a number of ways. Advancement opportunities for groundskeepers depend to a great extent on where the individual is on the career ladder. A head groundskeeper at a college might move up to that same position for a minor league team. A great achievement in this field is to become the head groundskeeper for a major league grounds crew.

Head groundskeepers who are already established can get ahead by becoming a consultant. When another franchise is burdened with dead grass, a rocky infield, or a water-logged outfield, the groundskeeper can rent out his or her skills as an athletic turf troubleshooter.

Toma's greatest rescue mission occured late in the 1981 NFL season. The soon-to-be Super Bowl champion San Francisco 49ers were almost unable to play football in Candlestick Park. Two weeks of record rainfall had caused disastrous mudslides in northern California. The 49ers' home field was a sloppy mess when Toma arrived on the scene. "When I left San Francisco, the grounds crew showered me with gifts," Toma says. "I got a plaque from the city. They called me the Sod God."

In professional sports, where the difference between winning and losing translates into dollar signs, the home field advantage is an important edge. When seeking a job at the pro level, the groundskeeper who can be devious with the field will have a leg up on the competition. Any team worth its salt will seek to employ an individual who can make use of all the little tricks of partisan groundskeeping.

Toma calls this practice "groundskeeping by deceit," and as the head groundskeeper for the Kansas City Athletics from 1956 to 1967, he was one of the masters. If the Kansas City third baseman couldn't field, the grass in front of him was slanted to make balls go foul. If the fielders were slow, the grass was grown higher. If the pitcher threw a sinker, a little extra hosing in front of the plate was helpful. If the other team could run, he'd pour sand around first base to ensure bad footing.

One of Toma's favorite stories involves Ted Williams, the great Boston Red Sox hitter. Williams liked the batter's box to have clay mixed into the dirt, which enabled him to dig his spikes in and really get a toehold. When Williams came to Kansas City and asked for more clay in the batter's box, what did Toma give him? "Pure sand," Toma says with a grin.

WHERE THE GRASS IS GREENER

It is imperative to a career in this field that individuals have personal experience in making grass grow. Toma is best known for growing grass. From 1958 to 1972, Kansas City's Municipal Stadium, which Toma maintained, was a turf mecca. The story is told that former New York Jets coach Weeb Ewbank surveyed the Municipal turf before one Saturday afternoon workout and announced, "This field looks too beautiful to practice on," and made his team work out on the sidelines.

On the football practice field, Toma often throws rye-grass seed out in the middle of the field before practice. He calls this technique "cleating in." "The players are your equipment," he says. "They push the seed into the field with their cleats."

When the Royals baseball team moved into a synthetic-surfaced stadium in 1972, Toma continued his growth as a sports-turf specialist by conducting experiments on every patch of natural turf allotted to him. At Royals Stadium, the bull pens are natural grass. The right-field bullpen is Derby rye mixed with zoysia. The rye grass provides color in the spring and fall, when zoysia is dormant. The left-field bullpen serves as a trial plot for Hound Dog, a tall fescue, that Toma is testing for durability.

He has a calendar on his bulletin board on which he keeps daily records for his field: every seeding, every watering, every application of chemicals, plus a daily weather record, taken from his own instruments, is noted.

Toma pours over trade journals, always on the lookout for new techniques and new strains of grass. He attends turf management conferences, and when grass won't grow the way he wants it to, he consults top agronomists from a dozen universities, specialists in pesticides, herbicides, and soil management. "That's the trouble with groundskeepers today," he says. "They don't want to go to the agronomists for help."

THE REAL GREEN

Factors affecting earnings include the groundskeeper's experience, expertise, and professional reputation. Other determining factors include the geographic location, type of field, and prestige of the team's venue. Individuals may be paid a straight fee for each game they work, or they may receive a salary for the year-round upkeep of the field.

The head groundskeeper for a minor league baseball field usually earns about $20,000 a year. The crew members are often students from local high schools who earn an hourly minimum wage. The head grounds-keeper at a major league park can earn about $150,000, or "about what a good plumber makes," according to Frankie Albohn, the former Yankee Stadium turfmeister.

Toma, for his part, would rather not divulge his earnings. "People think I make a fortune," he says, "but there's no money in it." Instead, Toma prefers to discuss the lack of respect afforded his profession.

"If someone in the front office needs a new typewriter, they get it," says Toma. "But if the groundskeeper needs a new lawn mower, he can't get it. Unless something happens, like if the owner has a doubleheader sold out and it's raining. They get jumpy. Suddenly they'll do anything. They'll rent a helicopter to dry off the field! But they won't spend money on the sunny day for good drainage. The groundskeeper is the dirt of the organization."

STRANGE BUT TRUE

The weirdest memorabilia request ever came after Super Bowl XXX when NFL turf supervisor George Toma gave Cowboy running back Emmitt Smith a patch of Sun Devil Stadium grass—and Smith asked Toma to sign it. Toma autographed the sod in white spray paint. "Sweet!" Smith said. "I want you to take care of my lawn."

"You're second in line," Toma said. "Bo Jackson keeps bugging me to do his."

SIDELINE

An increase in the number of golf courses has created bright prospects for jobs relating to golf course maintenance. Some 40 universities, like Penn State and the University of Maryland, offer a turf management pro-gram. Scholarships for turf management–minded students are available by contacting the Golf Course Superintendents Association of America.

This association provides services for students who intend to make their career in the golf industry. After graduating with a bachelor's degree, an individual may become an assistant golf course superintendent with a starting salary of about $25,000. A golf course superintendent makes in the range of $70,000 to $120,000.

ADDRESS BOOK

Golf Course Superintendents Association of America
1421 Research Park Drive
Lawrence, Kansas 66049
913/841-2240

Sports Turf Managers Association
P.O. Box 809119
Chicago, Illinois 60680
312/644-6610

Careers in Team Admin- istration

F ront office management is one of the most highly sought-after positions in the sports industry. Most franchises have positions for between 25 and 50 employees. This includes the front office personnel as well as the administrative support staff.

As of this writing, the four major sports leagues consist of 112 teams: 30 in the National Football League, 29 in the National Basketball Association, 28 in major league baseball, and 26 in the National Hockey League.

Doing the math optimistically, that translates to about 3,500 total jobs available nationwide at the major league level. Of course, this number is increased when including teams in related leagues or minor leagues.

In baseball, for instance, there are three classes of minor leagues, from Triple A to Single A; in football, there is the World League of American Football, the Arena Football League, and the Canadian Football League; in basketball, the Continental Basketball Association and the United States Basketball League; in hockey, the International Hockey League and the American Hockey League.

Team administration is a prestigious and high-profile career, and thus one of the most difficult areas to break into. But there are positions for a select few individuals who demonstrate the dedication and perseverance it takes to reach the front office. The rewards for the grueling hours and moderate pay can be a fast-paced and satisfying career.

The front office draws from a talent pool of individuals with a wide range of knowledge in the areas of player development, ticket sales, travel schedules, community relations, and equipment purchases. All these people play an important role in the success of the sports franchise.

TEAM PRESIDENT

The president of a sports franchise is the team's chief executive. Since sports is big business, the individual must possess the same managerial skills and corporate qualifications that are required of any Fortune 500 company president.

The sports team president is responsible for the overall financial well-being of the franchise. The person in this job will oversee many departments within the entire organization, including marketing, sponsorship, ticket sales, advertising, accounting, public relations, and community relations.

The president's main function is to increase paid attendance. By drawing fans to the stadium, the team will ultimately profit. Revenue will be generated through ticket sales and other turnstile-related activities, like selling concessions and souvenirs. In addition, sold-out arenas can translate into higher broadcasting rights and more lucrative licensing fees.

"We're in the business of entertainment," says Susan O'Malley, president of the NBA's Washington Bullets. "Our job is to make sure that people who buy tickets have a fun time and are treated as guests in our building. If they're treated right, they'll probably come back again."

PUTTING FANNIES IN THE SEATS

As part of this function, the president will formulate a strategy to encourage fans to attend games. If the team is winning, the job is relatively simple. But if the team is struggling on the field, putting fannies in the seats can be an exciting challenge.

The president must have experience in marketing and promotions in order to design special events that encourage fans to come out to the ballpark. Give-away promotions like cap day and poster night are popular, however, these singular events address only one-time attendees.

The president's main job encompasses cultivating more long-term support from within the community. This involves securing affluent corporate fans who purchase season tickets and luxury suites, also known as sky-boxes. Luxury boxes are an important additional revenue source, commanding as much as $250,000 per season. These potential corporate customers are often discovered when the team president gives speeches or appears at functions on behalf of the organization. To this end, the president will be expected to develop a strong and positive public image.

THE GREAT O'MALLEY

When Susan O'Malley was appointed president of the Washington Bullets in 1991, she became the first woman to head an NBA franchise—at the age of 29. Her distinction as one of the highest ranking women in sports is an advantage on the banquet circuit. O'Malley is in great demand as a speaker throughout the Washington, D.C./Baltimore area. "People never expect to see a five-foot-tall woman walk in and represent a basketball team," she says.

It's been a meteoric rise to the top of the organization for the talented Maryland native. "I've always wanted to do this," says O'Malley, now 34. In junior high school, O'Malley received a B-plus grade on an essay she wrote about what she wanted to be when she grew up—head of a pro sports team. "My teacher said it was good," O'Malley says, "but not very realistic."

She concedes that family connections helped her get in the door. Abe Pollin, the team's owner, is a close friend of O'Malley's father, Peter, who was president of the NHL's Washington Capitals. "I got the job because my father was good friends with Abe Pollin," she says. "But I like to think I moved up the ladder because of my own accomplishments."

O'Malley graduated in 1983 from St. Mary's (Md.) College, where she got a bachelor's degree in business and finance. She worked for an advertising firm for three years, then joined the Bullets during the 1986-87 season as director of advertising. Her duties included the development of new advertising campaigns, as well as placement and exposure of existing campaigns. One year later she was bumped up to director of marketing, and in 1988 was named executive vice president.

As the team's executive vice president for two seasons, O'Malley saw her philosophy of proactive service to the customer bear strong results. Her nurturing of season ticket holders, combined with her savvy marketing experience, has had a huge payoff: soaring attendance.

In her first season at the helm, the team experienced the largest ticket revenue year in the history of the franchise. In addition, the club achieved the highest renewal rate of season tickets ever by a Bullets franchise, which includes the year following the 1977-78 championship season.

HOW DOES SHE DO IT?

For years, mediocre teams like the Bullets relied on giveaways and other promotions to boost attendance at games against other laggards. But O'Malley decided to actively promote games against high-profile teams and make them sellouts.

As the Bullets increased their number of sellouts, fans were encouraged to purchase "ten packs"—tickets for the most popular 10 games of the season—to ensure not missing out on the big ones. During the 1994-95 season, the Bullets set a record with 20 sellouts in 42 home dates. The sellouts, in turn, prompted others to buy season tickets. At the time, O'Malley's decision to promote already popular matchups was ground-breaking in the NBA, but the strategy is now copied throughout the league.

When O'Malley took over, the season ticket renewal rate was a dismal 60 percent. To combat fan apathy, O'Malley started a monthly newsletter, initiated staff calls to ticket holders, sent holiday cards, and organized player receptions. Over the past five years, season ticket renewals have run at an average of 90 percent, an extraordinary figure for a team that finished the 1994-95 season with the NBA's second-worst record.

According to published reports, the Bullets lost about $4 million in the 1987-88 season before O'Malley took over. By the end of the 1994-95 season, the team earned about $1.5 million on revenues of about $33 million. Radio revenue alone is up 68 percent since O'Malley brought production in-house and seized internal control of advertising sales.

Now team owner Abe Pollin has put O'Malley in charge of raising revenue for the new $180 million arena he's planning to build in downtown Washington, D.C. The 23,000-seat arena is expected to open in time for the beginning of the 1997–98 Season. A state-of-the-art facility to draw fans, coupled with O'Malley's shrewd marketing strategies, should give the Bullets' owner a financial slam dunk.

SPOTLIGHT

Andy MacPhail,
president, Chicago Cubs

Andy MacPhail may have been destined for a successful career in major league baseball. His grandfather, Larry, who was elected to the Hall of Fame in 1978, won the 1941 National League pennant as general manager of the Brooklyn Dodgers and the 1947 World Series as the New York Yankees' chief executive. His father, Lee, was the general manager of the

Baltimore Orioles and Yankees; a special assistant to commissioner William Eckert; and the American League president who ruled that George Brett's pine-tar smudged home run should stand.

As a senior at Dickinson (Pa.) College, where he was a right fielder on the baseball team, Andy wrote letters to the 24 major league teams. After graduating in 1976, he landed a job as business manager of the Chicago Cubs' Bradenton rookie team in the Gulf Coast League. In 1977 he moved to Chicago as an assistant in the Cubs' parks operations department and joined the player development department the following year. He also held the titles of assistant director of player development and assistant director of scouting before leaving the Cubs in 1982. That year he became assistant general manager for the Houston Astros, a position he held until 1985, when the Twins hired him as the vice-president of player personnel. Prior to the 1987 season, at age 32, he was promoted to general manager.

The boy-wonder general manager won the World Series in his first year at Minnesota, and again in 1991. Two championships in five years is an amazing achievement for a small-market team. But the seasons in between proved difficult. When the team was playing poorly, the local press dubbed the young executive Andy MacFail.

"My father gave me a sense of perspective," says MacPhail, now 42. "If baseball becomes your sole focus, you can only expect life to be a rough roller coaster because that's how the game's designed. I try to read a lot of biographies, and my problems, compared with those [Winston] Churchill was facing in 1945, don't amount to anything. That's helpful when you're in last place, and people are writing that you shouldn't have your job."

In 1991, MacPhail was honored as major league Executive of the Year for his role in building the team that in one season went from last place to World Series champions. What makes MacPhail proudest about 1991 is that the Twins didn't make a trade all season. Three players were signed as free-agents prior to opening day; the organization's minor league system provided the rest. "In 1987, it was a mad scramble," says MacPhail. "In 1991, it was validation of a true baseball organization. I take more pride in 1991."

After nine years and two World Series championships with the Twins, he joined the Cubs as president in 1994. MacPhail's past success should follow him to Chicago, as will his principled approach to baseball management.

"The players can talk with me anytime about the state of the game, contracts, the Democratic candidates for President. The only thing I won't talk to them about is the lineup. Do that, you doom yourself. Everybody has full autonomy. The price they pay is full accountability."

SUCCESS STORY

Michael Rowe,
president, New Jersey Nets

Michael Rowe comes to the Nets with over 16 years experience working with the New Jersey Sports and Exposition Authority, the parent agency of the Meadowlands Sports Complex in East Rutherford, New Jersey.

After graduating from Seton Hall with a bachelor's degree in sociology and a master's in public administration from Rider College, Rowe served the state in Trenton from 1972 to 1979. While there he met Robert Mulcahy, who at the time was the governor's chief of staff. When the sports authority was organized in 1979, Mulcahy took Rowe along to help with the transition. Between 1979 and 1987, Rowe advanced from Mulcahy's assistant to the position of general manager, where he supervised 150 full-time and 2,500 part-time employees.

As general manager of Giants Stadium and Continental Arena for the past eight years, part of his duties was to participate in negotiations of leases with the Nets, Devils, Giants, Jets, college basketball, college football, World Cup soccer, and numerous special events, including rock concerts, papal visits, circuses, and ice shows.

Rowe, 46, has three times been named "facility manager of the year" by *Performance* magazine, a respected trade publication. It's the curious twist of his career path that he went from landlord at the sports authority to one of its tenants as the head of the Nets.

GENERAL MANAGER

The most important person in the front office is the general manager. He or she is responsible for handling all daily business activities of the team. Duties might include hiring and firing, promotion, supervising scouting, searching for a new arena site, making trades (presumably after consulting with the manager), and negotiating contracts with players.

All professional sports teams, from major leagues to minor leagues, employ a general manager. The main job function—to oversee all sports-related activities of the team—remains the same at each level. But general managers working with minor league teams may also be required to perform additional duties such as overseeing the souvenir booths or organizing the ticket office.

General managers of major league teams are responsible for the quality of the product. In sports this translates into fielding a successful and entertaining team. The individual is expected to accumulate a roster of quality players through shrewd trades, free-agent signings, and by drafting blue-chip prospects.

To accomplish this goal, the general manager must have a close working relationship with the department heads who fall under his or her supervision: scouting, player personnel development, minor league operations, and the coaching staff, to name just a few. The ability to surround yourself with qualified people, and the skill to tap into their knowledge, is a quality possessed by all who are successful in this field.

KNOW THE BUSINESS

A general manager of a professional team will be expected to have a complete understanding of the specific sport he or she is working in. Some general managers were athletes prior to obtaining a job within the organization. But athletic prowess is not a prerequisite for the position. What is necessary is astute business acumen.

A knowledge of business operations can only be acquired through experience. An individual may gain this experience by working in an administrative capacity at a lower level within the organization. Some current general managers began their career in scouting or player development, minor league operations, marketing or promotions, or business administration before earning the title of assistant general manager. The assistant general manager is instrumental in the negotiation of major league contracts as well as assisting in the daily operation of the major league team.

Another avenue of advancement toward becoming a GM is to serve the franchise as administrative assistant to the general manager. The individual in this position is instrumental in helping the general manager with the daily operation of the team. As in any corporate organization, paperwork can be an all-consuming proposition. The assistant is expected to oversee the administrative paperwork, allowing the GM to concentrate on a myriad of other responsiblities.

A BENGAL BUNGLE

In the sports business, personnel is a commodity to be bought, sold, and traded for. Whenever such a transaction takes place, the league office requires that proper forms be completed and filed on deadline. This function is performed by the assistant. The individual is expected to complete forms regarding player contracts, trades, personnel movement (such as minor league call-ups or demotions) waivers, disabled list, and releases.

To be sure, the completion of paperwork does not decide the winner of a pennant. But in 1988 the Detroit Tigers learned firsthand the importance of proper administration. Late in the season, the Tigers were in first place, but their lead over the Boston Red Sox in the American League's Eastern division grew tenuous. The Tigers had led the division longer than any other team, taking over first place on June 20, but with Kirk Gibson lost to free agency the year before, the team needed an additional offensive boost.

On August 31st, one day before the trading deadline, Detroit would acquire veteran outfielder Fred Lynn in a last-ditch effort to provide some sorely needed punch. Baseball rules specifically state that a player who is not on a team's 40-man roster by September 1st may not participate in the postseason.

Unfortunately, the Tigers' front office staff did not file the appropriate papers with the league office until a few minutes after midnight the next day. Because the Lynn paperwork reached the league office officially on September 2nd, had the Tigers qualified for the postseason, Lynn would not have been eligible to play in the playoffs or World Series. While Detroit finished the season in second place by one game, rendering the point moot, the team's embarassment was beyond dispute.

THE PAY-OFF

An individual who reaches the position of general manager will be well paid. Salaries range from around $50,000 a year at the minor league level to upwards of $1 million in the major leagues. General managers with a proven track record in the minors can advance their careers by moving up to the majors. Big league GMs can receive promotions in the form of job offers from more prestigious teams.

While a formal education is not required to become a general manager, a college degree is extremely helpful in this fiercely competitive field. Aspiring GM candidates who have a major in sports management will come in the door at a higher job level than applicants who don't. Other educational areas of importance include business administration, law, communications, and marketing.

EAT, SLEEP, AND DRINK SPORTS

General managers of major league teams are in a position of power and prestige. When the team is successful, the general manager will be applauded for his or her efforts. Conversely, the GM is forced to shoulder a heavy burden when a team performs poorly. The blame is not always justified. Many factors can inhibit the general manager's ability to carry out a strategic game plan.

The most significant hurdle faced by the general manager is the pressure created by financial constraints placed upon the office by the team owner and the league. In the face of escalating player salaries, the owner may hold the reins on the team's monetary budget for player and staff payroll. In addition, the salary cap currently imposed in basketball and football often severely limits the machinations available to a team's general manager.

The general manager works tirelessly to build a popular and successful team. The individual literally has no time off. A good GM must keep up-to-date on the activities of all players in the sport. This requires stamina and an intense drive to be the best. General managers need to be self-confident and possess the ability to make informed decisions quickly. For the lucky few, the reward is a championship.

A REAL DEAL

The New York Yankees' acquisition of Detroit Tiger slugger Cecil Fielder is an ideal example of the difficulties general managers face in wheeling and dealing for superstars. While there were preliminary discussions held with the Tigers, the trade for Fielder was consummated just hours before the July 31 midnight trading deadline.

"When you're talking about marquee players, these types of deals take time and usually get done in the winter," says Yankees general manager Bob Watson. "At first, it was just an inquiry."

But at 2 p.m. on July 31, Detroit general manager Randy Smith called Watson to ask if the Yankees were still interested in Fielder. The answer was a resounding yes. "The needs of a team can change very quickly," says Watson. "Randy called and we each agreed to put together a proposal."

Further complicating the process was the fact that Yankees owner George Steinbrenner was in Atlanta as part of his U.S. Olympic Committee duties. Yet, hours later, Steinbrenner gave his blessing to go ahead with more substantive talks.

Watson, along with assistant GM Brian Cashman, major league administrator Tom May, and baseball operations assistant Gene Keohane, ordered pizza and settled in for a long night. They discussed a variety of possible proposals, and came up with alternative counterproposals.

When the fax machine rang at 6:15, it was the Tigers making an offer. Watson and his crew mulled it over before arriving at an alternative of

Ruben Sierra, pitching prospect Matt Drews, and cash. The deal breaker would be convincing Fielder to rework his contract and defer salary.

But Fielder, who was playing a game that night, would be unavailable until after 11:00 p.m. So around 10:15, a proposal was sent to Fielder's agent, Bob Gilhooley. Less than an hour later the fax rang again, this time from Gilhooley, approving a $2 million deferment. With the approval of Steinbrenner and Tigers owner Mike Illitch, the deal was done.

TIPSHEET

- Attend a college or university that offers a degree in sports management. This core cirriculum is growing in popularity and is now offered at schools across the country.

- Try to obtain a college internship with a pro team at any level. This will provide a training ground and a wealth of contacts.

- Apply for any clerical or low-status job with a major league team. Get your foot in the door, keep your eyes and ears open, and learn the inner workings of an organization.

- Enroll in seminars and workshops to develop a network; join trade associations and sports-related organizations to gain insight and guidance from people working in the field.

REAL-LIFE ADVICE

Lou Lamoriello,
general manager, New Jersey Devils

Wayne Gretzky once called the New Jersey Devils "a Mickey Mouse organization." The franchise had indeed been the doormat of the National Hockey League. But the team's fortunes turned around as soon as Lamoriello was hired as general manager in 1987. He engineered a series of shrewd trades, astute draft picks, and free-agent signings. By 1995, Lamoriello had rebuilt the Devils into Stanley Cup champions.

personality sketch

Knowledge of sports; organized and supervisory; ability to handle stress; competent negotiator; good communication skills; detail-oriented; sound decision-maker.

He had come from a winning background at Providence College. In 15 seasons as hockey coach, the Friars compiled an impressive .578 winning percentage (248-179-13) and qualified for ten postseason tournaments, including a 1983 Final Four appearance in his last season.

He then spent five years as the school's athletic director. He was responsible for administration of 22 varsity teams and for the operation of all athletic facilities. Lamoriello's decision to hire Rick Pitino as head coach helped propel Providence's rise to national basketball prominence. The Friars made a memorable run in the 1987 NCAA tournament, reaching the Final Four in Lamoriello's last season before joining the Devils.

He was also a founder of the Hockey East Association and was elected commissioner of the seven-team league that, under his direction, became one of the most prestigious hockey conferences in the country.

Lamoriello was a member of Providence's varsity hockey and baseball teams as an undergraduate and served as assistant coach of both the hockey and baseball teams immediately following graduation.

"I don't believe that anyone should compete against anyone else, except when it's a team competing against another team collectively. I think you should compete against yourself to do the best you possibly can and to do what you think is right with the knowledge you have available and the people you surround yourself with. Because if you don't respect their knowledge and what they have to give, they shouldn't be there.

"The worst thing you can ever do is allow the media or the fans to influence your decisions. These are emotional people when it comes to what they critique, and I respect them tremendously. But if they influence your decision, then you're not making the right decision, because you're doing it for the wrong reasons.

"When I came to the Devils, people didn't give [the players] their due. I could not accept walking into the office and having people here who were used to losing, who were being satisfied with a good performance. It's something that's in my personality, but it's what I believe in. If you're going to do something, do it to the utmost degree you can. Then let the winning take care of itself."

SPOTLIGHT

David Dombrowski,
general manager, Florida Marlins

Dombrowski decided while attending Western Michigan that he wanted to be a baseball general manager. He had interviewed Chicago White Sox general manager Roland Hemond while doing research for a paper on the role of the general manager in baseball. Hemond had suggested he job-hunt at the winter meetings, held in Honolulu in December 1977.

Dombrowski, then a senior, rearranged his exam schedule so he could attend the meetings and flew to Waikiki at his own expense. When he returned to his hotel room after lying on the beach, he learned that the White Sox wanted to meet with him immediately.

"I was sandy, and in my cut-offs and asked if I could shower and change, but they said to come right away," Dombrowski says. He met with the team's director of baseball operations. "I told them I'd do anything," Dombrowski says. "I'd move cartons, shovel sidewalks, type. I just wanted to get my foot in the door."

Dombrowski was offered a job, but he still had one semester remaining at Western Michigan. "When I told my mother I wanted to take the job, she didn't talk to me for three days," says Dombrowski, the first in his family to attend college. Dombrowski agreed to a compromise; he would finish his accounting major by going to night school.

He accepted the job and immediately negotiated his first baseball contract, persuading the Sox to give him an $8,000 salary, one grand more than their intial offer. In January 1978 at age 21, he began his career as an administrative assistant in their minor league and scouting department. "I was a glorified gofer," says Dombrowski, now 40.

His first-year duties included everything from filing to making travel arrangements for spring training to operating the scoreboard to driving Bill Veeck, the team owner, home after games. Dombrowski handled every task thrown his way, worked well with others, and earned the respect of everyone in the organization.

The following year, 1979, he became assistant director of player development. By the spring of 1981 he had been promoted to director of player development, a position he held for less than a year before becoming assistant general manager at age 26.

As the right-hand man to general manager Roland Hemond, Dombrowski was responsible for administering all minor league operations and coordinating the team's scouting operations. He negotiated contracts and helped the general manager prepare for the draft.

A typical day began before 8 a.m., when he would meet with Hemond to look over the daily box scores and discuss other teams' players whom they might consider trading for. Upon arriving at Comiskey Park, Dombrowski listened to the tape-recorded reports phoned in by each of the Sox's minor league managers after the previous night's games. He kept extensive files on all Sox minor league personnel and blue-chip prospects in other organizations. After paying some minor league bills, he would meet with the scouts for a player evaluation meeting.

Dombrowski's star was rising like a comet. In 1986, the Montreal Expos hired him to oversee their minor league system, and by the following year he was promoted to assistant to the general manager. In 1988 he was named vice president of player personnel; at age 32, he was the youngest decision-maker in the major leagues. In 1990 the Expos made him their general manager. His dream had become reality.

In September of 1991, the expansion team Florida Marlins, who would join the National League in 1993, hired Dombrowski as executive vice president and general manager.

SPOTLIGHT

Ellen Harrigan,
assistant to the general manager, Baltimore Orioles

As the administrative assistant to the general manager, Harrigan is instrumental in helping Orioles' GM Pat Gillick with the daily operation of the team. She is well qualified for the position. Harrigan began her baseball career 15 years ago, and after rising up through the minor leagues, she's finally achieved her goal of reaching the majors.

"I wanted to get to the big leagues because that was my dream," says Harrigan, 33. "But I didn't want it to be because I'm a woman. I wanted it to be because I have the tools."

Harrigan earned membership into the old-boys club because she paid her dues. Hired in the early 1980s by the Toronto Blue Jays as a junior secretary, she was promoted through the ranks, and in 1990 she was appointed general manager of the St. Catharines (Ontario) Blue Jays.

In the world of baseball, hiring a female general manager was a radical move. Said Gord Ash, who at the time was Toronto's assistant general manager and Harrigan's boss, "A number of men who are general managers don't have playing experience and have done very well. What it takes to be a general manager at the major league level is determination and hard work and the ability to learn, and that is not defined by sex."

Even more revolutionary was the fact that Harrigan was presiding over the only all-female front office in professional sports. A short time after ascending to general manager, Harrigan brought in as assistant GM Marilyn Finn, who had been the promotions director of a local AM/FM station and cohost of a hard-rock morning show. The hiring of secretary Eleanor Bowman, whose son was the clubhouse manager, completed the formation of the all-female team.

From June through September, which are the months of the short-season Class A New York-Penn League, Harrigan and her staff worked from morning till midnight at Community Park in St. Catharines, a city on Ontario's Niagara Peninsula. Although she worked hard all day, Harrigan says her job really began by 6 p.m. on game night. That's when she would get busy organizing the 30 high school kids who ran the ticket office, concession stands, and souvenir booths.

Not until the seventh inning would she finally sit down for the first time all night. She was too busy supervising the souvenir stands, throwing delinquents who were sitting on the centerfield scoreboard out of the park, tasting new ice cream flavors, settling a shouting match between a husband and wife, and offering a fan a can of bug spray.

A key to Harrigan's success was her ability to be perceived as one of the guys. Players often asked her advice about girls. "I look at them as my little brothers," she says. "A lot of times they just ask me questions about dating."

But a six-foot-tall, red-haired Irish woman is still vulnerable to sexist Neanderthals, and Harrigan has encountered her share. There was the time in the St. Catharines clubhouse when a player strolled over to her without a towel on, just to see her reaction. "I looked him in the eye, answered his question, and pretended as if nothing happened," she says.

Harrigan has always displayed an ability to confront any problem with confidence and determination. Those are the traits that got her noticed with the Blue Jays, and she earned the respect of Toronto general manager Pat Gillick. When Gillick left Toronto, his assistant, Gord Ash, was bumped up to the general manager's office. And when Gillick landed in Baltimore with the Orioles, he made sure to bring Harrigan with him.

SUCCESS STORY

Bill Larsen,
general manager, Kane County Cougars

Larsen oversees the daily operation of the Cougars, the Florida Marlins' Class A affiliate. The Cougars perennially rank among the top 20 in attendance among all minor league baseball teams.

Before coming to the Cougars, Larsen was the general manager of the Rockford Expos of the Class A Midwest League for two years. There, he befriended then-Montreal Expos general manager Dave Dombrowski. When Dombrowski became the GM of the Florida Marlins his first task was developing a farm system. He contacted his buddy Larsen. The

Cougars, who for two years had been associated with the Baltimore Orioles, now have been the Marlins' rookie league team since October 1992.

DIRECTOR OF COMMUNITY RELATIONS

A professional sports team is considered to be a public trust, as well as an integral part of the fabric of the city in which it's based. With such a trust comes responsibilities, and pro teams cannot shirk them.

Developing and maintaining a good rapport with the fan base is vital to the ongoing success of any team. Whether they're reaching out to the people of a city through an annual blood drive or by collecting food to help feed the hungry, these teams do their best to extend their goodwill wherever possible, in the hope that they can help build a better community.

To be sure, magnanimity in sports also serves the team's self-interest. Community affairs—whether it be association with charities through team fund-raising efforts or personal appearances by players at local civic groups—will help create a positive image for the team, which is always beneficial when marketing a product to the public. An organization that can establish the perception of genuine concern and commitment to the community will sell more tickets.

THE FUTURE IS NOW

The director of community relations is responsible for developing and implementing public service programs for the team. Programs vary depending on the sport, but most professional leagues stress building a better future.

The New York Yankees play baseball from April into October, but the team's strong commitment to the community lasts year-round. Supporting the educational advancement of neighborhood children is the team's uppermost goal. Since its establishment in 1973, the Yankee Foundation has raised over $3 million for educational, athletic, and recreational programs for the city's young people. And for nearly 20 years, the Yankees have sponsored a college football game in association with the New York Urban League. This has helped provide more than $1.6 million in college tuition funds for financially strapped families.

The team's dedication to the future is also on display in the neighborhood surrounding Yankee Stadium. The Field of Dreams project is designed to renovate at least six neighborhood playing fields, and during the 1996 season, the team hosted 28 baseball clinics at Yankee Stadium for New York City–area kids. Nearly 3,000 youngsters participated in the clinics, which featured baseball instruction from Yankee coaches. The ballclub also distributes complimentary tickets for local nonprofit organizations—according to Brian Smith, the Yankees' director of community relations, the Bombers donated over 30,000 free tickets to organizations during the 1996 World Series–championship season.

Careers in the Community

Individuals who wish to pursue a career in community relations will be fortunate to learn that there are opportunities within every professional sports team. Internships are plentiful in this area, and enthusiastic workers who demonstrate a penchant for organization will fourish. The talent to juggle many projects simultaneously is imperative in this job, as is a personality suited to dealing with the public.

While a college degree is not required for a career in community relations, employers looking to fill available jobs seek candidates with a pleasant telephone manner, competent writing skills, and innovative thinking when it comes to developing programs.

Few positions open in a community relations department that are not low paying. Most organizations prefer to hire entry-level people, train them according to team specification, and promote from within. Generally, members of this department are overworked and underpaid.

ATHLETES IN ACTION

The league offices of the four major sports initiate national service programs that each team is expected to carry out. This creates much work for the community relations staff.

Major league baseball has recently implemented its RBI Program (Reviving Baseball in the Inner Cities), which uses baseball themes to teach reading, writing, and mathematics. To participate, students must maintain a high attendance record at school and demonstrate scholastic effort and good citizenship.

The majority of pro sports teams contractually require its players to do a certain amount of personal appearances. Most athletes enjoy lending a helping hand. Former New York Yankees catcher Jim Leyritz, who is now with the Texas Rangers, for instance, devoted much of his time and energy to the Kids of Harlem RBI. "I've lived a charmed life," he says, "and now that I'm at a high level, it's nice to give back and have a positive influence on these kids."

The National Basketball Association requires all 29 clubs to participate in its Team-Up program. This program, a joint effort of the league and the Players Association, utilizes the popularity of NBA players in helping to motivate young people to perform community service work.

The players appear at school assemblies and talk about the benefits of helping your community. The NBA offers the students an incentive for doing a community service-oriented project and then reporting back its positive results. At the program's completion, five lucky schools will be selected to be profiled in a segment aired on NBA's television show, "Inside Stuff."

THE PUBLIC SERVANTS

A typical community relations department consists of three or four people. An affairs coordinator and an assistant—who earn an annual salary ranging from $18,000 to $27,000— perform the role of liaison between the team, its players, and local organizations. In the case of the Team-Up program, the coordinator and assistant developed a questionnaire and mailed it to local schools in order to gauge their interest. They then recruited willing players they believed would best complement the program.

The role of the community relations manager is to develop and coordinate a wide range of programs and to ensure that these programs are executed properly. For this, the manager may make between $28,000 and $37,000 a year. Continuing with the Team-Up program example, the manager will coach the player on the points of the message to be presented during the assembly. The manager will then travel with the player to the school, not only to ensure timely arrival, but also to act as a representative of the organization and the league.

LENDING A HELPING HAND

While the Atlanta Hawks are winning on the hardwood, the Hawks organization is winning in the community. In addition to implementing service programs, community relations departments act as a fund-raising committee for worthy charities as well. The Hawks successfully aid numerous charities, nonprofit organizations, schools, and youth groups in the Atlanta area.

The purpose of the Atlanta Hawks Foundation is to create fund-raising events that will benefit worthy charities. With such annual events as the Lenny Wilkens golf and tennis tournament, the community relations staff is kept bustling. The staff works tirelessly to put on a good show and raise money. Duties include reserving a golf course, inviting other celebrities to attend, and approaching local businesses to ask for their involvement. This may include a contribution of services in kind as well as an appeal to sponsors to donate hard cash.

Tying all these efforts together is the community relations director. This individual must be a successful and innovative fund-raiser. Corporate executives are invited to black-tie events every other week. Gaining the attention of those who pull the purse strings is a challenge. The ability to raise money is therefore often dependent on the attractiveness of the event itself.

According to Dan Taylor, the director of community affairs for the Atlanta Hawks, "You've got to figure out how to set your event apart from all the others. Reserve a unique location and get big-name celebrities to attend. A well-known emcee to host the event is important," he adds, "and so is booking recognized talent as the entertainment."

In order to be effective, the individual in this position must know the needs of the community. This may require extensive research to gather information about the team's constituency, or it may be accomplished simply by mailing out questionnaires to local schools and civic groups. Most important is reaching out to the community on a personal level.

"You've got to get out and meet people," says Taylor. "People do business with the other people they enjoy being around. When it comes to fund raising, we're all doing similar jobs. You need to build relationships with people, and you can do that in a number of different ways. It doesn't even have to be in a business setting; it can be on the golf course or on the tennis court."

SPOTLIGHT

Dan Taylor,
director of community affairs, Atlanta Hawks

Now entering his eighth year with the Hawks, Taylor serves in the dual role of senior director of ticket sales and community affairs. As director of ticket sales, he develops and implements programs to generate ticket sales. He is responsible for maintaining customer service for season ticket holders, coordinating group nights and special post-game activities, as well as overseeing direct mail and advertising efforts.

A business administration graduate of Ouchita (Ark.) Baptist University, Taylor worked in commerical banking and real estate in Phoenix before joining the Hawks organization.

"I played hoops at a small college in Arkansas and even got a try out with the Phoenix Suns. When I didn't make it, I knew I wouldn't become an NBA player. I started selling real estate in Phoenix. One time I'm doing a deal—trying to get together a buyer and seller for a piece of property— and throughout the transaction there's this one particular gentleman involved. He'd been watching me work and determined what my skill sets were, and we enjoyed one another's company. After the deal closes, he looks me right in the eye and says, 'You're in the wrong business; you should work in the NBA.'

"The man's name is Ted Podleski; he'd worked for the Phoenix Suns and the Los Angeles Clippers. He gave me advice and said I could use his name. I began by writing letters to every team in the NBA. I received no offers. If I got a response, the message said no openings. Some teams didn't even send back a note saying they'd received my resume at all. I went through this process three times. On the third go-around, I received a call from [Hawks' president] Stan Kasten.

"If you've ever had an opportunity to meet Stan Kasten you know that everything is very brief and to the point. He said I don't have any openings, but anybody that knows Ted Podleski is worth talking to. If you're ever in town I'd love to meet you. I packed my bags and moved from Phoenix to Atlanta. No job, no place to live. I got to Atlanta, called Stan Kasten's office, told him I was in town, and got an appointment to see him the next morning at nine o'clock. I was so excited that I got there well before nine.

"That next morning Stan brought me into his office and said, 'Tell me again why you're here?' I said I wanted to work for him. He got up from his desk, walked out of his office, and I was left sitting there. Five minutes later he came back with the executive vice president. I was told that after the playoffs ended I could have a job selling season tickets and groups sales on straight commission. When I took the job, of course, everybody I knew thought I was nuts. It was the mid 1980s, when commercial real estate was booming. I had built up contacts and business relations over the years. Why leave a stable career to go sell tickets for straight commission? Because a job in the NBA was my dream.

"When I hire trainees, first and foremost, I'm looking for personable people. The sports business is jammed with highly intelligent, aggressive people. They know how to represent themselves and they know how to go about getting a job. If I'm interviewing someone, they've already met the job description requirements to get in the door. I'll talk with that person to determine if he or she can represent themselves in the most positive, personable manner possible. I'm looking for someone who will fit in and who the staff will enjoy working with. Then I probe a bit further to learn their career aspirations, what skill sets they own, and to determine if they can help the team."

SUCCESS STORY

Romy Barrett,
community relations manager, Chicago Wolves

Barrett handles player and mascot appearances, educational programs, special events, and charitable contributions. She also spearheaded the Wolves first educational endeavor, "Read to Success," a reading incentive program in suburban Chicago libraries. Prior to joining the Wolves, Barrett spent three years in the National Basketball Association as the player programs supervisor for the Detroit Pistons. With the Pistons, she handled media relations for player appearances and community relations programs, as well as coordinated the Pistons Speakers Bureau, which made over 600 presentations to 30,000 students each year. Barrett, a Detroit native, graduated from Michigan State University with a degree in communications.

TICKET OPERATIONS MANAGER

What do search committees look for when they go recruiting for a ticket operations manager? A trade publication recently listed this classified advertisement offering a position at a major NCAA Division I institution:

Ticket Operations Manager. The University of Nebraska is seeking candidates who will be responsible for personal supervision, procedure development, and financial accountability of the athletic ticket office. The individual in this job will oversee the distribution and sales of tickets for athletic events, as well as establish ticket inventory controls and provide summary ticket sales reports.

Bachelor's degree plus four years of related experience, preferably in a ticket or athletic office, is required. Supervisory and management experience necessary. Excellent organizational and communications skills essential. Computerized ticketing systems experience preferred. Evenings and weekends required. (Don't bother applying; the job has been filled!)

Ticket managers serve various functions depending on the drawing power of the team. An individual working for a minor league team may be responsible for everything that occurs in the ticket office. These duties include the distribution of tickets, mailings to season ticket holders, and handling the monthly financial statements.

At small colleges, where the ticket office may not be automated or computerized, all work must be done by hand. In this case, the ticket manager will be expected to address the hundreds of mailing envelopes used for ticket transactions.

The more popular teams require a larger ticket office to process the mind-boggling number of requests. Ticket managers of professional sports teams supervise a personnel staff. Six full-time employees work in the ticket office for the NFL's Chicago Bears; the manager and an assistant manager, three customer service representatives, and a union ticket seller.

GOOD FOR ONE ADMITTANCE

Ticket sales are the life blood of any sports franchise. Therefore, season ticket sales are extremely important to the overall financial health of the organization. Members of the ticket office are required to service the accounts of each season ticket holder, ensuring that payments are made and seat locations are improved whenever possible.

The ticket office staff works year-round. Even with the Bears' success—Chicago's Soldier Field has been sold out for the past ten years—members of the ticket office, unlike the players, do not have an off-season.

Beginning in March, the office invoices some 16,000 season ticket holders. The Bears have two payment deadlines; one in April, the other in May. Season tickets are mailed out in mid-July to accounts with no outstanding balance. Invariably, many blocks of tickets are returned due to a change of address. The ticket office is responsible for keeping an up-to-date list of all season ticket holders.

The Bears also maintain a policy of holding back tickets. Each year on June 1st, the team conducts an individual game sale. Lasting throughout the month of June and into mid-July, between 3,000 and 4,000 tickets per game are made available to single game purchasers. This policy is advantageous for fans, but creates more work for the ticket office staff. To combat the mad rush, the ticket office hires two interns during the summer to process the thousands of additional mail-order ticket requests.

Once the season begins, the duties take on a dramatically different role. Game day tasks comprise a large portion of the ticket staff's responsibilities. These duties can range from locating a complimentary ticket for a local dignitary to placating the disgruntled fan who inevitably shows up at the reservations booth in need of a replacement ticket because the one that was supposed to be left for him is nowhere to be found.

Ticket offices in the majority of metropolitan cities, including Chicago, employ a union ticket seller who is responsible for selling tickets the day or night of the event. All stadiums and arenas have scheduled hours in which fans may purchase tickets. Most venues have by now implemented a computer software program to make the job of assigning seats an easier task.

There is no margin for error in this job. At the end of the shift, the ticket seller's cash register must balance out. To ensure that it does, a simple system of checks and balances is in place. The seller is given a specific number of tickets; he or she must account for a certain amount of money due. Unused tickets must be returned.

The ticket seller should also know how to authorize credit card purchases and must always be on the lookout for counterfeit vouchers. Other duties performed by this union employee may be working the will call or reservations window. Free passes issued by the team are left here, as are tickets purchased by fans in advance of the game but not yet picked up.

WRITE YOUR OWN TICKET

Once an individual has gotten in the door of a ticket office, advancement opportunities can be plentiful. Most ticket managers begin at the least glamorous entry level position of all, the customer service representative. The individual in this job is expected to work the mailing machine. If a bulk mailing is necessary, he or she will also deal with the mailing house. The post garners an annual starting salary of between $18,000 and $22,000.

The customer service rep also acts as a type of traffic manager for tickets. This involves grunt work. All tickets going in and out of the office must be accounted for. Blocks of tickets coming back from the printer may total in the tens of thousands. Each and every one must be counted, logged in, and placed in a drawer by alphabetical order according to the buyer's last name. It's not unusual for someone performing this unenviable task to wear a pair of doctor's rubber gloves. Raw hands may lead to nasty paper cuts.

The assistant ticket manager earns a salary of about $28,000 to $34,000 a year. Responsibilities include handling all lost and stolen tickets, group ticket sales, house tickets, and players' complimentary tickets. The assistant manager often travels with the team to road games. He or she stays at the hotel with the team and responds to players' requests for extra tickets for family or friends. For this, the individual needs good communication skills in order to forge a relationship with the other team's ticket manager.

Since the Bears' ticket office is in charge of all ushers and security on game day, the assistant manager must contract with security and usher firms to provide the necessary personnel. The assistant will also work closely with the ticket manager to execute the actual physical ticket design. The Bears recently held an art contest to design season tickets for the NFL's 75th season and for the tenth anniversary of the team's Super Bowl championship.

The ticket manager is the boss of the whole operation. A ballpark salary for this position ranges from $48,000 to $54,000 per year, but earnings vary considerably. The stadium's seating capacity and the individual's experience are two important determining factors.

The main function of the ticket manager is to oversee the financial accountability of the office. For the Bears, this requires personally supervising the flow of tens of millions of dollars. All monies are electronically transfered via computer to the appropriate team bank accounts.

A strong educational background is required of a person who's rolling in dough—even if it belongs to other people. Possible degrees include business administration and accounting. Courses to study should stress mathematics and bookkeeping. George McCaskey, who earned a law degree from Arizona State University, has been the Bears' ticket manager since 1991. He had held several part-time jobs with the team since the age of 14. To be sure, you don't give this job to just anybody—the McCaskey family owns the Bears.

DOLE OUT THE BOUNTY

Ticket managers, to some extent, control the stadium seating chart. Because they determine who gets in and who sits where, they are extremely popular people. To deter abuse of power, ticket office rules forbid the acceptance of gifts from fans.

This isn't meant to imply that a ticket office is without largesse. Chief among the perks doled out by a benevolent team management is complimentary tickets to home and away games for you and a guest. But the bountiful fruit—indeed, the juicy tidbit that no ticket office member wants you to know—is the trading of tickets for automobiles.

It's called the auto dealers' ticket account, and it's accepted practice throughout the league in every sport. Working in conjunction with the team's marketing department, some office staffers are allowed to purchase for each game a limited number of tickets, say four, for barter with a local car dealership. The ticket price is charged against the employee's wages through payroll deduction. (The average price of four tickets is about $100.)

In return, the individual receives free use of a car, including insurance, for a whole year. If the dealer requests four tickets for each of the eight home games, the team employee incurs a cost of less than $1,000 in return for some $5,000 worth of services. Car dealers must be satisfied with the arrangement, or they wouldn't continue to participate. For their part, the car dealership owners receive a trip on the team plane to an away game.

WORKING THE TURNSTILES

The ticket office is a service job, and people who work in this area must enjoy helping others. During a game, the myriad of problems that occur in the stadium come through the ticket office. Members of the staff are trained to be of immediate assistance or will know how to direct the problem to the appropriate person. Often times, staffers are only able to catch a small portion of each home game due to these types of responsiblities.

Ticket personnel should have strong verbal and written skills. During any given year a popular team may receive as many as 1,000 telephone calls from season ticket accounts. These calls can be someone voicing a complaint, making a recommendation, or a season ticket holder simply intersted in discussing the team's performance. It is this attention to customer service that allows a team to build and maintain a satisfied season ticket base even when the team encounters a rocky season or two.

A HISTORY LESSON

Memorable sports events have on occasion drawn remarkably feeble crowds. In 1938 at Cincinnati's Crosley Field, a mere 5,814 spectators were in attendance for the first of Johnny Vander Meer's record two consecutive no-hitters. And in Hershey, Pennsylvania on March 2, 1962, Wilt Chamberlain's 100-point game was witnessed by only 4,124 people (several million fans now claim to have been in the stadium for that one).

REAL-LIFE ADVICE

Amy Baranko,
assistant ticket manager, Chicago Bears

Baranko is in her sixth season with the Bears. Her duties include assisting with ticket sales and distribution and overseeing The Bears Share Ticket Donation Program and the fan assistance booths. Baranko interned for the athletic department at the University of Notre Dame in 1989 and

1990. She received her master's of business administration from Lake Forest (Ill.) Graduate School of Management.

"After college I came to Chicago and worked for a year as a model. Knowing that a modeling career wasn't going to last forever, I volunteered to work as an intern for Score International Sports, a marketing company that sells sponsorships for tennis and golf tournaments. While at Score I sent out resumes. Mine basically looked like any other, but what got people to notice my resume was the cover letter. I wrote that I would work for you for free for a specific period of time. That's what my boss here at the Bears said caught his eye, that I would work for free. I figured if they didn't like me after that, fine. But I was confident I would prove myself.

"I was hired as a customer service representative, and I went to graduate school at night for two years to get my master's in business administration. When our assistant ticket manager retired, it was good timing for me. The Bears asked me to stay on as the assistant manager. I don't think the M.B.A. was necessary for the job—quite frankly, I don't use much of what I learned at business school—but it helped to give me more credibility. And I plan to use that knowledge eventually.

"I hire about 20 people for our fan assistance program. All of the people are interested in sports. Most of them have other jobs. They come in knowing that it's a ten-day-a-year job, and it'll give a bit of visibility and see if you like it. Last year we offered three of those people full-time jobs."

SUCCESS STORY

Ashleigh Bizzelle,
director of box office operations, Orlando Magic

Now in her tenth year with the Orlando Magic, Ashleigh Bizzelle is responsible for all box office operations for the franchise. She came to the Magic from the Zev Bufman Theatre Partnership. She started in 1978 as box office manager for Bufman's Orlando Theater and in 1981 began managing both the Orlando and St. Petersburg theater operations.

Prior to joining the Bufman organization, she served as the ticket manager for the Miami Floridians, a franchise of the former American Basketball Association. Bizzelle also spent five years as assistant manager for the Miami Dolphins. During that period she assisted in developing the NFL club's subscription policies and procedures.

She gained her early box office experience while working as the assistant box office manager for the Orange Bowl Committee, and with the minor league baseball Class A Miami Marlins, where she first worked with Pat Williams, the current president and general manager of the Magic.

ADDRESS BOOK

Box Office Management
International, Inc.
250 West 57th Street
New York, NY 10107
212/581-0600

Protix
4513 Vernon Boulevard
Madison, WI 53705
800/550-9705
(Full-service ticketing
company)

Select Ticketing Systems, Inc.
344 West Genesee Street
Syracuse, NY 13201
315/479-6663
(Computerized in-house ticketing management company)

Ticketmaster
3701 Wilshire Boulevard
Los Angeles, CA 90010
213/381-2000
(Leading independent ticket
services company)

EQUIPMENT MANAGER

A professional sports team employs an equipment manager to perform two very important functions: to make sure the players have equipment that works and to supervise the locker room activities.

First the equipment. The individual's main responsibility is the purchase, maintenance, and inventory of all gear required by the players and coaches. Equipment varies depending on the sport. In football, it covers the gamut from shoulder pads to tackling dummies. In baseball, it includes everything from pitching machines to rosin bags.

Prior to each game or practice, equipment must be checked for reliability and performance. If gear is in poor condition it must be repaired in time for practice. If something breaks during a game, the equipment manager will be expected to fix it on the spot, or at least be sure to have a suitable replacement in stock.

If a piece of apparatus is broken it must be replaced. In this case the equipment manager is responsible for initiating a purchase order request. To this end, the individual will participate in determining budgets and be held accountable for adhering to it.

The person in this job will also monitor the distribution of equipment and maintain adequate levels of inventory. If gear is handed out to team personnel, it must be reclaimed later. Since the equipment manager is inundated with requests, he or she must develop an inventory control program. This may be as simple as a sign-out sheet.

Travel complicates the equipment manager's job, especially in terms of the method used to keep track of supplies. Whenever the team goes on the road to play away games, the equipment must come along. An individual working for a pro team will usually have one or two assistants. The equipment and clubhouse manager supervises the assistants as they prepare to transport the equipment to away games. This involves loading trucks that go to the airport, then unpacking and distributing gear to each individual's locker. When the team travels back home, the process is reversed.

LAUNDRY DUTY

Knowledge of gear is only one element of the job. The equipment manager will also be responsible for the overall cleanliness of the equipment. Equipment cleanliness extends to the locker room facilities and the players' uniforms.

The equipment manager, with the help of his or her assistants, if any, will be required to perform laundry duties. Dirty socks, smelly sweatshirts, grass-stained uniforms, and the like need to be washed, dried, folded, and replaced in each players' individual locker.

This is not a glamorous job, nor is it routine. The equipment manager works long hours, often putting in at least 15-hour days that begin before 9 a.m. and last until midnight. He or she is expected to work during all games and practices, as well as being required to travel with the team.

A position of this type offers an individual who loves sports the opportunity to be part of a team. Equipment managers usually cite the comraderie they develop with players and coaches, as well as seeing the success of their efforts as the most rewarding or enjoyable part of their profession.

EQUIPPED FOR SUCCESS

Employment prospects are limited. Whenever the rare job opportunity arises, it's usually snatched up by an insider (read nepotism). Consider this example: Rob Cucuzza has run the New York Yankees clubhouse for nine straight seasons. His father, Lou Cucuzza Sr., has been running the visitors' clubhouse for 21 consecutive years and is assisted by his son, Lou Jr.

The majority of equipment managers do not need a college education. But the limited number of opportunities at the major league level, coupled with the fierce competition among candidates, may cause some pro teams to require a bachelor's degree in physical education or sports management. To be sure, a working knowledge of equipment room procedures is mandatory.

The salary range for equipment managers varies greatly, depending upon the individual's experience and the prestige of the team for which he or she works. Individuals who work for a professional team can earn from $25,000 to $50,000 a year. An equipment manager at a top-ranked university will make about $30,000; at smaller schools $20,000. Besides college athletics, the person will also be responsible for the upkeep of equipment for physical education classes, intramural sports, and all campus recreational activities. Individuals that are certified by the Athletic Equipment Managers Association will be able to command a salary on the higher end of the spectrum.

To become certified, a member must be 21 years old, have either a college degree with two years paid nonstudent employment in equipment management or 1,800 hours of student management experience, or five years paid nonstudent employment in athletic equipment management and a high school degree. Candidates must then pass the certification examination, which covers the areas of purchasing, fitting, maintenance, administration and organization, management and professional relations, and accountability.

A HISTORY LESSON

A team's equipment manager cannot win or lose games. But only a properly equipped team will be able to perform to the best of its ability. The 1934 NFL Championship Game, dubbed "The Sneakers Game," is the closest an equipment manager ever came to glory.

When members of the Chicago Bears and New York Giants arrived at the Polo Grounds in New York, they immediately knew the contest would be a slip-and-slide affair. The field was covered with ice, and footing was treacherous.

The elements surely favored the visiting team from Chicago. The Bronko Nagurski–led Bears possessed a devasting straight-ahead offensive rushing game. The Giants, by contrast, were more of a finesse team that favored outside running and cuts against the grain.

True to form, the Bears held a 10-3 halftime lead. Frustrated Giants coach Steve Owen dispatched equipment manager Abe Cohen in search of shoes that he hoped would give his players better footing on the icy field. Cohen returned with bags full of sneakers—and just in the nick of time.

The Bears had extended the lead to 13-3 early in the fourth quarter. That's when the Giants players switched from football cleats to basketball sneakers to give them much-needed traction. Suddenly able to cut and turn, the Giants scored 27 unanswered points in the final ten minutes and captured their first NFL title with a 30-13 victory.

USING YOUR HEAD

Since its inception in 1969, the National Operating Committee on Standards for Athletic Equipment has been a leading force in the effort to improve athletic equipment and, as a result, reduce injuries. Some of the committee's efforts include the development of test standards for football helmets. The N.O.C.S.A.E. manual suggests observing the following guidelines when inspecting helmets:

1. Check that helmet fit conforms with manufacturer's instructions and procedures.

2. Examine shell for cracks, particulary noting any cracks around ear holes (where most cracks start) and replace any shells that have cracked. DO NOT USE A HELMET WITH A CRACKED SHELL.

3. Examine all mounting rivets, screws, velcro and snaps for breakage, distortion, and/or looseness. Repair as necessary.

4. Replace face mask if bare metal is showing, if there is a broken weld, or if the mask is grossly misshapen.

5. Examine for helmet completeness, and replace any parts that have become damaged, such as sweatbands, interior parts, nose snubbers, and chin straps.

6. Replace jaw pads when damaged. Check for proper installation and fit.

7. Examine chin strap for proper adjustment, and inspect to see if it is broken or stretched out of shape; also inspect the hardware to see if it needs replacement.

8. Never allow anyone to sit on helmets. This practice could crush or deform the helmet.

TIPSHEET

- ⓤ While in high school, volunteer as the equipment manager for a team during the fall and spring.

- ⓤ During the summer, try to get a job at a sporting goods store or an equipment manufacturer to familiarize yourself with the tools of the trade.

- ⓤ Attend a college that offers a degree in sports management. Work as equipment manager for one of your school's athletic teams.

- ⓤ Try to get internships in the field.

- ⓤ Make valuable contacts by attending trade seminars.

SUCCESS STORY

Mike Davidson,
equipment manager, Kansas City Chiefs

Davidson has served as the equipment manager for the NFL's Chiefs since 1989. Before coming to Kansas City, he spent five years as assistant equipment manager for the Cleveland Browns. He is responsible for the outfitting of the team's players and coaches, as well as the purchasing and maintaining of the club's equipment.

The 40-year-old Davidson joined the Browns in 1984 and assisted with the club's equipment purchasing, inventory, maintenance, and travel arrangements. Prior to taking the Browns position, he was a marketing education coordinator for two years at Thomas W. Harvey High School in Painesville, Ohio, and had worked as an occupational work adjustment coordinator at Kimble Middle Schools in Stow, Ohio from 1979 to 1983.

Davidson is a 1978 graduate of Bowling Green State University in Ohio with a bachelor of sciene in education. He currently serves as certification secretary and comptroller of the Athletic Equipment Managers Association.

personality sketch

Knowledge of sports and athletic equipment; ability to be inventive when making repairs; organized and detail-oriented; reliable.

ADDRESS BOOK

*Athletic Equipment
Managers Association*
6224 Hester Road
Oxford, OH 45056
513/523-2362

*National Operating
Committee on Standards
for Athletic Equipment*
P.O. Box 12290
Overland Park, KS 66282

TRAVELING SECRETARY

Travel is not too much of a problem for a college sports team. Modern transportation makes it possible to zip in and out of a town so quickly that a minimum of class work is missed. A college team usually arrives the day before a game and goes through a light practice at the gym, just loosening up and getting the feel of the place.

Travel is far worse in the pros. The clubs bounce around the country, popping in and out of cities, airports, buses, hotels, arenas, and time zones until the players don't know Boston from Phoenix except for the sunshine (or lack of it).

Such travel is seldom broadening. Athletes don't know what Boston is like. They've never seen the place. All they know is the road between the airport and the hotel and the hotel and the arena. Athletes fly in, go to bed, get up, play ball, and leave. The game itself is the easiest part of the whole season.

All professional sports teams, and some elite college programs, require the services of a personal travel agent. The traveling secretary is responsible for coordinating all details that relate to moving the team from one location to another in a timely and professional manner.

The main function performed by this individual is the handling of all arrangements for ground and air transportation. This includes making airline reservations, chartering buses, and booking blocks of hotel rooms. He or she must also accompany the team on road trips in order to tend to any special needs that should arise.

GET YOUR HEAD OUT OF THE CLOUDS

Moving a professional sports team from city to city is a complicated process. It's also an expensive one. A bus and driver must be chartered to take the team from the stadium to the airport so they can fly to the location of their next game. The club's equipment and personal luggage becomes the responsibility of the traveling secretary at this point.

When the airplane (keep fingers crossed on the equipment and luggage) reaches its destination and the team collects its belongings, another bus that is gassed up should be waiting outside the terminal ready to drive the squad to the hotel.

Once the traveling secretary ensures that each member of the team is checked in and each room is satisfactory, he or she will dole out the per diem checks, commonly referred to as meal money. After a few hours of shut-eye it's off to the arena on yet another bus.

The successful traveling secretary will confirm all reservations and schedules far in advance, as well as make contingency arrangements should the best laid plans go awry. The job is one big juggling act. Come to think of it, that guy on the Ed Sullivan show who kept eight plates spinning would have made a helluva traveling secretary.

BOSTON OR BUST

Moving a professional sports team from city to city is also an expensive operation. It costs real money to travel, even when purchasing airline tickets and hotel rooms at preferred group rates. Most teams have a travel budget. The traveling secretary will also be a competent negotiator. He or she will be expected to discover the best possible deals and always be on the lookout for an advantageous service upgrade.

The person in this job is ultimately charged with making sure that all team members get where they are supposed to be, on time, and with as little trouble as possible. The entire team needs to be made aware of all travel arrangements. Hint: distribute typed memos, tack signs on bulletin boards, and ask coaches to include a travel reminder in all player meetings.

An organized team is managed efficiently at all levels. An athlete, like any employee away on a business trip, needs to know the dates, times, and locations of all arrivals and departures, as well as hotel telephone numbers. This information must be readily available to everyone, and easily accessible by all. Players and coaches will appreciate the common courtesy and respect you display by your professionalism.

THE SKY'S THE LIMIT

Experience and training as a traveling secretary is much more important than education. If you've ever tried to make sense of a frequent-flyer mileage statement, you understand. A college degree is always useful, but if you don't love travel and can't read a map, why bother applying? A candidate for this job needs to be familiar with the travel industry. A knowledge of computer software now being used by airlines for on-line reservations can distinguish you from the rest of the pack.

Employment prospects for traveling secretaries are best in baseball, a sport that requires frequent travel. In other sports where road trips occur less frequently and are of shorter duration, there may not even be an official traveling secretary. Instead these duties will be handled by a member of the organization with other administrative responsibilities. The NBA trainers often double as travel coordinators.

An aspiring candidate for this job may have better luck breaking in with a minor league team, gaining the necessary experience, and working his or her way up the ladder. Salaries range from $18,000 to $60,000 depending on the person's qualifications, the sport, and the prestige of the team.

BLAST OFF

Once in the door, advancement opportunities improve for a traveling secretary. The person who performs this job with élan will prove to be detail-oriented, personable, and possess an uncanny ability to juggle many projects simultaneously. These are characteristics that all employers covet when seeking to hire an individual for a position of increased power.

In addition to moving up the corporate ladder within the team hierarchy, a traveling secretary may advance his or her career by implementing entrepreneurial skills. Dave Eyrise discovered an untapped market in sports relocation. Whenever an athlete is traded, that player has two days to report to his new team. There's hardly time to deal with the emotional shock of such a lifestyle change, much less see to the resulting complications. That traded player is now desperate to find a new place to live, needs to put his old house on the market, as well as pack his family for the cross-country move.

Eyrise is the founder and director of Athletes on the Move, a specialized sports relocation service that offers a personalized approach for athletes, coaches, and sports executives on the move. Eyrise has set up a network of the top 100 real estate brokers and relocation consultants that cover all aspects of the relocation business throughout the country and the world.

The traveling secretary is a special breed of person. The individual will be reliable and able to work well under intense pressure, as well as possess a wealth of energy and trouble-shooting skills. The travel industry is susceptible to mistakes and notorious for testing the limits of human patience. So one of the most important traits for the traveling secretary is self-esteem. Whenever a connecting flight is missed, or luggage is misplaced, or the hotel rooms are not yet ready —and it does happen on occasion—a little self-esteem can go a long way.

A HISTORY LESSON

The NBA's New York Knicks have to take extra-long road trips every season when an ice show takes over Madison Square Garden. Walt "Clyde" Frazier, the club's Hall of Fame guard who now serves as its radio broadcaster, reminisces of an especially wearying western swing during the 1969-70 season.

"We beat Detroit in the Garden by one point Christmas night, then caught a midnight flight to Los Angeles," he recalls. "We arrived at L.A. International Airport at 3:30 a.m. (6:30 am New York time). We lost by 12 points that night at The Forum. We were up at 6:45 am the next morning for a flight to Vancouver that arrived at 11:15 a.m. That night we beat Seattle by 2. We were rousted out of bed at 5:45 a.m. for a six-hour, three-stop flight to Phoenix and beat the Suns that night by 19. How, I don't know. We flew home, finishing off a trip of more than 7,000 miles. We changed our name from the Knicks to the Zombies."

TIPSHEET

① Test your interest in this field. A summer job at a travel agency would serve as a proving ground to measure if your interest is worth pursuing.

① Contact universities in your area that offer a sports management degree; inquire about training seminars, apprenticeships, internships, or work-study programs.

① If at college, see about getting some experience by offering to handle travel arrangements for some of the school's sports teams.

REAL-LIFE ADVICE

Bill DeLury,
traveling secretary, Los Angeles Dodgers

Bill DeLury has been working for the Dodgers for 46 years, the last 16 seasons as traveling secretary. He began his career in the Dodgers organization in 1950 as an entry level record keeper and over the next 15 years held various jobs within the team's department of minor league operations. By 1965 he had transferred into the ticket office, where he sold season tickets and performed other duties in group sales.

"First of all, you have to love baseball. Secondly, you can't mind traveling. After all, if you don't love travel, then get out of the baseball business.

"The traveling secretary is usually a person who came up within the organization. When the job becomes available, a team likes to hire an internal person, someone they already know. You can learn the job fundamentals with a minor league club. The lower levels use lots of bus travel, so you'd start out with a little less pressure.

> ## personality sketch
>
> *Loves to travel and interested in the industry; ability to juggle many projects simultaneously; energetic and a reliable troubleshooter; good communication skills; dependable under pressure.*

"In this job you depend on lots of other people. People from airlines to get planes in on time, hotel staff to have rooms ready for you, dispatchers to get buses at the stadium on time. With so many people involved, you have to make sure to get them the information they need to do their job, so you can do yours. If you write letters in advance, then call ahead the day before, you shouldn't have many problems.

"Things only work out right when they're done right. But there's always that one person you're depending on who drops the ball. Then you've got a problem. That's when you put Plan B into action. Whatever that plan is, you'd better have one. I have the home telephone numbers of all my people: the bus dispatchers, hotel reps, everyone. If the job is not done and I've got to get up at three o'clock in the morning, somebody's gonna get up with me.

"Players realize that when arrangements go right the whole year, it's because a lot of planning went into it. I truly think the players appreciate you. I'm always honest with the players. If they ask you a question or ask for your help with a problem, listen to them. If you think you might be able to help, tell them you'll see what you can do and get back to them right away.

"If you know you can't do it, tell them so right away. Don't B.S. the players by saying you'll try when you know damn well you can't do it. They'll respect you for that. You want the players to respect you. If you can earn their respect, then you've got it made."

Careers In Stadium Opera- tions

Sports facilities are the entertainment hub of most major cities. These stadiums and arenas are not just a venue for athletic contests, but are also center stage for a full spectrum of entertainment events that range from rock concerts to political conventions.

During the 1950s, large metropolitan cities erected stadiums in memory and honor of local war heroes from World War II. The people who staffed these facilities were appointed by the mayor or the governor. That's not true today, by and large, because in the era of professional athletics as big business, trained employees are needed to operate the facilities.

Stadiums that were hailed as architecural marvels when they opened in the early 1970s—Busch Stadium in St. Louis, Riverfront Stadium in Cincinnati, Three Rivers Stadium in Pittsburgh, and Veterans Stadium in Philadelphia—are modern symbols of our conspicuous construction. When they were built, these multipurpose facilities made perfect economic and engineering sense. They were designed in cookie-cutter fashion to hold 55,000 fans and house both baseball and football teams. They now seem antiquaited barely more than a generation later.

When Peter Ueberroth became baseball's commissioner after the 1984 Summer Olympic Games in Los Angeles, he initiated surveys about what was best for the business. The stadiums of the 1990s, with their grass fields, modest scale, and friendly old-time feeling that evoke the atmosphere of Wrigley Field and Fenway Park, stem directly from Ueberroth's surveys. Today sports has entered the era of the down-sized stadiums; single-tenant facilities that hold 40,000 fans. Baltimore's Oriole Park at Camden Yards, Cleveland's Jacobs Field, and Denver's Coors Field personify the term "cozy confines."

Employment opportunities are good for individuals interested in the field of stadium management. In 1992 alone, 14 arenas housing professional teams were built or refurbished. This trend should continue. Cities are actively vying for pro teams by luring them with state-of-the-art arenas. And those cities that already have a home team need to upgrade their facilities in order to keep the organization content.

The minor leagues are also experiencing a building boom. Since 1985, 76 minor league stadiums have been or are being built in the country. Attendance at minor league games is also on the rise, increasing to over 33 million in each of the last three years from 27 million in 1992, according to the National Association of Professional Baseball Leagues in St. Petersburg, Florida, which governs minor league teams nationwide. And that, industry experts say, underscores a move toward affordable, family-oriented entertainment.

The exciting area of facility management is one of the newest areas of opportunity within the sports industry. Under the umbrella of stadium operations is facility management, field maintenance, ticket sales, scoreboard operation, game production, and public address announcing.

EXECUTIVE DIRECTOR

The job of executive director of a sports complex is, in many ways, analagous to the job of landlord of an apartment building. The executive director is in charge of the day-to-day maintenance and operation of the facility. He or she must be a jack of all trades, with skills in business administration, contract negotiation, accounting, risk management, and marketing and public relations.

The main function performed by the executive director is to handle the booking of the building. Today's sports facilities—whether they're publicly or privately owned—are costly to erect and costly to maintain. The executive director is under intense pressure to attract revenue-generating events on the days when the permanent tenants are not scheduled to play games. Therefore, it's important that the individual in this position be able to call on a strong network of sports and entertainment promoters to faciliate the acquisition of bookings.

The director is also in charge of overseeing all the financial business of the venue. The individual will be expected to negotiate the terms of leases with franchises and other occupants who use the facility during the year. At a venue that has a pro sports team as a tenant, many dates are booked in advance. On the other available dates the director will rent the facility to a promoter and extract the best possible deal.

In addition to overseeing the use of the building, the executive director also caters to the needs and wants of the tenants. Those who rent the facility require a certain level of comfort and will expect a number of requests be met. This may include anything from the installation of additional lockers to a fresh coat of paint in the dugout. As the arbiter of all decisions relating to the facility, the executive director will approve or deny these requests.

On the flip side of the landlord-tenant relationship, the executive director is also responsible for the interaction between tenants. The majority of facilities house two sports teams—a stadium usually hosts a baseball and football team, arenas usually host a basketball and hockey team. The often conflicting needs of tenants translates into problems for the director. Tenant relations can become a sticky issue, and this is where the director really earns his or her pay. When outlining the following specific example, it's important to understand the behind-the-scenes mechanics.

SIBLING RIVALRY IN TWIN CITIES

The Hubert H. Humphrey Metrodome in Minneapolis, Minnesota is home to the NFL's Vikings and baseball's Twins. The Metrodome is seen as unique by stadia afficiandos who know it's the only facility to have hosted the World Series, the Super Bowl, and the NCAA basketball Final Four. What sports fans don't know, but is much more important to the stadium's survival, is that the publicly owned Metrodome is self supporting. According to Bill Lester, the Metrodome's executive director, the facility makes enough money through its leases with its tenants to pay for the debt service on the building and the operations costs, as well as to make capital improvements as necessary with no public tax dollars.

The Vikings are the big-ticket item for the Metrodome. The team pays the stadium authority $4.5 million a year in rent to play host for 10 events (two preseason exhibitions and eight regular season games). The Twins have a rental agreement that is dependent on attendance. The deal stipulates that each fan is worth $1.50 to the stadium authority. Based on league attendance records for 1994, the Twins paid $2.1 million in rent in 1994 because the team drew 1.4 million paying customers that year to its 81 home games.

Let's say the Vikings want their clubhouse refurbished and the request is approved. Hearing of this, the Twins demand equal treatment. It's only fair that both tenants receive the same attention. Or is it? Remember, the Vikings bring in twice as much money as the Twins do in 71 less event dates. There's an inherent conflict here, and the executive director must deal with such problems on a daily basis.

THE BUILDING BLOCKS

Educational requirements for this job vary from person to person. A degree in sports management is helpful, but not all individuals in the position have one. At the least, an executive director will have a college degree in either accounting, business administration, marketing, public relations, or the like.

The executive director should also have a working knowledge of contract law. All facilities have their own attorneys, but the executive director will usually write agreements and contracts, as well as interpret them, before an attorney steps in to okay the legalese.

Experience is significant in obtaining this type of position. Most individuals have a background in sports administration, business management, community planning, or other related aspects in facility management. An understanding of engineering terms and building equipment is necessary to communicate with staff members. Knowledge of agronomy or horticulture may also be useful so the director can be familiar with the different types of athletic turfs.

Other areas necessary for the hosting of an event include the procurement of the adequate insurance coverage, security personnel, concession staff, and parking arrangements. Even if the director is not personally responsible for securing these arrangements, the overall readiness of the venue is his or her primary responsibility.

ROCK SOLID PERSON

An executive director of a stadium or arena can earn an annual salary of between $65,000 and $100,000. It's interesting to note that top jobs at a public facility tend not to pay as much as the same job at a private facility. Conversely, the lower-level positions, i.e., union jobs, tend to pay well across the board.

An executive director is the highest-ranking official in stadium management, so advancement opportunities are limited. Promotion prospects include finding employment at a bigger, more prestigious facility; relocating to a multipurpose stadium that serves numerous tenants; obtaining a job at a facility management company that oversees several stadiums; or obtaining a top administrative job with one of the tenants.

Moving from stadium management into team administration is rare, but it can be done. "It's called going over to the dark side," quips Bill Lester, the man in charge of the Metrodome. "My predecessor here made the jump, but it doesn't happen very often. In this position you have to learn how to say NO, and people like to shoot the messenger. Stay a while and the team usually ends up hating you."

Michael Rowe and Rick Nafe are two recent examples of this unique accomplishment. Rowe, who had been the director of the Meadowlands Sports Complex, is currently the president of the NBA's New Jersey Nets. And Rick Nafe will be stepping down as executive director of the Tampa Sports Authority to assume the duties of vice president for the major league baseball expansion team, St. Petersburg Devil Rays.

The executive director has an unenviable position. The individual must provide both a safe and comfortable venue for the fans and generate revenue for the stadium, while simultaneously providing the tenant with an optimal arrangement that will allow both parties to maximize revenue. It is not uncommon for these two agendas to conflict.

An executive director is in many ways a politician. The individual must be a diplomat when dealing with demanding performers in the entertainment field. He or she must also be comfortable working on a daily basis with public officials. Another important characteristic for a person in this job is effective communication skills and the ability to maintain an even temper during a crisis.

All this may seem like a 24-hour-a-day job. Well, almost. During the sport season, the job actually takes up just seven days a week from 7 o'clock in the morning until midnight. There's plenty of time to sleep in the off-season, when the job becomes a regular ten-hour work day.

TIPSHEET

☺ You desperately need to set up an internship. Tell your employer you want to see all facets of stadium management. Sit in on staff meetings, be present during the preparation of the event, at the event itself, and at post-event activities. See it all.

◯ Get some experience first at a small venue; apply for jobs at a nighclub, concert hall, or theater before going after the big arenas and stadiums.

◯ Break into the large arenas slowly. Secure part-time jobs in one of the related areas such as parking, security, or concessions.

REAL-LIFE ADVICE

Bill Lester,
executive director, Metropolitan Sports Facilities Commission

The Metropolitan Sports Facilities Commission is a public entity that owns and operates the Metrodome in Minneapolis, Minnesota. In his role as executive director, Bill Lester oversees the day-to-day operation of the Metrodome, home to the Twins and Vikings. Lester is currently in his tenth year at the Metrodome.

personality sketch

Supervisory; organized; business-minded; detail-oriented; diplomatic; problem-solver.

He attended a small college in Montana, where he played on the football team while earning his degree in philosophy. He came to Minnesota to attend the seminary, which he did for two years before leaving to become a teacher and coach. Before arriving at the Metrodome, Lester worked for 12 years as a special assistant to the chairman of the metropolitan planning agency that was responsible for systems such as airports, sewers, and transportation.

"The agency I worked for reviewed the budget of the sports commission, so I was familiar with the sports commission and the people associated with it. When they started looking for an executive director, I figured they wanted someone who was an administrator, someone used to working with boards and commissions. At the interview I told them that if they were looking for someone who could repair the air-conditioning system I was not the right person. But if they were looking for an administrator who could hire and fire those people, and someone who could organize the various systems that constitute stadium management, then I was the right person.

"When I worked at the planning agency, we used to say process is our product. In this business you know that come hell or high water, on the 28th of October the Vikings will play the Chicago Bears here. There's closure and a sense of accomplishment when you put all the systems in place that will result in that game. We see our job as a gathering place where people come to create these tremendous events that become such an important part of the fabric of people's lives. These are chances to celebrate because you come to these events with people you care about and who care about you. Our job is to provide a clean, safe environment for these essential parts of the human existence to take place. That's the magic of the job. There's an energy and excitement to playing a part in such huge numbers of people's lives.

"In 1995, the Metrodome was booked on 305 days. As a publicly owned facility, we have an integral responsiblity to see that the public gets a return, not just use of it for pro sports. We wouldn't have the building if not for pro sports, but this also allows us to have charitable events, high school football, college baseball. Everything from roller skating in the corridors to having a clean, safe place for runners to run in our concourse on alternate nights during the winter.

"My advice to people interested in this field is don't look at a specific person in a specific job. Rather, look at what the services are that have to be delivered in order to put these events on, either on the team side or the building side. See where you might have an interest or a potential niche. Take the skills you already have in an area of your expertise, and then look where there's a fit. Look where your skills are, and where your interests and inclinations are, and then think broader than one specific job."

SPOTLIGHT

Bob Castronovo,
executive vice president and general manager,
Meadowlands Sports Complex

During his 15 years of service at the Meadowlands, Bob Castronovo has shaken the hand of Pope John Paul II and removed by hand from a candy dish all of the brown M & M's in accordance with the contract of rock group Van Halen.

Whether he's greeting the President of the United States (he's met them all since Nixon) or securing a helicopter for Elton John (the singer refuses to fly in all but one specific type), Castronovo orchestrates the proceeding with elan.

"You want to appease people," he says, "but still treat them in a way they won't lose respect for you."

In his current position with the New Jersey Sports & Exposition Authority, Castronovo runs Giants Stadium—the only stadium in the country that has two NFL teams as tenants—as well as the Continental Airlines Arena. A bustling place, the Meadowlands is home to the NFL's Giants and Jets, the NBA's Nets, the NHL's Devils, Rutgers football, Seton Hall basketball, many major outdoor rock concerts, and various touring shows, like Ice Capades and Ringling Brothers, Barnum & Bailey Circus.

Castronovo is well prepared to deal with screaming crowds—he was a high school teacher before joining the Meadowlands. He worked after school and on weekends as a part-time supervisor of ushers ("I needed extra money"). In 1981, he was offered the job of admissions manager, and he accepted. "People thought I was crazy," he says, "leaving the security of a tenured position. But I've always loved sports and entertainment, and this was something I wanted to pursue."

As admissions manager, Castronovo was in charge of about 100 ushers, 70 ticket takers, and 30 elevator operators. Once he had mastered the nuances of guest services, often called the front-of-the-house activities, he then set out to learn the back-of-the-house operations. He served the facility as an event manager for six years, then was promoted to director of adminstration in 1987. In this position he was dealing with contracts, insurance, and scheduling. Two years later he was named assistant general manager and, in 1995, to his current post as the man in charge.

Over the past few years, the Meadowlands has hosted the World Cup, the Stanley Cup, nearly two dozen outdoor concerts, the NCAA basketball Final Four, and the papal visit. Castronovo, who has a bachelor of arts in history/pre-law from Rutgers University and two master's degrees from Montclair State University (history and administration), admits that "because the buck stops with me, the pressure can be intense." Especially during certain types of rock concerts.

There was the time when Axl Rose, the lead singer of Guns N' Roses, didn't arrive for the show until well after midnight. "That's when this job isn't fun," says Castronovo. "You're worried because 70,000 kids are in the house waiting for him to come on stage. If he doesn't, you'll have big problems. I sweated a lot."

And for good reason. The next night, Rose was a no-show for the band's scheduled gig in Montreal. The fans trashed the building. Castronovo cites another nerve-racking experience that occured during a Grateful Dead concert. While the band was playing, a tornado touched down just a few miles away from the stadium. Whether or not the Deadheads were aware of the impending danger, Castronovo was forced to evacuate the field not once, but twice, during the show.

Inclement weather is a reoccuring problem for stadium managers. New Jersey hadn't had any rainfall for weeks leading up to the papal visit. Lo and behold, when Pope John Paul II arrived at Giants Stadium, the heavens opened up. "It rained like crazy that day," says Castronovo, "but the Pope stood out there for a couple of hours to greet all the people who made the event work. He said to me 'See, I've cured your drought.'"

SUCCESS STORY

Jerry Bell,
president, Minnesota Twins

Named the third president in the history of the Minnesota Twins in 1987, Jerry Bell is in his tenth year as chief executive of the organization. It is in that position that he is responsible for the business activity of the club.

Bell joined the Twins after serving as executive director of the Metropolitan Sports Facilities Commission, which operates the Metrodome. He joined the M.S.F.C. as assistant executive director upon the commission's inception in 1977.

Prior to becoming involved in professional sports, Bell's background was in the park planning and construction business. He served as chief park planner for the Twin Cities Metropolitan Council and was involved in the construction of 47 parks, an 18-hole golf course, two ice arenas, and numerous other park and recreation facilities throughout the Twin Cities metropolitan area.

ADDRESS BOOK

Facilities Publications

Agent & Manager
650 First Avenue
New York, NY 10016
212/532-4150

Amusement Business
49 Music Square West
Nashville, TN 37203
615/321-4250

Athletic Business
1846 Hoffman Street
Madison, WI 53704
608/249-0186

STADIUM MANAGER

If the executive director is like a landlord, the stadium manager is the building superintendent. The individual in this position is responsible for overseeing everything about the physical facility, from the locker room to the playing field.

The stadium manager makes sure that the game clock, scoreboard, and public address system is working; that the field is marked properly, the basket is 10 feet high, the goal posts are the right width apart; the seats are clean, all security guards, ushers, and ticket takers are in place, and that the band performing the halftime show gets off the field on time.

The stadium manager, sometimes called the building manager, is also responsible for all physical and mechanical aspects of the facility. This includes a familiarity with the technical features and mechanical operation of the plant, as well as the maintenance of equipment and machinery. The manager is also in charge of all field maintenance crews such as the groundskeepers, the setup and teardown crews, as well as all custodial operations.

An important function of the stadium manager is the supervision of facility employees. These can include ushers, security, maintenance personnel, electricians, and sound and lighting technicians. The individual is responsible for directing the activities of the employees and making sure everyone does their jobs properly to ensure the most efficient operation.

The stadium manger is required to keep the facility clean and in good condition, making sure repairs are made when needed. One of the most important functions of the stadium manager is to handle all the problems and crises that occur within the scope of the job. An individual who can solve problems quickly, calmly, and effectively will be successful in this job.

FROM ALLEY-OOP TO ZAMBONI

Ever wonder how an arena is able to host two sporting events in a day, each with a different surface? One such day could start with a basketball game at 1:30 p.m. on the hardwood, followed by a hockey game at 7:30 p.m. on the ice. After the basketball game ends, the court must be removed and replaced by ice. And the seating configuration—especially the choice seats around the playing surface—must be rearranged.

John Fett, who for decades was the building manager at the old Chicago Stadium, is a tear-down, set-up legend in the field. He was an Air Corps pilot in World War II and once managed movie theaters owned by the Wirtz family, who own the stadium, as well as the Bulls and the Blackhawks. Here's how it worked: After the Bulls' afternoon game had been completed, Fett took charge of the 20 or so men who must ready the Stadium for the evening's hockey game. The workers stack chairs, sweep debris, coil wires, roll carpets, and prepare to remove the 255 sections of basketball court and dozens of black eight-by four-foot sheets of plywood resting under the court and atop the ice. Fett oversees the Stadium's metamorphosis from basketball court to hockey arena—and vice versa—in as little as three hours.

In addition to preparing the field for play, the stadium manager is also responsible for trouble-shooting in a crisis. During halftime of the 1996 NCAA men's basketball final, it seemed as if the Continental Arena roof had sprung a leak. This could have been a major embarassment for the Meadowlands Sports Complex, not to mention potential danger for players and spectators.

Large water droplets fell from the 129-foot-high ceiling and splashed off the south end of the court near the foul line. Bob Castronovo, then the arena's general manager, assigned workers to mop up the floor and dispatched a work crew to climb the catwalks high above the rafters in hopes of locating the source of the problem.

Crew members discovered that the roof was not leaking after all. The culprit was condensation from an air vent. Workers wrapped a towel around the offending vent—called an air diffuser—to contain the moisture, and no more water reached the court. Although the start of the second half was delayed briefly, play was not interrupted because of the drips.

INDUSTRIAL STRENGTH STAFF

Educational requirements for this job vary from person to person. A degree in sports management is helpful, but not all individuals in the position have one. At the least, a stadium manager will have a college degree in either accounting, business administration, marketing, public relations, or the like.

It's not mandatory for individuals in this position to be a building engineer. The stadium manager is not required to be an expert in heating, air-conditioning, or plumbing. But he or she will be expected to possess knowledge of industrial terms and have a general understanding of how equipment works. Should a piece of equipment ever be damaged and in some way affect a game, the media will bombard the stadium manager with questions. The individual in this position needs to know a little bit of what's going on in order to provide the answers.

The stadium manager can earn an annual salary of between $45,000 and $65,000. Variables depend on the type of facility and the person in the job. Factors regarding the facility include the size and location of the venue and the number of tenants. The stadium manager of a large, multipurpose facility located in a metropolitan area will earn more than an individual working at a single-tenant arena. The manager's experience, as well as the assumption of added responsiblity, will also determine earnings.

Experience is significant in obtaining this type of position. Most individuals have a background in sports administration, business management, community planning, or other related aspects in facility management. Other areas of experience necessary for someone in this position include the deployment and management of personnel in the security, concessions, parking, and cleanup functions.

An understanding of the technical aspects of the stadium is helpful, but not always required. At larger facilities the stadium manager will be assisted by a building maintenance supervisor and a field maintenance supervisor. Each supervisor earns an annual salary between $35,000 and $45,000 and will manage a small staff.

The building maintenance supervisor is in charge of the structural maintenance of the stadium and all capital improvements. He or she usually has an engineering background and will oversee a staff of electricians that handle the day-to-day functioning of all electrical systems as well as the air-conditioning units. The field maintenance supervisor oversees all duties performed by the grounds crew. He or she is expected to secure contracts with companies that handle the parking lots, the concession stands, and all cleanup functions.

STADIUMS' ROLE IN THE MILLENNIUM

Outside of sports, the stadium manager plays an important role in the community by overseeing the upkeep and maintenance of a facility. A well-operated stadium will attract other revenue-generating events such as musical concerts and business conventions. This contributes to the financial health of the city, as well as its cultural vibrancy, and its civic pride.

Jack Murphy Stadium in San Diego, California was built in 1967 at a cost of $27 million. Today that cost would be $200 million. A city-operated facility like Jack Murphy Stadium is an asset to the community. It's vital to the city that the stadium be keep in good working condition to service its numerous tenants.

"We're probably the busiest multipurpose, natural turf stadium in the country," says Steve Shushan, the assistant stadium manager of Jack Murphy Stadium. "Our goal is to be self-sufficient and not require any subsidies from the city. And, of course, to turn a profit."

To this end, facilities are implementing a strategy of utilizing the stadium as convention center. Jack Murphy Stadium has opened its doors to religious congregations such as the Jehovah's Witnesses, and in 1995 played host to the Alcoholics Anonymous convention. "It didn't help our beer sales," laughs Shushan, who then quickly adds "but it brought a lot of people into the city. A convention like that can draw over 50,000, so it fills up the hotel rooms and people spend money in the city."

To maximize revenues, the stadium rents its parking lot as much as possible. The Murph, as it's affectionately known, boasts the second largest parking lot in the country, with over 18,500 parking spaces. Among his numerous responsibilities inside the stadium, Shushan also oversees the rental of the parking lot. During an average year, 250 events will be held in the Jack Murphy Stadium parking lot. These events include boxing matches, motor sports racing, circuses, three-on-three basketball tournaments, automobile shows—anything that people can do on asphalt.

It's an exciting, rewarding, yet very stressful profession. "It's like running a little city," says Shushan. "All the problems that a city has— trash, recycling, traffic, noise pollution—are issues we have to deal with on a daily basis. And as a city-operated facility, we had to institute a no-smoking policy in the seating areas of the stadium. That was revolutionary because we were the first multitenant facility to institute the policy."

TIPSHEET

- ① Experience is your ally in this competitive field. Try to obtain an internship at a small theater or a supper club. Then volunteer for a part-time job at a stadium or arena.

- ① You're more apt to be considered for an available full-time job if you're already a known commodity. Look for part-time positions at a sports complex in areas such as security, parking, ushers, ticket takers, and concessions.

- ① Set yourself apart from the crowd. Learn as much as possible about how a stadium operates; become familar with equipment and machinery.

REAL-LIFE ADVICE

Steve Shushan,
assistant stadium manager, Jack Murphy Stadium

As assistant stadium manager, Steve Shushan is responsible for facility operations, finances, and contracts for San Diego's Jack Murphy Stadium, home to the Padres, Chargers, San Diego State University Aztecs, and the Holiday Bowl. Before working in his current position, Shushan was the stadium's business manager. His background is bolstered by two decades of administrative and management experience with the city of San Diego.

> ## personality sketch
>
> *Organized; good communication skills; supervisory; trouble-shooting ability; calm demeanor.*

"If you like sports and entertainment I think this is the job for you. There is no typical day at the stadium. One day may include talking to a promoter who is interested in bringing in an event; another day you're dealing with a production company that wants to use your facility for filming a commercial. This diversity is something I really love. You're not going into a job and just crunching numbers. You're dealing with day-to-day problems, and it's fun.

"The cons of the job is that it's very stressful. You're pulled in numerous directions. One of our goals is to have a facility that is profit making. But if you put on a concert, you may get complaints from the city council, from the citizens, saying this will create problems. So you have to deal with that fine balance and walk a tightrope. Do we host an event that may create a problem, but will get us $250,000? Yes we do. But we try to minimize the problems as best we can. We work with security and work with the police, so there aren't any problems in the surrounding areas and people can't jump on you the next day.

"If you asked me, 'How does one get into the facility management field?' Lots of persistence and luck. There's many related industries that are involved in putting on an event at a stadium, such as the food concessionaire, parking, and security. Those jobs usually open on a part-time basis, where you could have a regular job during the day and at night maybe take a job as a security guard or with the food concessionaire. This way you're getting a foot in the door, and people are seeing your face. So when a position does open up, you'll have a better opportunity if you've already worked in the stadium.

"The skills that I feel are essential are, first of all, you need to be thick-skinned and have a lot of self-confidence. You're going to be jumped on from all different angles—the media, the tenants, the citizens. You can't take it personally. You need to be confident in what you're doing and how you're doing the job. You need good business management and organizational skills. The saying, 'You're only as good as the people under you,' I agree with 100 percent. You need to develop a good organizational structure and a high-performing team. That takes practice and knowledge in having good organizational skills.

"You need good marketing, advertising, and public relations skills. I can't say enough about good public relations. If you can't present yourself well and speak well for the facility—you're dead. You also need good negotiating skills. You negotiate not only with the people under you, but with the supervisors in getting a job done; with the unions who come to you about salary increases; and with the tenants, who are always demanding improvements."

SPOTLIGHT

Bill Squires,
general manager, Walt Disney World Sports Complex

When the Walt Disney company broke ground on a new sports complex in March 1996, they hired Bill Squires to run it. In his position as general manager, Squires oversees the new Disney complex in Florida, the crown jewel being a 7,500-seat baseball stadium that will become the spring training site for the Atlanta Braves starting in 1998 and the home of the rookie league team.

The complex will also include a 5,000-seat field house, a 5,000-seat arena for track and field, four general purpose fields, four softball fields, 12 clay tennis courts with seating for 2,000 fans, several Little League baseball fields, five sand volleyball courts, and an All-Star sports cafe. "What I find exciting is I'll be in on this from the start," says Squires.

Prior to joining The Mouse, Squires worked for the New Jersey Sports and Exposition Authority as director of Giants Stadium operations. At the Meadowlands he was responsible for making sure the stadium was ready for football games and a wide range of other events, including rock concerts and papal visits.

A 1975 graduate of the U.S. Military Academy, Squires left the active service in 1987 to take a job as head of operations at Yankee Stadium. He came to the Meadowlands in a similar capacity in 1990.

"As a kid, the Yankees were my favorite baseball team and the Giants were my favorite football team," he says. "Now that I've had a chance to work with both of them, people said, 'What are you going to do next to top that?' Going to Disney World might be it."

ADDRESS BOOK

International Association of Auditorium Managers
4425 West Airport Freeway
Irving, TX 75062
214/255-8020

Stadium Managers Association
875 Kings Highway
Woodbury, NJ 08096
609/384-6287

EVENTS COORDINATOR

The events coordinator of a sports facility performs many of the same functions as a theatrical stage manager. The individual in this position will act in the capacity of stadium representative—serving as a liaison between the tenants, leasees, building staff, promoter, and facility management—with responsibility for organizing and overseeing the readiness of the field.

The events coordinator is in charge of scheduling and coordinating all on-field events. He or she will have varied responsibilities depending on the size of the facility and the specific event being held. Within the scope of the job, the coordinator must communicate requests to the building staff and follow-up to ensure the successful completion of projects.

The person in this job is very visible during the pre-game, halftime, and post-game activities. Duties may include providing the anthem singer with musical accompaniment or a wireless microphone. If the microphone is not operational, the events coordinator will assign an electrician or sound technician to fix or replace it.

The events coordinator is very active during a game. The individual is expected to handle all emergencies and problems that may occur. If the hockey rink's ice is not firm enough, the events coordinator will assign a plant manager or building engineer to adjust the chiller machines (the equipment that freezes the ice).

Another duty performed by the events coordinator is the supervision of all part-time workers that comprise the event staff. Personnel includes ushers, ticket takers, parking attendants, security guards, concessionaires, and custodians. The events coordinator works closely with the crews at the facility to ensure that everyone is doing their jobs properly.

At some of the larger, multipurpose facilities, the events coordinator may also be required to handle all the bookings for nonmajor tenant events. In this role, the person will oversee all aspects of the event, from the initial inquiry about stadium availability, to interfacing with the promoter's staff, to inception of the event, and right up through to the actual staging of the event. The coordinator will also arrange for the setup prior to the event and the teardown following the event.

GO SITE-SEEING

Employment prospects are good for events coordinators. Almost every community has a public facility, whether it be a stadium, an arena, or a convention center. Add to this the emerging trend of maximizing the facility's user-friendliness, and that equals available opportunity. Coupled with a healthy turnover rate—events coordinators frequently go on to better-paying positions—an interested and persistent individual should be able to get a foot in the door.

An internship is the most important training one can have to break into this field. While a college degree in sports management or administration is helpful, it's not a requirment to landing a position as an events coordinator. When hiring for a staff position, the facility manager is most interested in a candidate's experience. The majority of sports facilities offer internship opportunities.

Internships are also available at big corporations that specialize in managing sports facilities. Companies such as Ogden Entertainment and Leisure Management International offer stadium owners a comprehensive service of venue management in the hopes of providing a more efficient and profitable facility. The firms bring in their own personnel to fill the key positions, which means they control numerous jobs in the industry.

Facilities managed by Ogden Entertainment include Arrowhead Pond in Anaheim, California; The Great Western Forum in Inglewood, California; Hartford Civic Center in Connecticut; Rosemont Horizon in Illinois; and Target Center in Minneapolis, Minnesota. Sites run by Leisure Management International include Miami Arena in Florida; The Pyramid Arena in Memphis, Tennessee; and The Summit in Houston, Texas.

EDIFICE COMPLEX

The events coordinator can earn an annual salary in the range of $35,000 to $45,000, but wages can be augmented with lots of overtime pay. The events coordinator is relegated to long hours, ensuring that the team or event for which he or she is responsible runs smoothly. This requires being the first person at the venue in the morning and the last one to leave in the evening. It also requires a tremendous amount of overtime, as these events are commonly held at night or on weekends.

What are the dos and don'ts for an events coordinator? Says Rick Nafe, who for 12 years served as president of the Stadium Managers Association, "Do be enthusiastic. Do not watch the clock. Do not worry about weekends and holidays." A dubious testimonial, but a realistic one. The events coordinator puts in long hours and should expect to be working when everyone else is playing. Still, say events coordinators we talked to, the variety of duties is extremely stimulating.

TIPSHEET

- Getting that first job in facility management takes persistence. But once you're in, advancement to better-paying positions is a snap.

- An internship at a sports complex will give you needed experience, and it also indicates that you're serious about working in the field.

- Don't be too proud to accept a low-level job. Once you're in the business you'll hear of interesting job openings throughout the industry network.

- A terrific job can become available at any moment. But it's in another state. The freedom to relocate is key to one's upper mobility.

REAL-LIFE ADVICE

Gary Groves,
special events coordinator, Anaheim Stadium

In his position at Anaheim Stadium, Gary Groves is respon-sible for the organization of all events in the 70,000-seat facility as well as the accompanying 105,000-square-foot exhibition center. He acts as liaison between the stadium and the Anaheim Angels, in additional to other tenants, including the Freedom Bowl and the Disney Land Pigskin Classic.

Before joining Anaheim Stadium, Groves served as assistant facility director and events coordinator for the Portland Exposition Center, a small multipurpose facility in Maine.

personality sketch

Excellent interpersonal communication skills; detail-oriented; ability to delegate tasks and organize follow-ups; cool under pressure.

"After working at the Portland Exposition Center for a year an a half, later my boss informed me that he was a finalist for a job at another facility. I was happy for him, but at the same time I was confused inside. If he left two things could happen. I could be promoted to his job as director, or another director would come in and want their own assistant and I'd be out on the street. So I started thumbing through this trade magazine, *Amusement Business*, and there was a posting for the events coordinator at Anaheim Stadium. I always wanted to work for a facility that housed a professional team and here it is, a great opportunity to get back out to California. So I applied for it.

"The people from Anaheim Stadium called me. They said they wanted me to interview for the job, but the first round of interviews would have to be by telephone because they couldn't fly me out. I told them I was going to pay my own way to come out and see them in person. I felt it was important for me to see them and see how the facility was run and the people who were there. So I flew out on my own, and to sum it up, I got the position.

"I've been fortunate with the experiences and job opportunities that I've had, but I felt like I made them happen. I took an aggressive approach. I took the initiative by flying out there on my own. That separated me from the others that applied. You get out and do whatever you can to get in. If you have a full-time job and you have to work at a facility part time, then do it.

"At Anaheim Stadium we're presently looking at about 210 event days per year, so there's a big commitment there. In my job I'm dealing with people who lease the facility. It takes a lot of time. You're working events that happen at night and on the weekends. It's a sacrifice you have to make. You get a lot of self-gratification. There's no better feeling when you've worked hard to produce an event and it goes off safely, and people had a good experience.

"What we look for in terms of skills when we go to hire, it's not so much what experience you have, but it's really how you fit into our facility. It's how you deal with people, especially difficult people. It's all about your ability to manipulate behavior. You have crowds of 60,000 people coming to an event; you can't have total chaos."

ADDRESS BOOK

Leisure Management International
11 Greenway Plaza
Houston, TX 77046
713/623-4583

Ogden Entertainment Services
Two Pennsylvania Plaza
New York, NY 10121
212/868-6000

SCOREBOARD OPERATOR

As the batter steps up to home plate, a baseball fan can glance at the stadium's scoreboard and, in an instant, see that player's photograph, read his hitting statistics, learn how he's doing in this game, and how he's fared against this pitcher during his career. The scoreboard information you take for granted all comes from a glass-enclosed booth located high above the action.

personality sketch

Understanding of sports and an uncanny ability to concentrate; knowledge of computers, graphic design, and script writing.

Some members of the scoreboard operation team are responsible for inputting numerical data such as the number of balls, strikes, runs, hits, and outs. Others keep track of game scores from around the country and update them as needed.

Assistant directors and video assistants are responsible for producing five hours of live entertainment for each of the season's 81 home games. They write scripts for 15 to 20 video features for daily use on the Diamond Vision.

"Everything is scripted," says John Franzone, who as the New York Yankees' director of video and broadcasting operations, is the man in charge of running the Yankee Stadium scoreboard. "The videos, player intros, the music between innings, advertisements, even the trivia quiz. It's all scripted."

The preparation begins at 9 o'clock in the morning when the assistant directors and video assistants begin scripting the production for the scoreboard's opening number when fans enter the stadium at 6 o'clock that evening. Production time is cut in half for day games, when the gates open at 11:30 a.m. On those days, the staff begins production at 7 a.m.

Franzone, now in his 10th season with the Bronx Bombers, points out that the scoreboard should react to the game action like a loyal hometown fan: leading the cheers, providing useful factoids, testing fans' memory, and even taunting the opposition. "It's an electronic world, an MTV world," Franzone says. "People look to the scoreboard for information and entertainment."

Author's Note: Franzone has since left the Yankees' organization to run the scoreboard system at Walt Disney World Sports Complex.

YOUR NAME IN LIGHTS

Stadium scoreboards have come a long way since the days when a man peered through an opening in the board and slipped a wooden block number in a slot next to the inning to indicate runs scored. These days, it seems every major league ballpark and professional arena sports a fancy scoreboard. Fortunately for those who wish to become scoreboard operators, progress translates into greater employment opportunities.

It takes several people to operate all of the different scoreboards that are currently in use. At Yankee Stadium, an 11-person staff comprises the full scoreboard team. The Yankee Stadium scoreboard, installed in 1982, is actually a multifaceted information-display system. The centerpiece is the Diamond Vision screen, which shows specially produced videos, live game action, instant replays, color stills of players, and typed messages.

The Matrix board is filled with stats and cleverly designed artwork. This board also keeps count of balls and strikes and records the number of outs for each half inning. The Line scoreboard tallies the up-to-the-minute line score, noting runs, hits, and errors as they happen. The Out of Town scoreboard provides periodic updates of all scheduled games being played that day.

In this high-tech age where information is a commodity, the members of the scoreboard operations crew are the ultimate information brokers. While no formal education is required to operate a scoreboard, the requisite training is necessary to successfully manage it. Classes on computer graphics and data entry are helpful, as are courses that teach script writing.

Hands-on experience is vital whether it is obtained through internship or by assisting an experienced scoreboard operator.

Individuals interested in the field of scoreboard operation should volunteer to work at high school games. Once an individual feels comfortable working the scoreboard under game conditions, he or she should contact local teams to volunteer his or her services.

KNOW THE SCORE

Earnings for scoreboard operators vary greatly. Factors determining earnings include whether the operator is working a sophisticated scoreboard at the major league level or a simpler board at the college or minor league level.

An individual working a basic Line scoreboard that tracks the progress of a college game is likely to be a student who pockets an extra $25 spending money. At the minor league level, however, the person might be a retired coach who earns $150 per game.

A head scoreboard operator in charge of a new-fangled major league system can earn in the range of $35,000 to $50,000 a year. Earning power may be upwardly affected by the operator's reputation. Top operators are recognized by winning an award from the Information Display and Entertainment Assocation (IDEA). This group develops programming for scoreboards in stadiums and arenas throughout the United States. Winning an IDEA award will never be likened to winning the Oscar for Best Picture at the Academy Awards. But the IDEA awards do honor deserving members of the field, and these individuals may be highly sought after. Three of the most prestigious awards include Best Video Board Display, Best Matrix Board Display, and an award citing Honorary Excellence. The trophy for Honorary Excellence is bestowed upon the team whose scoreboard displays and entertainment are consistently of the highest quality.

PUSH THE RIGHT BUTTONS

Head scoreboard operators can advance their careers by receiving job promotions from minor league teams to major league teams. Advancement opportunities are also available through relocation from small market teams to large market teams in more prestigious cities.

When breaking into the business, it is most common to move up from within the organization. Individuals who can handle inputting numbers on the Line scoreboard and the Out of Town scoreboard may earn a promotion to Matrix board or Diamond Vision screen. From there, a person can work towards becoming an assistant director or video assistant, and then be next in line when and if a higher-level job becomes available.

A JOB YOU CAN COUNT ON

Individuals aspiring to become scoreboard operators must have an uncanny ability to concentrate. The operator must never lose track of the count or the number of outs in an inning. Failure to do so will result in keen embarassment. "There are no time-outs for us," Franzone says. "When the television goes on a commerical break, that's when we're really cookin'."

A qualified operator should have a thorough knowledge of the sport and be able to anticipate events before they occur. During a game, there's split-second timing involved, with photographs and statistics gracing the board in rapid-fire sequence. It does get chaotic. And often times, an event happens on the field that requires a member of the scoreboard crew to improvise. Franzone recalls the time when he looked at a graphic on the scoreboard and said to his staff in amazement, "How'd that get up there?"

Also important is the talent to create an entertaining diversion for fans when the game on the field slows down. A personal favorite is the Bunyan-esque bat that swings across the center field scoreboard, each swat leaving in its wake the words, "We want a hit!"

TIPSHEET

- Ⓤ Enroll in basic computing classes to reach a level of comfort when working with keyboards and display screens.

- Ⓤ Gain a thorough understanding of all sports so as to anticipate events before they occur.

- Ⓤ Attend as many sporting events as possible and pay attention to the scoreboard's role before, during, and after the game. This will provide you with a good source of ideas.

- Ⓤ Get as much experience as you can. Offer to act as the scoreboard operator for high school sporting events, especially basketball, to determine if you maintain composure under fire.

☺ Contact amateur and professional teams for entry-level positions. Getting your foot in the door is important because most scoreboard jobs are "inside hires."

ADDRESS BOOK

Daktronics, Inc.
331 32nd Avenue
Brookings, SD 57006
605/692-6145
(Designer and manufacturer of
electronic scoreboards)

Display Solutions
6301 Best Friend Road
Norcross, GA 30017
800/541-9593

(Designer of outdoor video
systems)

*Information & Display
Systems, Inc.*
11222-2 St. Johns Industrial
Parkway
Jacksonville, FL 32246
904/645-8697

GAME PRODUCTION MANAGER

It's been said that music calms the savage beast. And when combined with the fast-paced, unpredictable tempo of sports, music also excites and invigorates.

The popular melodies you hear blaring from the stadium's sound system are brought to you courtesy of the game production manager. Working much like a silent disc jockey, this individual psyches up the crowd by spinning tunes before and after the game, between innings, periods, or quarters, and during other long breaks in the action.

The person in this job will be expected to have an encyclopedic knowledge of popular music. At most stadiums and arenas the production manager may choose the music for the playlist. At others, a slight restriction may be imposed, which calls for the production manager to work with a superior in compiling the list of songs.

Once the playlist is developed, a written song schedule may be followed. The production manager at the Metrodome in Minnesota, for example, is required to play "We're Gonna Win Twins" when the team takes the field and after each victory. Once an individual in this job has proven restraint, he or she may then be allowed to exercise some ad-libbing skills. This aspect of the job requires knowing when it is an appropriate time to use special sound effects.

The game production manager is responsible for giving cues to an engineer who controls the soundboard. During a hockey game, when a particularly violent collision occurs, you may hear the sound of teeth rattling. To accomplish the effect, the production manager and engineer must work closely together and be able to communicate ideas quickly.

A production manager and engineer at the major league level will earn between $25,000 and $35,000 per year, depending on experience and stadium prestige. A game production manager with additional responsibilities in the marketing and promotions departments, for instance, can expect to earn on the high end of this spectrum.

Although no educational requirement is needed for this job, some type of internship or apprenticeship is recommended. Unless a team is willing to provide on-the-job training, it's doubtful that you will be hired without previous experience.

JOCK ROCK

Professional and college teams throughout the country use music to get the crowd fired up to fever pitch. One foot-stomping tune that resonates in stadiums and arenas is "Rock and Roll, Part 2" by Gary Glitter. This popular hit from the 1960s has once again returned to the top of the charts with a bullet, thanks to its heavy play at sporting events.

The song's national coming-out party occured during the 1991 World Series at the Metrodome in Minnesota. It was played over the public address system when the home team scored a run. It really stoked the crowd by letting them chant "Hey" in unison on every other fourth beat.

It had originally become popular in the Twin Cities in the spring of 1990 when the North Stars reached the Stanley Cup finals. When the Twins reached the American League playoffs, Joe Johnston, then the team's game production manager, decided to play the number.

"It's a crowd pleaser, a real rally song," Johnston says. "The fans automatically related to the music, and when they yelled 'Hey!' and the homer hankies flew, it was awesome."

Another sports rally song that is at least semi-awesome is "We Will Rock You/We Are the Champions" by the rock group Queen, which is sung at a number of stadiums.

Most rewarding for the production manager is the rare occasion when one of his selections becomes the team's theme song. The pop song most associated with a baseball team is the 1979 hit "We Are Family," by the Philadelphia-born vocal quartet of sisters who recorded under the same of Sister Sledge.

This tune became the theme song of the 1979 World Champion Pittsburgh Pirates, led by Willie "Pops" Stargell. It was regularly heard over the sound system at Pittsburgh's Three Rivers Stadium and on boom boxes in the Pirates clubhouse.

REAL-LIFE ADVICE

Wayne Petersen,
game production manager, Minnesota Twins

Wayne Petersen has worked for the Minnesota Twins since 1987. He began as an intern in the club's marketing and promotions department while working towards his master's degree in sports administration from Mancato (Minn.) State University. Upon graduating, he was hired for a full-time position. In addition to his duties as game production manager, Petersen has also served the club in the capacity of advertising and broadcast manager.

"The game production staff coordinates a schedule of half-inning breaks with Ron Newman, who's been our organist for over 18 years. The script might call for organ music after the bottom of the third inning or for canned taped music after the top of the fourth. I'll usually schedule 66-percent of the half innings for canned music and one-third for organ.

"During the game we're all communicating on head sets. If something happens impromtu, the organist usually has to take it. The flow of the game will dictate the music we play. A tight ballgame is a different scenario than a blowout. During a tight game the crowd is much more likely to respond; they're already in the game. You can get them out of their seats and on their feet by playing upbeat, high-energy-level music.

"The type of crowd at the ballpark will also determine the music we play. Wednesday nights are senior nights and Sunday afternoons tend to be more families with young kids. We'll try to appease those crowds by laying off the high-volume stuff and rely more on the organist.

"Actually, a lot of what we play is dictated by our own players. During batting practice we'll roll a music reel and often times the players have suggested some of the songs we play. Some players actually give us a written list of what music they like to hear when they come up to bat. Paul Molitor is a huge Bruce Springsteen fan. So every time Molitor comes up to bat we play "Born to Run." Marty Cordova is a huge fan of the movie "Mission: Impossible," so when he comes up we play that theme song.

"I don't really think Molitor got his 3,000th hit because we psyched him up, but we're definitely helping the cause. We're not working against them, we're working with them. Whatever the players want, we're happy to oblige."

PUBLIC ADDRESS ANNOUNCER

The public address announcer acts much like the master of ceremonies of the event. The individual's main function is to announce all pertinent information before, during, and after the game. Some announcers merely state the information in an authoritative tone. Others have unique styles or enthusiastic phrasings that they use to excite the crowd. Whatever your style, you must possess a clear and pleasant speaking voice.

personality sketch

Public speaking experience good communication skills; clear speaking voice; knowledge of foreign pronunciations

The public address announcer's job begins a few hours before the event. During this time, the individual collects information about each team, including the roster of names and the particular lineups to be used for that game. The announcer must be sure to pronounce all names correctly. Most teams include a pronunciation guide in the media booklet, but if you are still unsure, enter the locker room and ask the player personally.

Depending on the event, the public address announcer may explain the stadium ground rules, warn spectators about interfering with play, introduce a celebrity to take part in a pre-game ceremony, and ask the audience to rise as an entertainer sings the national anthem. An individual in this job will then announce the starting lineups and the officials.

During a baseball game the PA announcer introduces each batter as he approaches the plate and each new pitcher as he enters the ballgame. During a football game, the PA announcer acts more as a basic play-by-play announcer, identifying the ballcarrier, the yards gained, who made the tackle or recovered the fumble, as well as announcing the current down and yardage needed for a first down.

While there are people who do this as a full-time job, most freelance on a part-time basis. Individuals may work for more than one facility. Positions may be located throughout the country in any city that hosts a team.

YOUR ATTENTION PLEASE

The majority of public address announcers got their start as high school students working for their local teams, or in college. A bachelor's degree in speech communications is not required, but a comfortable pulic speaking manner is essential to becoming successful in this field.

A pleasant speaking voice is not a prerequisite for this position. Indeed, some of the most successful annonuncers, like Rex Barney, possess a voice of pedestrian quality. But the good announcers have staying power because they become part of the stadium experience. Anyone who has ever attended a Baltimore Orioles game will remember Barney's reaction whenever a foul ball was caught by someone in the stands: "Give that fan a contract."

Several avenues are available for a PA announcer to advance his or her career. An announcer working freelance for a team in the low minor leagues may be hired for a full-time position by a team in the high minors. Or an announcer working in the minors may be promoted to the major leagues. Another way to seek promotion is by jumping to a more presti-gious team or to a multi-purpose stadium with several tenants who require the talents of an announcer.

Many factors determine what a PA announcer can earn. These factors include the amount of work the individual does as well as the prestige of the teams and stadiums in which he or she works. An experienced freelance announcer can earn somewhere around $100 a game at the major college level, while a top-notch announcer in the major leagues may command in the range of $250 to $500 per game. Announcers with name-recogintion value can negotiate their own contracts.

THE VOICE OF REASON

Bob Sheppard has been the Yankee Stadium public address announcer since 1951, Joe DiMaggio's last year and Mickey Mantle's first. Sheppard's voice is the Stadium voice in our heads, the one that echoes from the deep caverns behind the right-field grandstands and rolls away toward the monuments in left-centerfield. Sheppard has seen the great years in the Bronx, the not-so-great, and the God-awful. Name a Stadium memory, and he introduced it.

"I'm not here to comment," says Sheppard. "I'm not here to be emotional. My style behind the microphone is considered old-fashioned. Some of my younger colleagues are saying 'Kirrr-bee Puck-ettt!!!!' I'm more restrained."

Sheppard relaxes by reading a novel in his tiny glass-enclosed box up behind home plate. He breaks away from his reading to make an entry in his box score. Then, in his inimitable style, he announces the next player's arrival at the plate.

"Now batting . . . Number Twelve . . . Wade Boggs. Number Twelve." With Sheppard at the microphone, the name is spoken like some sort of deity, with the bookend numbers on either side. Amazingly, he makes people hear both "g"s in "Boggs."

"I don't think I pause before consonants," says Sheppard, who also announces the Giants' football games over at the Meadowlands, "but I do want the vowels to be heard. Vowels and diphthongs are the open sounds, the beautiful sounds in the language. Consonants give intelligence to speech—the 't's, 'g's, 'd's, and 's's. They provide crispness and clarity."

FROM CICERO TO THE BIG 0

If you get the feeling that Sheppard lends a dignity and a professorial air to the proceedings, you're absolutely correct. He has been a professor of speech at St. John's University, in Queens, New York, even longer than he has been announcing. His course, "Introduction to Speech," is mandatory for all St. John's undergraduates. Students get into voice, diction, oral interpretation, and public speaking.

After picking up a master's degree in speech at Columbia, he came back to teach at his alma mater in the late forties. He drifted into announcing with the football Yankees, a club in the NFL-rival All-America Football Conference, who played their games at Yankee Stadium.

"The field hasn't changed much since Demosthenes and Cicero, but there's much less oratory than America once heard," Sheppard says. "The age of William Jennings Bryan is gone. We've become a lazy-tongued people."

THE NAME GAME

Sheppard normally stays out of the clubhouse, but whenever a new player with an unfamiliar name turns up, he tries to have a personal consultation about pronunciation. When rookie Mike Pagliarulo joined the Yankees in 1984, Sheppard approached him and asked the obvious question. According to Sheppard, Pagliarulo replied, "You know the opera Pagliacci? Same thing. Pahlyarulo."

When asked to name some of his favorite names, Sheppard goes into announcing mode: "Jose Valdivielso. Salome Barojas. Harmon Killebrew always had a nice flow to it. Alvaro Espinoza. Mickey Klutts. Goose Gossage you can make sound like a fastball. Some names are euphonic, some are not. Steve Sax is sharp and hard, a tough name."

STRANGE BUT TRUE

Sheppard doesn't travel much due to his busy schedule. But a few years ago, while the Yankees were on an extended road trip, he and his wife went to Fenway Park for the first time. His opposite number, the distinguished Sherm Feller, persuaded Sheppard to do a guest inning in the middle of the game.

Sheppard came on unannounced, and his first batter, by chance, was a familiar erstwhile Yankee who had moved along to the California Angels a year or two before.

"Now batt-ing for the Angels," Sheppard announced, "Number Forty-four . . . the right fielder . . . Reggie Jack-son. Number Forty-four."

Stunned, Reggie stepped back from the plate and dropped his bat on the ground. The first place he looked was straight up.

A SOPRANO IN THE CHORUS

In 1993, one of baseball's longest streaks came to an end as Sherry Davis of the San Francisco Giants became major-league baseball's first full-time female public address announcer, handling all 81 home games at Candlestick Park.

Davis, who is single and in her early 40s, got the job after trying out against 498 other candidates, only seven of them women. "I really did it on a lark," says Davis, a legal secretary and longtime Giants fanatic who called in sick that day. "I figured the worst that could happen is that I'd get to spend a spring day at Candlestick Park."

When her turn came, Davis, who had done some radio-commerial voiceovers, said, "Good afternoon, baseball fans. Welcome to Candlestick Park!"—and got a round of applause from the other candidates. She also got the job.

"Her voice is soothing, but there's a punch to it that generates excitement," said a Giants executive who helped pick Davis.

Davis earns $75 for every game, and she negotiated a makeup schedule with her law bosses for time lost announcing day games during the week. She also gets her own parking space and free popcorn in the press box, where she will be working.

She sees her selection as a, well, giant step for women. "I think it affects the way jobs are viewed," she says.

Careers in Sports Marketing and Public Relations

The field of sports marketing and public relations is an intriguing, and often overlooked, industry. The majority of people searching for employment in the sports field concentrate their efforts solely toward landing a job with a professional team or league. This is a terrible mistake. Falling under the larger umbrella of sports marketing, the areas of corporate sponsorship, special events, and licensed merchandise provide diverse career opportunities, offering interaction in both the sports and business worlds.

The mutual codependency between athletics and business is a cozy relationship. Sports fans today want bigger events, leading to rising costs not covered by the traditional means of revenue, such as ticket sales. Almost 35 percent of all professional teams are now charging at least $100,000 a year for luxury box suites, compared with about 2 percent just one decade ago. The revenue generated from corporate suites now equals that of overall ticket sales.

This fact alone speaks volumes as to who the venue, the team, and the sport are addressing. And business, which faces mounting competition, is forced to find new avenues to market their names, products, and services. Sports marketing agencies began selling the concept of corporate sponsorships in the mid-1970s. The idea took root during the 1980s and has blossomed in the '90s. In 1994, according to International

Events Group, a research firm that tracks sports sponsorships, the number of corporate sponsors has now reached over 3,500 and continues to escalate.

Marketing professionals are needed to protect the company's investment in sports. Corporate America spends nearly $25 billion annually on sports advertising, sponsorships, and related special events. The three largest companies accounted for $1.25 billion alone: General Motors ($445 million), Philip Morris ($405 million), and Anheuser-Busch ($400 million).

Prosperity is also being enjoyed by the leagues, who sell hundreds of millions of dollars' worth of licensed merchandise, ranging from team jerseys to trading cards to helmet-shaped umbrellas. Due to savvy marketers, sports is now awash in logos and brand names. When was the last time you heard someone use the word "sneakers?" Now they're called athletic shoes, and they confer status the way automobiles did during the 1950s, when America was coming of age.

In 1917, the Converse Rubber Company introduced a basketball sneaker. Several years later a former pro player named Chuck Taylor began driving around the country giving clinics and selling the Converse All-Stars out of the trunk of his car. In 1936 Converse honored Chuck Taylor by naming the sneaker after him.

Today, the desire for the hottest in sports attire and footwear has grown out of control. Thousands of American teens have a pair of athletic shoes in his closet that cost one hundred bucks. And the world is following our lead. In 1991, Nike registered international sales of $450 million. In 1992, that figure was over $1 billion. All serious athletic companies are now looking overseas as a source of new profitable markets.

Sports has grown out of all proportion to the rest of society. Many college football coaches earn more than the president of their university. The lowliest rookie in baseball is being paid more than the President of the United States. Not surprisingly, with so much money up for grabs, the employment landscape is sown with new opportunities in marketing, promotions, public relations, and licensed merchandise.

DIRECTOR OF PROMOTIONS

The director of promotions for a sports team is responsible for keeping the club in the public eye. The individual is in charge of building an interest in the team and thereby increasing the team's visibility. A person in this position needs to be a genetic cross between P. T. Barnum and Bill Gates.

To accomplish the aforementioned goal, the promotions director will be expected to develop unique promotions in order to attract attention from the media and the general public, as well as from potential advertisers. These promotions may include contests or special events that will provide fans attending the game an additional entertainment value.

Promotions may involve the team acting in an independent fashion, such as a baseball team giving away balls, bats, or caps. Other situations may require the promotion director to devise a "tie-in," which is a promotional idea involving a local advertiser or community organization. A commonly used "tie-in" is a radio station giving away free tickets to the first caller. Additional avenues where promotional opportunities can be explored include event sponsorship and athlete appearances.

Bill Giles, the owner of the Philadelphia Phillies, noted wryly that when his father was the president of the Cincinnati Reds, from 1937 to 1950, "marketing consisted of a one-inch ad on the sports page and a sign at the stadium that read 'Game Tonight.'"

Today's promotions techniques—such as market research, consumer profiles, and customer surveys—are proactive. The successful promotions director will be required to target the audience the team is attempting to reach and then determine the most appropriate, efficient, and productive ways to attract the attention of that audience. To this end, the individual working for a small franchise will often be expected to supervise research on demographics as well as on audience and community needs.

The director must bring all promotional ideas and projects to the team owner. If the project is approved, the promotions director will determine the appropriate implementation methods for the program. This may include deciding on the best time of year to execute the promotion, as well as its duration. A contest, for instance, will also require the hiring of outside personnel to handle any mailings such as coupon redemption and distribution of prizes. While the director will not personally oversee these functions, he or she is ultimately responsible for a smooth running program.

BUSH LEAGUE BONANZA

For a creative individual in the field of promotions, minor league baseball is a dream come true. Franchises are most often located in rural cities. The community is proud of its team, and the fans are loyal. The game is often a significant social event on the town calendar, and a family atmosphere pervades the ballpark and its surroundings. It's not unusual to find bush league ballparks hosting community events like an outfield egg-toss, three-legged race around the bases, or a cow-milking contest at home plate.

Mike Veeck, the son of the late Chicago White Sox owner-impresario Bill Veeck, is president and part owner of the St. Paul (Minn.) Saints, arguably the most successful minor-league ball club in the country. In its first two years of existence, 1993 and 1994, the team filled 98 percent of the 6,300 seats at Midway Stadium—the third highest occupancy rate in pro baseball, behind the Toronto Blue Jays and the Baltimore Orioles. Veeck's experience as a promoter is the reason for the team's success.

Veeck (rhymes with "wreck") first gained attention as the director of promotions for the White Sox. In 1979, he organized a "Disco Demolition Night," at which he set fire to hundreds of Donna Summer records and other disco paraphernalia in center field between games of a doubleheader. The bonfire ruined the grass and caused the Sox to forfeit the second game, effectively laying the foundation for Veeck's subsequent exile from major league baseball. He's never looked back.

"Independent baseball is definitely the wave of the future," says Veeck, who is currently riding atop the crest.

Several Saints players have gone on to the major leagues in recent years, including New York Mets shortstop Rey Ordonez, who played for Veeck in 1993. Darryl Strawberry, cast onto baseball's scrap heap, began 1996 in St. Paul, yet finished the season sipping champagne with the World Series-champion New York Yankees.

Whenever a Saints player is purchased by a major league team, the Saints get paid a finder's fee, in effect. The fee, often hefty, is still the most practical and risk-free method pro teams have of acquiring established young talent. The major leagues have begun to rely less on their minor league system—operating a minor league affiliate costs big money and there's no assurance that a bush leaguer will develop into major league material—and more on the independent teams.

"It makes a lot more sense to have me develop the talent," says Veeck, "and then sell it to them at a reasonable price."

PROMOTIONAL MATERIAL

Employment prospects are terrific in the growing field of marketing and promotions. Individuals who aspire to a sports promotions position may find jobs in any city that hosts a sports team, from Elmira (N.Y.) to Escondido (Ca.), Eau Claire (Wis.) to El Campo (Tex.).

Employment opportunities exist in team marketing within the areas of ticket sales, promotional events, corporate sponsorships, team licensing, and research. This research may include tracking the effectiveness of advertising and promotional campaigns, as well as analyzing demographics in order to more efficiently market the franchise.

Since ticket sales and sponsorships are the lifeblood of any franchise, it is vital for those working for the team to gain experience in a sales-related position. Whether it be the sale of season tickets, luxury boxes, group functions, or advertising time, most new marketing and promotions employees work in one of these departments. It wasn't always this way, however.

"When I started out everything was public relations," says Rich Israel, director of marketing for the NFL's San Diego Chargers. "There were only three or four of us in marketing—in the entire league of 28 teams. When we went to the PR meetings and got together, we couldn't even fill a table for lunch. Now it's all changed. They're called marketing and PR meetings and there's more people in marketing than PR."

Earnings for a promotions director can range from $25,000 to $125,000. Factors that determine an individual's salary include the experience and reputation of that person, as well as the location and prestige of the organization that he or she works for.

Depending on the size and structure of the organization, the promotions director may work alone or may supervise a small staff of assistants. The individual may also function in association with members of other departments, such as advertising, public relations or publicity, marketing, and community relations.

Career advancement opportunities may be found in these related areas, as well as within the community at large. Another function performed by a promotions director includes acting as the team's spokesperson and attending community or industry events on behalf of the organization. Valuable contacts are often forged at such events and may lead to more lucrative positions.

The majority of individuals working today as a promotions director have earned a marketing degree from a four-year college. Organizations searching for a promotions director will place much emphasis on educational requirements, experience, and a proven track record. At lower levels within a promotions department, however, applicants need only demonstrate enthusiasm, interest in the field, and moderate experience.

Experience may be obtained through an internship at a marketing and public relations company, by volunteering to work for the promotions department at a local radio or television station, or by getting a summer job with a minor league sports organization.

LIKE FATHER, LIKE SON

Or, if you're like Mike Veeck, you learn about sports promotions at the feet of the master, his father, Bill Veeck. Veeck, who died in 1986, was an iconoclast who learned the game at the hotdog stand in Chicago's Wrigley Field, where his father was general manager of the Cubs. Later, Bill himself became general manager of the then minor league Milwaukee Brewers.

Veeck sent a midget to bat, invented the exploding scoreboard, integrated the American League, put players' names on their uniforms, and produced the first baseball team to surpass the two-million mark in fan attendance (the 1948 Cleveland Indians). Veeck owned three different A.L. teams at various times: the Indians, White Sox, and St. Louis Browns.

After World War II Veeck brought Cleveland a pennant in 1948. His promotions brought in fans and he brought in the players, including Lary Doby, the league's first black player and 42-year-old rookie Satchel Paige. In the early 1950s, Veeck tried to save the Browns. Some of his gimmicks were outrageous, such as sending midget Eddie Gaedel to pinch-hit (he walked) and having the fans manage a game by holding up decision cards. As White Sox owner he gave the team its first pennant in forty years in 1959.

The midget incident warrants a closer look. Eddie Gaedel, who was a 26-year-old Chicago theatrical midget, was announced as a St. Louis Browns pinch hitter to lead off the bottom of the first inning in the second game of a double-header against the Detroit Tigers on August 19, 1951.

The scene was one of the most hilarious in baseball history. The 3-foot, 7-inch Gaedel wore uniform No. 1/8. When the announcer introduced him as a pinch hitter (replacing Frank Saucier), Gaedel bounded out of the dugout swinging three toy bats. His one-and-a-half-inch strike zone was so low that Tiger catcher Bob Swift knelt behind him. Left-hander Bob (Sugar) Cain, trying not to laugh, walked him on four pitches, whereupon Gaedel was replaced by a pinch runner (Jim Delsing) and scampered off the field.

Veeck had signed Gaedel earlier that day to a single-game contract for $100 plus expenses. He made his first appearance between games of the double-header when he popped out of a huge papier-mâché birthday cake that had been rolled onto the field in celebration of the American League's 50th anniversary.

Indignant over the stunt, AL President William Harridge warned other teams against the use of midgets and ordered the walk expunged from the record books. Fortunately, Gaedel's name and plate appearance remains in the Baseball Encyclopedia.

NOW PITCHING: MARCEL MARCEAU

The son has learned his lessons well. Mike Veeck's St. Paul (Minn.) Saints play in Midway Stadium, which is located just seven miles away from the Metrodome, home to the American League's major league baseball team, the Minnesota Twins. Despite the huge difference in stadium seating capacity, the Saints sometimes outdraw the Twins. "This is the hottest ticket in town," Veeck claims.

Fans enjoy the Saints games because they never know what to expect. One of Veeck's unforgettable schemes was "Mime Night." He hired mimes to re-create close plays with the idea of orchestrating instant replays through pantomime. What Veeck hadn't realized was that midwesterners loathe mimes. The resulting confusion was nowhere near the notoriety caused by his infamous Disco Demolition Night, but the fans' reaction was certainly memorable nonetheless.

"They were throwing everything that wasn't nailed down at the mimes, who left tearfully in the fifth inning," says Veeck. "They even got the mimes to talk back. It was quite undignified."

Somewhere Bill Veeck was smiling.

TIPSHEET

- Ⓓ Hands-on experience in promotions is vital. While you're still in high school, try to find a part-time or summer job with a local sports marketing company.

- Ⓓ College internships provide a valuable training ground and the opportunity to make important contacts. Ask your professors if the college has any connections.

- Ⓓ Break into the field slowly. The pay won't be very good at first, but the experience you receive will be worthwhile in the long run.

- Ⓓ Once you have some practical skills, begin sending your resume to sports teams and leagues, as well as major companies and businesses that you know are involved in sports.

- Ⓓ When applying for a job be sure your methods are creative and unique. Remember, you're looking for a promotions position. Prospective employers are apt to be searching for a distinctive individual, one capable of standing out from the crowd. If you can't promote yourself, the theory goes, you can't promote a team or product.

REAL-LIFE ADVICE

Rich Israel,
director of marketing, San Diego Chargers

Rich Israel joined the NFL's Chargers in January 1979 as director of advertising and promotions and maintained that position until he became director of marketing in 1984. Prior to joining the Chargers, he served as promotions manager for the San Diego Friars of World Team Tennis.

personality sketch

Creative imagination; excellent verbal skills; knowledge of sports.

"The best way to get into the business is one of three ways. One, intern without pay. It's a great opportunity, though not everyone is in a position to it; but if you can, it's a good way to learn about sports. Second is telemarketing. Most of the people who work for me now started in telemarketing. It's tough, but we don't look for professional telemarketers. We want enthusiastic people who want to get into sports, and then we teach them telemarketing. We bring in an outside consultant to provide professional telemarketing training. We'd rather have enthusiastic people representing us than somebody reading from a boilerplate. Third is commission sales. Anytime you're willing to walk in and say to somebody 'No risk to you; just give me a chance. I can sell for you; I can bring in revenue,' that's another way to break in.

"When I got into this business, everything was public relations. That's what got the league where it is, and they do a great job. The NFL is a PR machine. Now the trend in sports is toward marketing. Not to say that PR isn't part of marketing, but in the NFL, marketing really stands alone. Media relations is a huge part of what we do. Keeping the networks happy—when they're paying the kind of money they're paying—is extremely important.

"Another point, and you've heard it before, is the importance of networking. Every job opportunity I've received—unsolicited, over the last few years—I can trace almost every one to people I know. Not just people I do business with, but usually the people I become good friends with who call me up. Those contacts are critical, so don't ever sell yourself short when you're told of the importance of networking; no question it's valuable."

SPOTLIGHT

Pam Harris,
vice president/marketing, New York Knicks

Now in her sixth season with the Knicks, Pam Harris has greatly expanded and refined the team's extensive marketing efforts. Following four years as the Knicks' director of marketing, Harris was promoted to vice president in June 1995.

In her current position, Harris continues to oversee all the club's marketing efforts, including game entertainment, team advertising, sponsor-related promotions, and community service programs. Harris also plays a role in developing the Knicks' ticket sales strategy and building value into being a season ticketholder.

"Those fans are our shareholders. They are the lifeblood of the team," says Harris. "We need to make sure they enjoy themselves and feel they have invested wisely."

One key goal in the marketing of the Knicks is to help create new businesses that address the need for a deeper association between fans and the team. One such program is the Knicks Out of Bounds Club for children, in conjunction with Modell's sporting goods stores, which features merchandise gifts and a quarterly newsletter, geared towards kids of all ages. Another expanding project is the popular Knicks Road Trips, which enables fans to accompany the team to exciting away games.

"Pam is one of the brightest marketing minds in the business," says Knicks president and general manager Ernie Grunfeld. "She has a unique understanding of the sophisticated tastes and high standards of our fans. She's been able to develop the team's marketing efforts with a flair and excitement that New York and the whole NBA have come to expect."

Community service is an important part of the Knicks' mission. "Together with sponsors, we try to invest resources and energy into programs that will make a difference in the community," says Harris. "Like many urban areas, this city has many pressing social issues. We have an obligation to give back."

Harris has over a decade of marketing and advertising experience. Prior to joining the Knicks in the summer of 1991, she was a brand manager on the Excedrin product line at Bristol-Myers Squibb. Before that, she worked on Close-Up toothpaste and Pond's cold cream at Cheesebrough-Pond's. She began her career in account management at Grey Advertising.

Harris received a bachelor of arts in international relations from Stanford University and a master of business administration from the Wharton School of Business at the University of Pennsylvania.

SUCCESS STORY

Jim Loria,
director of marketing, Kansas City Blades

As marketing and public relations director for the Blades since 1990, Jim Loria is responsible for designing and implementing all team promotions, as well as creating and selling sponsorship packages. His additional duties include administering and overseeing all marketing and community relations programs, as well as media and public relations activities.

Loria was the recipient of the first-ever International Hockey League Marketing Director of the Year award for the 1992-93 season. Prior to joining the Blades, he worked for Western Hockey League teams in Billings (Montana), Regina (Saskatchewan), and Spokane (Washington). He was named the WHL executive of the year following the 1987–88 season. He was also a front office executive for five years with the Washington Capitals of the NHL.

DIRECTOR OF PUBLIC RELATIONS

The director of public relations is the individual most involved with the media. He or she handles specific game day requests, arranges interviews, and provides statistics. In some cases, the PR director will also accommodate the visiting teams' needs in these areas.

The director of public relations, sometimes sporting the title of "team publicist" or "director of media relations," puts out each season a handy-sized press guide containing all pertinent information about the club, including player biographies and records. Often this guide doubles as a yearbook and is sold to the fans. The publicist also churns out press releases and aids writers and broadcasters at each home game, furnishing pre-game notes, half-time and final box scores, and a "running play-by-play"—a score-by-score account of the action.

People who work in this field are personable and skillful at developing and maintaining relationships. A member of the public relations staff must have a fluent knowledge of sports and an understanding of the media industry.

PUBLICITY ADVISORY

This is a very time-consuming job. The PR Director usually works about 16 hours on game day. He or she arrives early in the morning and, for an evening contest, departs as late as midnight.

The typical day begins by writing press releases as necessary to cover the news as it unfolds. Some topics that need to be addressed by the media are player injury reports, biographical information, and performance statistics. The public relations staff may also manage player appearances at post-game press conferences, as well as be responsible for arranging appearances for athletes at public events and orchestrating community programs.

To prepare for an upcoming game, the public relations staff will be expected to produce a press kit. The press kit contains additional information specific to the opposing team for that night's game. This may include statistics on how your team's batters fare against this particular pitcher or what the other team's win-loss record is in your home ballpark.

Prior to the start of a home game, the main duty performed by the PR staff is the distribution of press passes and credentials to appropriate media outlets. During home games, the director of public relations is required to manage the press box. Other responsibilities include servicing the press in any way, whether it be making seating assignments, following up that telephone lines are properly installed for a writer's computer modem, or distributing media guides to out-of-town journalists.

After the game, the PR director arranges for and conducts press conferences. This may involve being a sort of mediator during a debate. The PR director will decide who asks questions and call on that person. After the question has been asked, the director will then rephrase the question so that the athlete and the entire room are aware of what is being asked. The individual in this position must be sensitive to the needs of both the player and the media. The PR director tries not to antagonize the media, but at the same time cannot allow the press conference to run all night.

CAN YOU RELATE?

Team publicists come from varied backgrounds. Most have earned a college degree in communications or journalism and will have spent a great deal of time working in the office of the sports information director. Others may have educational training in marketing, promotions, or English. But whatever the individual's college major, common to all who work in public relations is the ability to write well.

Public relations is generally a low-paying field, especially considering the large number of hours that one puts in. A main reason for the relatively unattractive pay scale is the basic economic law of supply and demand. The growing number of people eager to work in this field drives salaries down.

Earnings vary greatly depending on the type of job. Salaries in public relations can range from $18,000 at an entry level position to well over

$65,000 as the director of public relations for a professional sports team. Other variables include the individual's experience, expertise, and level of responsibilities, as well as the reputation and popularity of the particular team or league it competes in. Most mid-level PR professionals can expect to earn between $28,000 to $40,000 a year.

Employment prospects are fair in public relations, but individuals interested in this field must be willing to start at the bottom. Guidance in resume writing and help in obtaining internships is available from the Public Relations Society of America. Be forewarned, however, that entry-level positions such as public relations assistant are not glamorous jobs.

The assistant's main function is to maintain and update the team's game-by-game scrapbook. Nonetheless, these low-level jobs do provide an opportunity to rub elbows with athletes, team administrators, and media professionals. Only by developing a network of contacts can a PR assistant expect to advance his or her career.

Career advancement can come in many ways. An individual working for a college may advance his or her career by joining a minor league team, and then eventually work for a pro team. Someone already working at the pro level can jump to a more prestigious team. The director of public relations for a pro team may find advancement prospects by serving as PR director for an entire pro league or college conference.

Opportunities are available if you're motivated and alert to the possibilities. Says Tom Ambrose, vice president of public relations for the NBA's Phoenix Suns, "People say that timing is everything, but positioning runs a close second. Improve yourself in your chosen field, and put yourself in the best possible position to seize an opportunity when it comes along."

COLLEGE SPORTS INFORMATION DIRECTOR

The best training ground for becoming a public relations director for a professional sports team is by working as a sports information director. The sports information director (SID) is responsible for public relations at the collegiate level. The individual in this position will educate the media and the public about college sports teams and its players.

Most SIDs are required to oversee the publicity activities for all the school's sports teams. The big-time universities, however, assign a different SID to handle each of the major sports. Although the overall scope of functions vary depending on the size and prestige of the school, a SID's main duties remain the same regardless of the school's stature.

The SID will be expected to schedule television, radio, and newspaper interviews for coaches and athletes. The individual will write news releases, media guides, and playoff brochures. On non-game days, sports information directors attend practices, prepare advance material, and process requests for credentials.

On game day, the SID will attend athletic events and see to it that the media has the information it needs. The individual will also manage access to the press box and coordinate news conferences. As the game is in progress, the SID maintains up-to-date statistics for the media and the NCAA.

"You couldn't do this job without being sports-minded," says Fred Nuesch, secretary of the College Sports Information Directors of America and longtime SID at Texas A&M University at Kingsville. "No two days are alike. It's seven days a week, lots of night work and weekends, and lots of travel."

The majority of SIDs have a degree in journalism or communications. Salaries usually range from $20,000 to $35,000. Higher earnings are not unheard of, but the well-paying posts are located at the major college level in high-profile sports. Such jobs are hard to come by.

Every university sports program and collegiate conference office employs a media relations or sports information director. Here's an advertisement that appeared during the summer of 1996 for a typical entry-level position:

"Assistant Media Relations Director. The Big Sky Conference is seeking candidates who will be the primary contact for volleyball and women's basketball in addition to other sports to be determined. Duties will include weekly releases and other pertinent administration of assigned sports including design and layout of conference media guides. Weekend and evening work required. Requires bachelor's degree in journalism, communications or related field. We desire at least two years' experience in sports information office or related setting with hands-on experience with desktop publishing (PageMaker) and other PC applications. Salary is $20,000–$23,000."

TIPSHEET

- Gain writing experience by working during summers or part-time at a local newspaper.

- Get involved with the college sports information director's office. The SID's office will open your eyes as to the variety of responsibilities and duties performed when handling an event.

- An internship in the public relations department of a minor league team would be valuable experience on a small scale.

Ⓘ Join trade associations and attend seminars; they are useful when trying to develop a network of contacts.

REAL-LIFE ADVICE

Marilyn Van Dyke,
national media relations manager, Upper Deck

In her five years with Upper Deck, Marilyn Van Dyke has been responsible for securing and maximizing national media attention for the company's sports-related memorabilia. Her main job functions are to orchestrate public relations activities, such as celebrity and athlete appearances, to initiate media coverage of company events, and to generate brand awareness of company products.

personality sketch

Skillful writer; excellent communicator; sensitive to media deadlines; tireless worker; ability to work on many projects simultaneously; knowledge of sports.

Van Dyke attended Luther College in Iowa, where she received a bachelor of arts in psychology and theology in 1976. Her first job after graduation was as a receptionist with the Minnesota Kicks of the North American Soccer League. Six months later she was promoted to public relations assistant. She also served as community relations manager for the NASL's Dallas Tornado before being hired by The Playboy Clubs, where she spent six years as director of promotions and media relations. In 1986, she started her own promotions and entertainment consulting agency, then spent nearly three years as director of public relations for the California Special Olympics before arriving at Upper Deck.

"I was always a big sports fan, but I didn't know anything about soccer. I was looking for a job, and when I saw an ad that said you could work for a sports organization, I jumped on it. The ad didn't say the job was as a receptionist, but I wanted in, and I was willing to start at the bottom.

"Once I got in, I offered to do anything. I made myself available for extra hours without pay, I showed high interest, and I was quickly able to gain knowledge of the sport. I would constantly ask if there was anyone who needed help. The PR person took me under his wing. He let me handle some minor media requests, answer some phone calls, and eventually I was kind of a go-between for the public and that department.

"The best advice I could give someone interested in public relations is to get a degree in journalism or communications. I have no public relations, journalism, or communications background. For me it was the job skills and the hands-on experience. I just fell into it, and I was lucky. It's easier to get a PR job if you're a good writer with a journalism degree. Writing is the key to being successful in PR. You have to put out press releases and advisories, and you need to write media guides.

"A person in this job needs to be assertive, somewhat aggressive, definitely bold, not shy, and extremely persistent. It's difficult breaking into the sports field. Everyone wants to be working for a sports team, but there's only a certain number of jobs. If you can financially swing it, I'd advise starting out as an intern. Anyone who interns has to be willing to do whatever is asked of them, even the grunt work. If you perform well, the likelihood is better and the odds are higher that you'll be kept on in some position.

"You also need to be passionate about your job. You can count on working lots of hours, so you should choose a field you're going to love. This is not an 8 to 5 job. It's at least 12 hours a day, with extra hours on game nights. If you don't believe in what you're doing, if you're not passionate about it, you won't be successful.

"You need to pay your dues, but the bottom line, what it all comes down to, is your relationship with the media. A PR person is responsible for getting as much information to the media as possible on a daily basis. You're constantly dealing with the press, whether it's in press conferences or in the press box, or pitching stories to try and get additional news coverage outside of the actual game reports.

"A PR person is only as valuable as the contacts they have. I have three business card holders and I still need another one! It's all who you know. It's imperative to build up media relationships so they know you and trust you. Nothing is off the record. You lay down your cards very carefully in how you want to disseminate your information. You try to keep everybody happy; you don't ever want to get members of the media mad at you."

SPOTLIGHT

Arthur Triche,
director of media relations, Atlanta Hawks

It's important to get involved as a volunteer at sporting events, the earlier in your career and the bigger the event the better. Arthur Triche says he wouldn't be with the Atlanta Hawks today if he hadn't made contacts through volunteer work.

As an eighth grader trying to make a few bucks delivering newspapers, he was making his stop at Tulane University one day when the football coach happened to be walking out of the building. "I asked him if I could be a ball boy, and he said, 'Sure, come back in August,'" says Triche.

Four years later, Tulane offered Triche a partial scholarship to stay on as a student manager for its basketball team. By his junior year, he was on full scholarship, jockeying duties as manager, student sports information assistant, and writer/editor for the school newspaper. Triche graduated from Tulane in 1983 with a bachelor of arts in communications and stayed on as assistant sports information director.

He later went on to fill similar positions at Louisiana State University and with the NFL's Detroit Lions before becoming public relations director for the Hawks in 1989, the first African American to hold that position in the NBA. Not surprisingly, Triche still does volunteer work and keeps making contacts. He has helped out at the 1984 Olympic Games in Los Angeles, three Super Bowls, three Final Fours, six NBA All-Star Games, and one NBA Final.

SUCCESS STORY

Tom Ambrose,
vice president of public relations,
Phoenix Suns

Tom Ambrose has been associated with the Suns for nearly 25 seasons. He graduated from Notre Dame in 1970 with a bachelor of arts degree in English. He then moved to Arizona, where he spent two years on the public relations staff of the Arizona Republic and the Phoenix Gazette. He joined the Suns in 1973 as public relations director and in 1987 was named the team's vice president of public relations.

ADDRESS BOOK

College Sports Information Directors of America
Campus Box 114A
Kingsville, TX 78363

Public Relations Society of America
33 Irving Place
New York, NY 10003
212/995-2230

SPORTS PUBLICIST

A team-oriented public relations professional is geared towards running the day-to-day press operation for the club. The individual goes through a similar routine, performing the same functions on a daily basis throughout the season—preparing game notes, fielding media requests, setting up interviews, etc. A professional sports team is assured of receiving steady press coverage. The team is an ever-changing story, and its fans want to read that story. Therefore, the media is required to come out to the ballpark.

By contrast, the sports publicist must be creative at all times in order to make news happen. The individual will be required to implement and coordinate strategies to get positive publicity regarding a client's image or event. He or she is in no position to sit back and wait for the media to come knocking on the door. The rare exception to this rule is if the publicist is representing a mega-star or working on an event that the whole world will be watching, like World Cup soccer or the Olympics.

A publicist in the sports industry may find employment opportunities in three different ways. The individual may work for a public relations firm handling athletes and sports-oriented events, as an in-house press agent for a sports-related company or athletic management agency, or be self-employed and work with a variety of clients and events.

SPIN DOCTORS

The main function performed by a publicist who works for an athlete is to manipulate a positive image for the client. Athletes command huge salaries based on talent, of course, but they can also increase their earnings exponentially by signing endorsement contracts and serving as a corporate spokesperson (just ask Michael Jordan about his relationship with Nike). To achieve this goal, the publicist will develop strategies to attain a positive image for the athlete.

Arranging for promotional work with children or setting up a charitable appearance may not generate significant revenue at first, but these activities create for the athlete an appearance of genuine goodwill. As part of the big picture, these promotional acts may prove beneficial by giving the athlete the necessary exposure that is a precursor to future ventures or campaigns that are lucrative. Building and maintaining a positive, professional image for the client, while simultaneously maximizing the athlete's marketing income, is the delicate balance that a publicist strives to accomplish.

Crisis management is another key element of the publicist's job. An athlete, like any public figure, will become a media target should a controversial event occur. "It's not a matter of if the media will cover you, but how and when," says Kathleen Hessert of Sports Media Challenge, a crisis communications firm for athletes. "The media goes thermonuclear when it catches onto a story."

Crisis management and dealing with the media are interrelated. And crisis planning and prevention go hand-in-hand with effective crisis management. A publicist should prepare the athlete well in advance as to the myriad of crisis possibilities, the alternatives, and appropriate responses in a media situation. Says Hessert: "In the Chinese language, the word 'crisis' is a combination of two words—opportunity or disaster—and that depends solely on how you respond to the situation."

ALERT THE MEDIA

A professional working to publicize a sports-related event serves as a liaison between the client and the media. When an event is scheduled to occur—such as an athlete's book signing or a sporting goods store's grand opening—the main function provided by the publicist is alerting the media. The successful publicist will make information easily accessible to all members of the press who may cover the event.

The most straightforward style of media alert is the press kit. The basic objective of any press kit is to provide the media with an outline of the event so that reporters can quickly decide if they wish to attend. The press kit contains brief biographies of all participants, a press release on the reason for (and significance of) the event, as well as a fact sheet of specifics that explain the where, why, when, who, and how of the event.

The extent of publicity generated by an event is directly proportional to the number of media people attending that event. Several factors determine the attractiveness of an event and, thereby, its success. The presence of a legendary sports celebrity will always draw a large gathering. Other crowd pleasers are the once-in-a-lifetime awards presentation or honors ceremony, as well as a giveaway promotion of souvenir items.

EAT YOUR HEART OUT, MR. ED

The business of sports publicity is an extremely competitive field. Look at the sports section of today's newspaper. Count the number of "must stories," i.e., articles covering the local pro teams. You'll notice there's not much space left over for feature stories on individuals or reports on the lesser sports. The biggest challenge faced by any sports publicist is getting publicity for an athlete or sport that doesn't get regular exposure.

"Harness racing is always fighting for column inches," says Tom Cosentino, the former director of public relations at Yonkers Raceway. "The media will cover the big stakes races, but to get some newspaper publicity on a Tuesday you have to find an angle that makes an editor say, 'Wow, now that's a good story.' Sometimes those stories are found by looking down the backstretch."

One such example is found with Manfred Hanover, an Ohio-bred trotter who came to race at Yonkers in the late 1980s. The pacer hadn't shown much potential during the previous year, but he arrived in New York coming off a series of big wins and performing better than expected. In the first race at Yonkers, Manfred Hanover set the track record. The next day Cosentino planned to write a program story about the horse's new-found success. What he got was a national story for Yonkers Raceway.

Cosentino approached the trainer of Manfred Hanover and inquired as to what, if anything, was being done differently to gain such positive results. The trainer expounded at length about new training techniques and different workout regiments. Cosentino listened patiently and took copious notes. Then he asked about the horse's diet. That was the $64,000 question.

As Cosentino recalls, "The trainer said the horse wasn't getting the proper nourishment and had developed some sort of electrolyte problem. So Manfred Hanover was drinking two to four quarts of Gatorade each day. As it turned out, the horse liked orange flavor the best."

Cosentino had his scoop, published the exclusive story, and then went after the national media. He contacted local sports columnists, the wire services, and television reporters. The press drank it up in droves. What started as a novel story had mushroomed into a media whirlwind. "Yonkers Raceway was the talk of the town," says Cosentino proudly. All because of a horse that quaffed Gatorade.

FACT SHEET

The majority of publicists who work in the sports industry are college graduates with degrees in public relations, marketing, communications, journalism, or sports administration. While there are still a number of old-time sports publicists hired years ago without college training, most firms currently require some type of college background.

Salaries for sports publicists vary greatly depending on the individual's reputation, experience, and level of responsibility, as well as the specific requirements set forth by the client. Some publicists may work on a retainer basis, trying to get publicity for the client every day, while others may be a fee-only publicist for the duration of a specific event. Other variables that determine earnings include the size, location, and prestige of the firm employing the publicist.

Annual salaries can range from $28,000 to over $100,000. Individuals just beginning their careers may earn even less than the aforementioned minimum, while those with a proven track record may command a sum in the high six figures. The highest paid publicists usually work for a celebrity superstar and act more in a capacity of personal manager.

Individuals employed by a publicity firm are not always responsible for bringing in new business. Those who do secure new clients will be compensated commensurately and be viewed favorably for promotions. Qualified, experienced, and successful sports publicists may advance their career by launching their own company.

Sports publicists who work independently will be expected to obtain their own clients. As in any business, publicists acquire new business through referrals and recruiting. A satisfied client may endorse his or her publicist when asked for a recommendation, but savvy marketers cannot survive on word-of-mouth alone. An innovative self-promoter will use the relatively small size of his or her company to advantage, citing the opportunity to provide personalized, quality service as well as the ability to give undivided attention to their client's needs.

A publicist will be expected to court the press and develop a trusting relationship with members of the broadcast and print media. An individual in this position will be expected to keep in constant contact with media personnel, apprising them of breaking news regarding a client. He or she will also arrange press conferences and interviews, as well as act as an information source for media queries and requests.

To be a successful publicist, an individual needs to possess excellent writing and communication skills. A great deal of time is spent composing press releases and talking on the telephone. He or she should be well liked, yet persistent; boldly aggressive, yet respectful. The best publicists are creative people who are capable not only of developing a unique concept, but who also have the organizational know-how to implement a program and possess the attention to detail necessary to nurture an idea into reality.

TIPSHEET

① Internships are invaluable experience and provide a network of contacts available nowhere else.

- ☺ Training programs within an established publicity firm are often difficult to land, but they can be had. Research the name of a personnel employee who is responsible for recruiting young talent. Write letters and be persistent.

- ☺ A foot in the door is your best bet to finding employment opportunities more to your liking. Don't be too proud to start at an entry-level position. Agencies often promote from within.

- ☺ Experience on a small scale will help you compile a proven track record. Think about working in publicity for the community theater or local organization.

REAL-LIFE ADVICE

Tom Cosentino,
principal, O'Leary & Cosentino Communications

In March 1996, Tom Cosentino helped launch O'Leary & Cosentino Communications, an independent sports publicity firm. With over ten years experience as a sports publicist, Cosentino is well prepared to service his broad-based clientele, which currently includes The Breeders Crown/Hambletonian Society (harness racing's championship series) and The Score Board, Inc., a publicly traded sports memorabilia company.

personality sketch

Creative thinker; skilled writer; personable communicator; knowledge of sports and understanding of athletes; organized; detail-oriented.

Cosentino worked as an intern in the New York Yankees' public relations department while attending St. John's University. He graduated in 1983 with a bachelor's degree in athletic administration and was subsequently hired by the Yankees as a media relations assistant. After a brief stint at a now-defunct sports statistical service, he was hired in 1985 as assistant public relations director at Yonkers Raceway. The following year he was promoted to PR director, a position he held for two years.

In 1988, Cosentino joined Lapin East-West, a sports and entertainment public relations agency. There he would handle such clients as The Ice Capades, Top Rank Boxing, and the National Hockey League's 75th anniversary celebration. During his seven-year tenure at Lapin, Cosentino would rise from account executive to account supervisor to general manager. In 1996, he formed O'Leary & Cosentino Communications. The company has offices in Morganville, New Jersey and White Plains, New York.

"The key to any job in sports is the internship. I wouldn't be where I am today if not for what I learned on the internship and how I applied myself. My dream was working for the Yankees, and there I was, working in the Yankee Stadium press box for Dave Righetti's no-hitter. The key is to do as much as possible, learn as much as possible, and keep asking for more.

"Some interns feel it's beneath them to cut out newspaper clippings and paste them in a scrapbook. I started out doing just that. But I did it well, and only then was I allowed to do more. By the end of the year I was helping to write the game notes and was on the phone speaking with the media.

"I don't believe the old saying that there's no such thing as bad publicity. There is bad publicity. Some publicists will do anything to get their client's name in the news. I don't believe in that. What I do believe in is that there's good publicity in everything. You can turn a negative into a positive. You have to work at it; you can't just do things from the seat of your pants. You need to think through your entire publicity campaign.

"The key to being a good publicist is your relationship with the press. On the agency side where you have many clients, my motto has always been that clients come and go, but the key to your business is your relationship with the press. You can never damage those relationships because you're always going to need to go back to those individuals in the future to pitch them stories.

"Let's say a client comes after you and says, 'I didn't like the way that piece was written; I want you to call the writer to complain.' Well, you have to weigh the options. It's ultimately your reputation on the line because you deal with the media. I'd say to that client, I can't do it; it's unprofessional.

"The practice I've always applied to my job is that if I felt a story didn't cover my client in the best possible light, I can't complain about it. The only way I can complain is if something is factually incorrect. Then I can go back and say something in a nice way. And usually, the writer or broadcaster will realize the mistake and then do a retraction piece. And that's more publicity."

SPOTLIGHT

Art Berke,
director of communications, *Sports Illustrated*

Art Berke has been involved at the highest level of the sports industry for two decades; holding public relations and promotions positions in various areas in the field. He can boast such prestigious positions as director of sports and prime time sales for ABC, press representative for ABC Sports, and associate director of information for the major league baseball commissioner's office. In his current job, Berke oversees all public relations and publicity activities for *Sports Illustrated*.

"*SI* doesn't really have any direct competition," he says, "so my main focus is enhancing the image of the magazine and publicizing its weekly contents, as well as books, calendars, television specials, and the whole range of what *SI* represents."

Berke began his career with aspirations to be a sportswriter. He attended Indiana University and graduated with a degree in journalism. He landed his first job, in New York in 1971, on the editorial staff of a weekly football newspaper called *Gridiron*. He next spent three years as the editor of sports encyclopedias for children, before being offered a job as assistant public relations director in baseball commissioner Bowie Kuhn's office.

"I made a decision that the next step would've been for me to be a PR director of a major league team," says Berke, "and that wasn't quite what I wanted to do. Basically I think the title now is better, it's called media relations director. Public relations is not just servicing the media; public relations is more a creative way of going at things."

Berke's next stop was at ABC Sports, where he worked in publicity for two Winter Olympics over four years: the 1984 Sarajevo Games and the 1988 Calgary Games. It was at those 1984 Games that Berke coordinated perhaps the greatest publicity coup in Olympic history. The idea occurred to him on the airplane trip to Sarajevo during a mental brainstorming session.

It hit like a thunderbolt. The network's Wide World of Sports programming opens with a heels-over-head tumbling ski jumper who personifies the agony of defeat. "I realized that guy was from Yugoslavia," Berke recalls, still barely able to contain his excitement over a decade later. When the plane touched down, Berke set out to find the most famous athlete that nobody knows.

Three days (and a number of interpreters) later, Berke was informed that Vinko Bogatei was working, ironically enough, as the starter at the ski jump event. Berke and the interpreter trudged up the mountainside and, out of breath, invited Bogatei to the ABC broadcast center for interviews. The media response was overwhelming.

"We had 25 major national print columnists and maybe 15 local television crews there," says Berke. "All of them were thinking 'This is one heck of a story.' But the biggest thrill for me," Berke adds, "was the following year when I received a Christmas card from Vinko Bogatei. He's a factory worker in Yugoslavia. I think he does understand, to some extent, that in this country he is a celebrity."

Yet another example of a good publicist turning a negative into a positive.

ADDRESS BOOK

Public Relations
Society of America
33 Irving Place
New York, NY 10003
212/995-2230

DIRECTOR OF CORPORATE SPORTS MARKETING

A corporate sports marketing director is responsible for developing and implementing strategies to enhance a company's image through an association with sports. Individuals may work on a national or local level. There is a wide array of duties within the scope of this job.

Corporate sports sponsorships are divided into four main areas: team sponsor, broadcast sponsor, title sponsor, and official sponsor. The director will be expected to oversee the coordination of marketing efforts in any one, or all, of these areas. The individual will also formulate budgets to provide adequate means for carrying out the marketing plan in a productive and efficient manner. To accomplish this, the director must be fluent in all four areas of corporate sports sponsorship.

Team sponsorship involves a company that seeks an advertising vehicle attaching its name to a recognized sports team. In the case of auto racing, the advertising vehicle is the vehicle itself. Over 3.5 million people each year attend stock car races alone, while some 185 million watch on television. Team sponsorship provides a tremendous opportunity for a company to build brand equity and expand the consumer franchise.

"It's the best marketing tool that I've been involved with in 15 years at Hershey," says Bob Fisher, director of marketing for the chocolatier. Hershey completed its first year of NASCAR sponsorship in 1995 and noted immediate results. "It has tremendous impact at retail," adds Fisher. "We almost presold displays and price features simply by having a NASCAR program that made sense to the retailer. We did business with customers we hadn't done business with [before]."

Team sponsorship as advertising campaign goes deeper than a decal stuck to a racing car. In order for these promotions to be successful, the programs must create in the minds of the consumer a strong symbiosis between the team and the sponsor. To this end, the sponsor must reinforce its relationship with the team. This is accomplished through cross-promotions and local marketing tie-ins.

GENTLEMAN, START YOUR ENGINES

Some years ago, Pepsi-Cola had developed a promotion to market its sponsorship of Don "The Snake" Prudomme, a drag racer who competes in the funny car category. The promotion, executed through a national fast-food restaurant chain, was a contest in which the winner would receive a ride in Prudomme's dragster. Now a Top Fuel dragster can reach a speed of 300 miles per hour and travel a quarter-mile distance in less than five seconds. A dragster leaves the starting line with a force five times greater than gravity—the same force needed by the space shuttle when it takes off from the launching pad at Cape Canaveral, Florida.

The contest was obviously designed to appeal to the younger generation, a target market that Pepsi is desperate to tap into. Says Ken Wuestenfeld, who at the time worked for the soft drink company as the point person for the contest, "All the marketing people got involved, and the ad agency, and Prudomme's agent. They all said we'd better make sure that the person who wins this contest is right. Well, it's not a perfect world. The winner was a 75-year-old grandmother. She had the ride of her life!"

Team sponsorship is rapidly growing as we approach the next century. The reason for the growth in team sponsorship is directly related to what's referred to in the field as market fragmentation. In layman's terms, market fragmentation means that the target audience is more detached and therefore more difficult to reach. The most frequently cited causes of fragmentation are declining brand loyalty and a glut of advertising that bombards an ever-increasingly skeptical consumer. The majority of marketers today strongly believe that team sponsorships will provide the solution to this changing market environment.

AND NOW, A WORD FROM OUR SPONSOR

The most common form of sponsorship is broadcast sponsor, which involves the purchase of commercial airtime during a television or radio broadcast of a sporting event. Any corporate franchise worth its salt has specific objectives in how best to create product awareness and, subsequently, build brand loyalty. This may be accomplished by increasing publicity and generating an overall feeling that the company understands the needs and wants of its target market.

"Corporate image is very important," says Wuestenfeld, now the national sales manager of Sara Lee. "The right marketing strategy can dramatically impact sales, goodwill, and market share of a company. The bottom line of making money is what we're all about, but how we are perceived by the general public is almost as important. Do people want to buy our products?"

A prime example of this is Cadillac's sponsorship of the America's Cup in 1992. Cadillac is an upscale market automobile, and the captive yachting audience that tuned in to watch the race is the ideal demographic market in which to promote Cadillacs.

The impact of corporate broadcast sponsorship on sporting events is impossible to overlook. The advent of television time-outs and other play stoppages woven into the action, like the two-minute warning, were created to appease the corporate sponsor and maximize their brand exposure during the game telecast. Individual sports leagues, buoyed by the ever-increasing rights fees paid by television, were only too happy to oblige with these "minor" changes in the flow of the game.

By making corporate sponsorship an appealing forum, and thereby generating more revenue through commercial advertising sales, the TV networks gained a controlling interest in what occurs on the field. Individual sports such as tennis and golf have changed their entire formats for determining who wins and who loses. Tennis has added the tie-breaker to settle sets ending at six-games-all. And golf completely overhauled its tournament scoring system from match play (each hole won counts as a point) to stroke play, which combines the 72-hole total score. This scoring system requires the viewer to wait until after the final hole is completed before a winner is crowned.

While these changes were made to enhance the excitement of sporting events for viewers, to be sure, television networks aren't in the business of titillation for charitable purposes. As the contests grew ever more exciting, resulting in increased ratings, television networks were able to justify charging a higher fee for the available advertising time. In short, everybody wins in the corporate-sports-broadcast-sponsorship game.

THE SPONSOR NAME GAME

The highest profile area is the title sponsor, in which a company attaches it name or brand name to an event or promotion. These corporate-sponsored events provide fans with the programming they want. In exchange for these telecasts, the consumer is constantly reminded of the product offered by the sponsoring company, usually through commercials.

(These commercials are not always of the traditional nature. Announcers for the Arizona Diamondbacks, who begin major league play in 1998 at Bank One Ballpark in Phoenix, will be required under a contract with the stadium's title sponsor to call every home run hit at the park "a Bank One boomer.")

One of the earliest examples of a corporate title sponsor dates back to the mid 1930s, when Gillette began sponsoring entire broadcasts of boxing matches. The company would purchase the broadcasting rights to the event and then sell this package to radio stations and (later) TV networks. As the years passed, Gillette was the company that the sporting public— a predominantly male audience—most associated with championship athletics. This corporate philosophy served Gillette well as the company sold more and more razors on its way to becoming the established international corporate giant it is today.

Some title sponsorships seem a bit incongruous. Take for example the Ironman Triathlon. Anheuser-Busch negotiated a contract to purchase the rights to this event, thereby earning the privilege to call it the Bud Lite Ironman Triathlon. Traditionalists scoff at such inane name-calling, as if a beer with fewer calories can help you train for a 2.4-mile swim, a 112-mile bicycle ride, and a 26.2-mile marathon run.

Many such incongruous marriages are consummated and last till-death-do-they-part. But sponsors beware: Don't assume that an investment of hundreds of millions of dollars is going to last your lifetime, let alone your children's lifetimes. The flavors of the decade change. Traditional family values rule. For example, take a few years ago, when the women's professional tennis tour found itself choking under a particularly dark smoke cloud.

GAME, SET, MATCH

The tour had enjoyed a long and successful relationship with Virginia Slims. The sponsorship began in 1970, at a time when Philip Morris was rolling out the Virginia Slims brand of cigarette marketed to women smokers. The company decided to bankroll the prize money for a tournament in Houston. The ensuing brand recognition gave Philip Morris the idea of tying their product to the sport. The fledgling women's tour welcomed the deep pockets of Philip Morris with open arms. Spurred by the cigarette company's financial backing, women's tennis caught fire. By 1994, players on the Virginia Slims tour competed in over 60 international events for some $25 million in purses.

But the recent spate of anti-smoking revisionism smacked the women's tour right in the catgut. Anti-smoking groups berated the tour for its silent endorsement of smoking (guilt by association) and called for the tour to sever its ties with the cigarette company. Of course, professional women's tennis players do not publicly endorse smoking. But when the volleys lobbed at the tour began to impact negatively on image—and therefore business—the tour backpedaled. Women's tennis, under continued scrutiny and facing intense pressure, snubbed out its dependency on cigarette money.

With the Virginia Slims sponsorship now gone, the Women's Tennis Association is at a crossroads of commercial expansion. "Philip Morris is essentially the history of women's tennis," says Philip de Picciotto, who directs the women's tennis division of Advantage International. "With Philip Morris uninvolved in the WTA tour, the game has a little bit of a void, but it also has an enormous opportunity." In October 1995, the Corel Corporation, a Canada-based computer graphics software firm, signed a three-year, $12 million sponsorship deal to create the COREL WTA Tour.

In spite of an occasional incongruous "tie-in," the title sponsorship trend continues to grow. Why? Because the ploy works. Currently, 14 of the 19 college bowl games are operating under an alias. Corporate name-plastering includes the Federal Express Orange Bowl, the Thrifty Car Rental Holiday Bowl, and the IBM OS/2 Fiesta Bowl. Even stadiums and arenas are getting into the act. The facility can generate millions of dollars each year just by changing its signage. Currently, five arenas housing NBA teams are sponsored by an airline company: the United Center, America West Arena, the Delta Center, US Airways Arena, and Continental Air-lines Arena. (But before you think, "Free peanuts," keep in mind the interests of the concessionaire.)

HERE'S THE PITCH

Official sponsor refers to the official supplier relationship, in which a company provides goods or services to a sporting event or organization for use and endorsement. This relationship is seen most often in the Olympics ("the official snow tire of the Jamaican bobsled team") and when an individual athlete, preferably with a high profile, endorses a particular product ("I use this jock itch medication so you should too.")

At the infancy of sports marketing, the use of an athlete as corporate pitchman embodied the whole of athletic sponsorship. Sports icons like golfer Arnold Palmer and NFL quarterback Joe Namath proved that athletes could indeed sell products. In addition, market research indicated that this caliber of athlete was an effective way to generate product awareness and, more important to advertisers, promote highly acceptable levels of consumer recall.

Today, it's almost a mandatory element of the entire sports marketing mix that sports heroes serve in multiple roles, not only as front men in advertising campaigns, but behind the scenes in order to effect primary objectives of the sports marketing program.

"The advertising campaign is nothing more than a three or four month snapshot that is retained, if you're lucky, for only six months by the consumer," says Sara Lee's Ken Wuestenfeld. "You've got to make these spokespersons real, you've got to have people meet them, and you've got to get them out into the local marketplace."

AND HE SCORES!

The best results occur when an athlete and the product have unified expectations and objectives; together they are stronger. As great a basketball player as Michael Jordan is, without Nike he would not be quite the marketing powerhouse (and vice versa). To this end, the company must have a clear business plan, and the athlete must be made aware of the specific role he or she is to play in that plan.

It's critical to a company entering into a paid endorsement relationship with an athlete that the athlete be held accountable. Consumers can tell when an athlete is behind a product versus when an athlete is just paying it lip service. Furthermore, the company must provide itself with an escape clause, especially when signing a long-term contract with an athlete, in case an unsavory incident should occur to jeopardize the athlete's marketability.

From a corporate perspective, the selection of an appropriate spokesperson is key because that athlete reflects the company he or she works for. An example of a successful national program was the Pepsi-Bo Jackson relationship. By contrast, an example of one that didn't work was the Pepsi-Mike Tyson coupling. When the heavyweight boxer was indicted on a rape conviction, the soft drink company was forced to abandon its costly advertising blitz.

"Those are the risks you take," says Wuestenfeld. "Athletes are expensive, and if an athlete has a turn for the worse, it creates a bad image for the company. Going forward, I look for corporate America to concentrate more on event sponsorship because of the Tyson incident."

VALUE-ADDED EMPLOYEES

Employment opportunities are excellent in corporate sports marketing. Says Sara Lee's Wuestenfeld, "In my former position at Pepsi, I was supported by ten marketing managers, their assistants, very often an advertising agency that was brought in, and we also received input from corporate headquarters. All told, each program involved maybe 50 to 100 people."

Corporations tend to hire applicants who have worked in an industry outside of sports. Companies look for people who have gained an understanding and appreciation of what it takes to be a successful marketer. Aspiring candidates need a broad base of knowledge in brand management, sales promotions, marketing strategies, product planning, and tournament operations. Also important to job applicants is the ability to write well, speak clearly and forcefully in public, and make persuasive presentations to clients.

Major corporations designate huge sums of money to the sports marketplace in order to promote their products or services directly to the customer. With so much money riding on the outcome of a marketing strategy, companies expect the programs to be promoted and executed with a high degree of professionalism. The mega-events implemented on an international scale are expensive—Sara Lee spent $40 million to become an official Olympic sponsor for the 1994 Games in Lillehammer. High-profile events on a national level are budgeted between $10 and $20 million.

Marketing directors who oversee such hefty budgets—and therefore shoulder much more responsibility and accountability—can earn an annual salary in the neighborhood of $250,000. That's certainly an exclusive neighborhood, and it doesn't include the negotiation of any supplemental income such as sales commissions, revenue-sharing, or other factors tied to corporate profitability. Marketing directors at smaller companies with less money earmarked for sports programs earn salaries in the range of $50,000 to $100,000. Says Wuestenfeld, "It's not how much money you make, but how much money is in your budget."

The companies devoting a large portion of the advertising budget to sports—beverage companies, automobile manufacturers, fast-food chains, and airlines are among the most frequent sponsors—do so because they know a particular demographic audience will be watching the event. If a company determines that this audience is within the target market for their product or service, then the additional possibility exists for cross-promotions, another key element that is an inherent factor of sports marketing.

SLAM-DUNK MARKETING

This idea of cross-promotions is well illustrated by Sara Lee's decision to sponsor the NCAA women's basketball Final Four. Sara Lee is a holding company of 50 to 60 operating businesses worldwide. The $13 billion organization, headquartered in Chicago, boasts such famous name brands as L'eggs, Hanes, Playtex, and Champion.

The Sara Lee food division understands its main customer base to consist of women 18- to 34-years-old. By sponsoring women's hoops, the company hopes to sell more than just marble cake and nylons. The Hanes division has updated its line of women's undergarments (Hanes Her Way), and the Champion division has extended its line of casual sportswear to include the active women's market. This cross-promotions strategy is an effective means to back into a target market.

These marketing programs don't come about by accident. Most companies have entire sales promotions or marketing departments that are focused specifically on landing the right programs for their company. These negotiations very often take several years, and once a deal is struck, the actual program or event may take between six months to one year to orchestrate and pull off. This provides a modicum of job security.

"These are not turnkey operations," says Wuestenfeld. "There's lots of behind-the-scenes work that can lead to careers. We have a staff in corporate of five people who are involved in sports marketing. But then we also have roughly 50 people or so in each one of the 50 to 60 operating companies that are involved in sports marketing. Think about it: Just in one corporation, we're talking about up to 2,500 jobs for people who spend a good portion of their time involved in sports marketing activities."

Sara Lee's sponsorship of the Ladies Professional Golf Association employs 60 people on a year-round basis. These individuals perform a host of functions, with no detail overlooked. According to Wuestenfeld, there's even a person who every three months is responsible for checking the greens at the golf course to ensure that when the tournament rolls around, the course is in good shape.

"The tournament represents the company," he says, "and it's televised on ESPN. We want to make sure we get the best play for our money."

TIPSHEET

- Attend a college or university that offers a degree in sports administration. Continue your education and earn a master's degree in marketing or business management.

- Obtain internships or part-time jobs at a corporation involved with sports marketing on a local level. Once a company has trained you, it's more likely to hire you down the road.

- Learn as much about the business as possible. Subscribe to trade publications like *Sport Marketing Quarterly*, attend seminars, and develop a network of contacts that may lead you to where the jobs are.

- While these jobs appear difficult to find, and even tougher to land, one must use a little imagination. Check the game-day program to find local sponsors who participate in sports advertising and sponsorship. Next time you attend a sporting event, buy a program and scan it for event sponsors.

- One of the best ways to break into this competitive field is to become an assistant to a marketing manager or an entry-level associate post. Volunteer your time and services, ask lots of questions, work hard, and learn the ropes.

REAL-LIFE ADVICE

Ken Wuestenfeld,
national sales manager, Sara Lee

Ken Wuestenfeld has over ten years of experience in sales and marketing with three Fortune 500 companies. He began his career with The

Carnation Company in St. Louis before moving to Phoenix to join PepsiCo, where he managed a $60-million business in the Arizona and Nevada territory.

In his current position with Sara Lee in Chicago, Wuestenfeld is responsible for sales and marketing activities of the top 100 chains carrying Sara Lee food products throughout the United States. During his career, he has been involved with a variety of corporate athletic sponsorships, including the PGA Phoenix Open, the Pepsi Hot Shot competition, and various collegiate events.

"Most people ask me, What's a guy who sells and markets cheesecake doing at a Chicago Bulls game? Well, Michael Jordan endorses underwear for Hanes, which is a division of Sara Lee. Throughout my career one common denominator seems to be prevalent: corporate sports marketing. Every company I've worked for has been involved in corporate sports marketing, and, quite frankly, it's becoming more and more of a focus for these organizations. Over the last four or five years it's become a focal point.

"There's a vast array of opportunities not necessarily related directly with the athletes or with teams in particular, but also all of these secondary, trickle-down opportunities. It's much like a pyramid. The teams and athletes are on top, but the career employment opportunity is really beneath that and on the local level. Local marketing is crucial to the success of any corporate program.

"Top management is not making the crucial decisions any more, which is good for people seeking employment. Decisions are being pushed down to the local level. The people we hire behind the scenes are vital. We're looking for people with unique backgrounds. They should have a little bit of business expertise and an understanding of what sports is all about. I don't mean watching a football game on Sunday. I mean understanding the ins and outs of organizations, how things are developed, how athletics is perceived in the marketplace.

"Sports marketing opportunities are abounding nationally and internationally for American companies. And I underline internationally. There's all new markets out there. You can bet by the year 2,000—Sara Lee included—we'll be penetrating these markets in these countries. And you can also bet that we'll be using local sports marketing to get our name out there. So don't just confine yourself to America, there's also huge opportunities internationally with big companies. Don't hesitate to contact either the human resources department or, more applicably, the director or vice president of marketing or sales promotion. That's where these activities take place."

ADDRESS BOOK

Sport Marketing Quarterly
P.O. Box 4425
Morgantown, WV 26504
304/599-3482

SPORTS MARKETING MANAGER

The sports marketing manager will execute the marketing concepts and programs utilized by the company, as well as devise marketing strategies and other business plans for the event or team they represent. Some managers may handle amateur sports while others are primarily concerned with a specific professional sport.

While the marketing director oversees the full implementation of the strategic game plan—focusing on rights acquisition and subsequent advertising sales—the company's marketing manager will concentrate on promotions and publicity.

The individual in this position is expected to pay close attention to the areas of hospitality, merchandising, licensing, and other techniques of corporate packaging. He or she is responsible for negotiating contracts with national wholesalers and local retailers and ensuring that these contracts are fulfilled. All of these functions must be performed in unison in order to effectively ensure a successful marketing program.

The sports marketing manager's main goal is to build strategic alliances in order to demonstrate distinctive characteristics of the company's product or service. As the manager of sports marketing for Gatorade, Cindy Sisson oversees the company's relationship with all professional and college teams in the northeastern United States. Her responsibilities include the negotiation of contracts with all professional basketball, baseball, football, and hockey teams, as well as major universities within that region.

QUENCHING A THIRST FOR MARKETING

Saying Gatorade is perceived as an icon in the active thirst market is like saying Santa Claus is somehow associated with Christmas. With sales in excess of $750 million, Gatorade is the undisputed worldwide leader of the isotonic beverage industry. As of this writing, Gatorade is the only company that owns an "official product category" sponsorship with teams in the four major professional sports leagues.

As an official sponsor at NFL, NHL, NBA, and major league baseball games, Gatorade is in the unique position of being the only company in the sports drink industry with a presence at the event. When a company is involved as an official sponsor, they are establishing tremendous brand awareness and invaluable name recognition. Building brand awareness, while not translating directly to sales, is critical in marketing.

In addition to ensuring the proper placement of Gatorade coolers on the sidelines—the traditional Gatorade dump on the winning coach is a publicity coup—Sisson educates the athletic community as to how Gatorade works in hopes of maintaining the company's 90-percent market share despite new competition from All-Sport and PowerAde.

"Sports marketing is primarily a service industry," says Sisson. "You've got to take care of your key influences. In my case, it's the coaches, the trainers, and the athletes."

GOING SPORTS MARKETING CRAZY

Sports marketing positions are available throughout the Fortune 500. Corporations from Avis to Zenith run promotions and advertising campaigns in conjunction with professional sports leagues. The NFL alone has some 125 major corporate sponsors. The odds of obtaining an internship within the sports marketing department of one of these companies is much more favorable than the possibility of joining the NFL's sports marketing arm.

Marketing professionals work incredibly long hours, and the pressure to succeed is intense in this competitive field. It's commonplace for a manager to work 70-plus-hour weeks and over 100 hours during the week of a scheduled event. Like most everything else in sports, these events take place at nights and on weekends.

A friendly warning: Marketers can suffer from burnout. To keep sane, take time out for yourself. This will also keep your ideas fresh.

Employment prospects are increasing in relation to corporate America's continued reliance on sports marketing. "Meaningful sponsor-recognition campaigns not only build corporate awareness but communicate a qualitative consumer message that the event is only possible through sponsor support," says Jackie Woodward, sports marketing director for McDonald's.

A prime example of such a campaign is McDonald's All-American High School Basketball games. These events, which bring together the country's top high school basketball prospects to showcase their talents, has developed into a solid television draw, as well as an important recruiting tool for college coaches.

More and more top sponsors like McDonald's, Coca-Cola, and Anheuser-Busch are dealing with the sports marketing duties in-house, rather than hiring outside agencies to handle the details. The creation of new sports marketing departments is a growing trend that bodes well for candidates just entering the field.

A PEEK INSIDE THE DOOR

It's not unusual to find up to 20 marketing professionals working within an in-house sports management division. Reporting to the corporate director of sports marketing is a staff of five to ten marketing managers. These managers ensure that the marketing programs run smoothly. The marketing managers earn between $50,000 and $100,000 a year, while the director may earn in the range of twice that amount. Assisting the marketing managers are a number of entry-level associates, who implement the decisions made by their superiors.

These well-educated, over-qualified associates perform much of the grunt work and earn a starting salary of about $25,000. In order to advance their career, an associate should be enthusiastic and hard-working. The individual should gain a thorough knowledge of the company, its products, and its goals. He or she should then keep an eye open for any positions that may become available higher up on the corporate food chain. Developing a network of contacts inside the company is vital to the upward mobility (and ultimate longevity) of lower-ranking employees.

"Realize sports marketing is primarily a sales job," says Gatorade's Sisson. "You're selling two things: either your product or your event and yourself. Always keep that game face on. You never know where your next opportunity is going to be."

TIPSHEET

- ① Volunteering your services is the best way to get noticed. When a professional sports team comes to town for a charitable event, approach the organizing committee and get involved.

- ① Consider obtaining some experience in a marketing field outside of sports. A marketing professional will have an easier time making a lateral move into the sports industry.

- ① Don't limit your job search to sports leagues, conferences, or teams. The odds of finding employment are better within the marketing department of a company that is an active corporate sports sponsor.

◍ Try to land an internship or a temporary position within a company's sports marketing division. Most companies have a policy of filling entry-level positions from among their interns.

REAL-LIFE ADVICE

Cindy Sisson,
sports marketing manager, Gatorade

As the manager of sports marketing for Gatorade, Cindy Sisson oversees the company's relationship with all professional and college teams in the northeastern United States. Her responsibilities include the negotiation of contracts with all professional basketball, baseball, football, and hockey teams, as well as major universities within

personality sketch

Ability to forge relationships and negotiate for services; organized; hard-working; personable; enthusiastic; responsive.

that region. Her duties also require her to handle national golf programs for the Ladies Professional Golf Association and the PGA of America, as well as national motor sports activities for NASCAR and IndyCar.

Before joining Gatorade, Sisson was the director of promotions for the LPGA, with responsibilities for all promotions, licensing activities, and special events. She has also served as a liaison to the International Olympic Committee for all National Olympic Committees in preparation for and during the 1984 Los Angeles Games. Sisson earned a bachelor of science degree in sports medicine from Pepperdine University and a master's degree in kinesiology from UCLA.

"I did not have a marketing degree. You don't really need a degree in marketing to become a sports marketer. But how I got into the business is that I became a volunteer. I volunteered to work for the 1984 Olympics and finally, after many, many hours, I was hired to work in the National Olympic Committees area. That was a fun job, but after the Olympics, what was I going to do next? I had just finished my master's and went to Europe to rest for six months. I came back and became a commodities broker. But while doing that, I volunteered for the Los Angeles Open for six years. That's how I got in the golf business. I met people and kept my face in front of these people. After volunteering for an LPGA event, I got hired by the LPGA. So volunteering at the local level really works.

"About the trend, being a former stockbroker, sports marketing is still in a bull market. This is evident by the industry changing dramatically, offering so many newsletters. These are imperative; there's plenty of job opportunities in there and you need to keep up on them. If your local library or university doesn't have these journals, tell them to get with it because there's great opportunities there.

"I receive so many resumes its frightening. I receive almost as many resumes as I do sponsorship proposals. Gatorade currently sponsors over 6,000 events a year; we probably receive 50,000 proposals a year. It's just as difficult for me to keep on top of the resumes as it is for proposals for sponsorships. One of the best I've ever seen came from a woman who sent out a picture of herself, and on the back was her biography like a baseball card. And that went around the whole office.

"So if you can be creative and think of an outrageous way to get your resume to rise to the top, I would encourage you to do that. And be creative when job hunting. Look inside your school university newspaper or [alumni] magazine; maybe there's some people that work at the company you're going to interview with. Call them in advance and say you're an alumnus. Because I don't know if I can even give 10 seconds to a resume. The only way I'll give attention to a resume is if it's a friend-of-a-friend type of thing; then I'll spend the time."

SPECIAL EVENTS MANAGER

A special events manager ensures that the sporting event runs smoothly and to the satisfaction of the corporate client. In this position, the individual will oversee all the details and logistics necessary to properly execute the event marketing plan. While specific functions vary depending on the scope of the event, the manager performs a variety of duties.

The events manager is responsible for determining the expected attendance, for choosing a suitable location, and then setting up press conferences to publicize the event. Once this has been accomplished, the individual must develop a plan of action. He or she will be expected to coordinate efforts with the in-house public relations and marketing departments, as well as with the ticket manager, food concessionaire, and security staff.

Special events management offers a wide array of services. "We call ourselves a sports marketing company," says Carl Thomas, founder and president of CAT Sports, a pioneer in the field of sports event marketing.

"We're really an event designer, an event developer, an event manager. We're a market research company, we're a sponsorship sales company, we're a public relations firm, we're an advertising agency, and we're a sponsorship sales outfit. We're a television packager."

The area of special events is an integral part of the sports marketing industry. It's high profile and is given big-budget attention. The types of special events that are executed cover all ends of the marketing spectrum in terms of public visibility, from the Olympic Games to local banquets held in honor of Little League championship teams.

MARKET YOURSELF

Sports and special events have become a fixture in American corporate marketing culture. Corporate America no longer needs to be convinced that special events should be part of their marketing mixture; companies already understand the importance of special events marketing. This is good news for job seekers.

Employment opportunities exist in sports marketing divisions of teams, facilities, and corporations. There are also companies whose sole purpose is to develop and implement special events for other organizations. International Management Group, ProServ, and Advantage International are the top three; but, literally, hundreds of sports marketing and management agencies exist—and most offer internships.

A college degree in sports management is not required to work in this competitive field. However, prospective employers are inundated with applications and seem to favor candidates who have demonstrated a serious interest in sports marketing. Individuals who don't have the appropriate education possess practical experience from the "school of hard knocks."

Practical work experience in sports events marketing can be gained in three areas: event, association, and corporation. The junior level sports marketing opportunity is found at the event site. This may mean working at a local golf tournament to make sure the banners are properly hung. The job will most likely be temporary and last only for the duration of the event. But don't be alarmed; from the planning stage of the event to its actual execution may take at least six months.

After working a few years at the event level, an individual may move up the ladder by obtaining a position with the association running that event. Continuing with our example, the lackey who hung banners at the golf tournament may then get a job with the golf association. This will most likely be a full-time position, with increased responsibility and exposure on a national scale.

Once our candidate has worked a few years for an association, the individual is now ready for the big time: corporate sports marketing. At this level, he or she will create marketing programs and review proposals developed by subordinates. At each stop—from event to association to corporation—our candidate's salary has doubled, as have all the perks that go hand-in-hand with career advancement.

MARKET RESOURCE

The successful sports event marketer is obligated to demonstrate to the client that they will receive a return on their investment. Objectives need to be set with each project to measure and track the potential success of a company's involvement. "You have to come to them with creative, effective programs that are well researched, that can be professionally executed, and will deliver on specific objectives," says Thomas.

The area of sports marketing special events requires strict management, administration, and logistics support. In the early stages, detailed strategic planning is conducted, in which the conception and development of an event takes place. This includes a thorough scouting report of the competition, a general review of financial and marketing issues to be addressed, as well as administrative concerns.

"Before we can do anything productive for a sponsor we have to understand what the company is trying to accomplish," says Doug Pirnie, marketing director at IMG. "No matter how organized the marketing plan is, it all boils down to the fact that they are trying to sell more of whatever it is they make. Research the company and understand how the business works, then you're in a much better position to help them use a special event or program in a way to meet their specific objectives."

When Advantage International participated with MasterCard to help the creditor with its World Cup soccer sponsorship program in 1994, Advantage first talked to member banks to learn more about the business before coming back to MasterCard with a proposal of specific programs.

"Don't get hung up on being strategists," says Harlan Stone, senior vice president of marketing & sales for Advantage International. "Roll up the sleeves. Work is often the most important part of the project. Clients would rather have a C idea with A+ execution than the reverse."

TIPSHEET

Ⓤ Volunteer to work at a local sporting event in any capacity. Get noticed and forge relationships that will help your future career goals.

- Gain knowledge of marketing, even if it's at a company that's not involved in sports. Marketing experience will give you a pronounced advantage when attempting a lateral move into the sports industry.

- Attempt to obtain an internship or a temporary position within a company's sports marketing division. Most companies have a policy of filling entry-level positions from among their interns.

- Constantly keep abreast of the ever-changing world of sports marketing. Read trade journals and newsletters such *as Sport Marketing Quarterly* to learn the latest.

REAL-LIFE ADVICE

Carl Thomas,
founder and president, CAT Sports

A pioneer in the field of sports events marketing, Carl Thomas and CAT Sports have developed, marketed, and managed sports event properties since 1982. The company's most prominent event is the Bud Lite Triathlon series. During the 1990s, CAT Sports has been the executive producer

personality sketch

Detail-oriented; troubleshooter; supervisory; delegatory; dogged determination.

of nearly 30 television shows, running the gamut from the nationally syndicated NFL Quarterback Challenge to a local triathlon show in Houston, Texas.

"What is marketing? It's sales promotion, advertising, and public relations. Marketing in the grand context of sports marketing is lots of different things.

"As you seek to find your place in a sports career, and if it's marketing, you need to understand what part of marketing you want to be in. You have to focus in on what you want to do in this great big arena of sports. And in the smaller segment of the arena called marketing, really focus in on what elements you want to move into.

"It's also important to know what you don't want to do. Particularly for those of you who are within a few years of graduating college and just getting your feet wet in your career path. Sometimes it's very difficult to understand what you want to do. A lot of times it's easier to know what you don't want. And by the process of elimination you begin to close in on the very elements that will ultimately appeal to you.

"If you're not absolutely committed to be in sports, don't love this industry, and are not willing to do anything you need to do to get into it and stay in it, you're not spending your [time] wisely. If on the other hand you are committed, you do love this industry, there's never been a better time to be in it. The industry is crying for creative, aggressive, smart, intelligent, articulate people. There's a place for you. Keep after it. And be bold."

SUCCESS STORY

Doug Pirnie,
marketing director, International Management Group

As a 20-year veteran of IMG, the largest sports management and marketing agency in the world, Doug Pirnie has responsibilities in the areas of corporate marketing, promotions, research, sales development, and publicity. During his career he has helped to develop national and international special events programs, evaluations procedures, and promotional tie-ins for a wide variety of corporate clients.

Pirnie began his career at Time, Inc. in 1969, as a publicity coordinator for *Sports Illustrated* magazine. He then moved to *Golf Digest* and *Tennis* magazines in 1972 as marketing coordinator. He joined IMG in 1976.

ADDRESS BOOK

Here's a Who's Who in Sports Marketing

Advantage International
1025 Thomas Jefferson
Street N.W.
Washington, DC 20007
202/333-3838

CAT Sports
5966 La Place Court
Carlsbad, CA 92008
619/438-8080

Championship Group
3690 North Peachtree Road
Atlanta, GA 30341
770/457-5777

*Clarion Performance
Properties*
Greenwich Office Park 5
Greenwich, CT 06831
203/862-6000

DelWilber & Associates
8201 Greensboro Drive
Mclean, VA 22102
703/749-9300

Golden Bear Sports
Management
11780 U.S. Highway One
North Palm Beach, FL 33408
407/626-3900

Integrated Sports International
One Meadowlands Plaza
East Rutherford, NJ 07073
201/507-1122

International Management
Group
One Erieview Plaza
Cleveland, OH 44114
216/522-1200

Muhlemann Marketing, Inc.
6000 Monroe Road
Charlotte, NC 28212
704/568-2520

Nike Sports Management
One Bowerman Drive
Beaverton, OR 97005
503/671-3074

Players, Inc.
2021 L Street, N.W.
Washington, DC 20036
202/463-2200

ProServ
1101 Wilson Boulevard
Arlington, VA 22209
703/276-3030

MARKETING DIRECTOR OF LICENSED MERCHANDISE

The marketing director of licensed merchandise is responsible for developing techniques for marketing sports apparel. The type of gear most commonly sold are jackets, hats, and jerseys emblazoned with a team's logo or insignia. In this position, the individual will also be expected to understand promotions, advertising, and public relations.

This is a burgeoning industry for professional and collegiate sports, as well as individual teams and schools. In 1995, the NBA signed on with 110 licensees; major league baseball had 440. That same year the NCAA had over 2,000 licensees; Penn State alone had 1,500 licensees. Total retail sales generated by the industry in 1995 was approximately $14 billion, according to Stu Crystal, the director of marketing for Starter, the leading sportswear company.

"In 1988, Starter did $60 million," he says. "In 1992, we did $282 million; in 1993, we did $356 million, and in 1994 we did approximately $400 million. Starter's market share is really very, very small, and we are the industry leader."

In the business of licensed merchandise, the marketing director must constantly strive to expand and open up new markets. As Starter's marketing manager, Crystal made the company known for creating young adult and teen fashions while maintaining its reputation of making what pro athletes and coaches wear on the field.

ON YOUR MARK

Unlike other sportswear companies, Starter built its brand by first emphasizing the authenticity of its licensed athletic wear and later promoting its name. Athletes and coaches would wear the garments during games, and consumers "wanted to wear what the pros wore," says Crystal, 37.

Demand was already strong in the inner-city neighborhoods. To further boost this demand, Starter broadened its product line from nylon jackets into hats, shirts, and other products.

"We went into fashion by taking authentic things and making them look like street wear," says Crystal.

Crystal has helped reinforce Starter's image and create consumer awareness by running television commercials on programming such as MTV and *The Fresh Prince of Bel Air*. Starter regularly spends over $15 million on advertising, according to Crystal. To cement its authentic-wear image, Starter airs spots during sporting events, uses stadium signage, and has even put its logo on ballboy shirts.

"We've maintained our cachet of being very cool, but our priority is our heritage of authenticity," Crystal says.

CUSTOMERS ARE YOUR CHUM

The marketing director will be expected to make decisions on which team apparel will prove to be most popular with consumers. In order to assure an appropriate inventory, the director is required to oversee staff personnel during the market research phase of the process. Specific demographic information about potential purchasers and their needs is valuable when addressing inventory concerns. In the retail game, overstocked is just as dangerous as understocked.

One of the main functions of the director is to negotiate contracts with sports teams and governing organizations in order to legally manufacture and sell licensed team products. All efforts performed by the marketing director are designed to attract more customers to buy your sportswear. It helps, of course, if the logo attached to the apparel represents a winning and exciting team. But as Crystal alluded to above, cool often takes precedent over winning.

After an NHL franchise was awarded to San Jose in May 1990, team marketing people from the city spent 13 months on consumer research before choosing San Jose's name, colors, and logos. Why a shark? "A shark immediately summons an image of aggression, speed, and strength," says San Jose vice president Matt Levine.

Levine went to chi-chi boutiques (Neiman-Marcus), department stores (Bloomingdale's), cataloguers (L.L. Bean), and sportswear companies (Starter), and asked, "What shades of blue sell best?" The answer he heard over and over was teal. Studies showed that by itself, teal appealed to women; when it was combined with black, men went for it too. After the logo was finally completed, it was introduced at a press conference conducted on the ice in San Jose.

"ESPN and CNN picked it up," says Levine. "It became a national story."

In the team's first season of 1991–92, national sales of Shark gear totaled over $150 million, an unprecedented figure for an NHL franchise. On the ice, however, San Jose was not faring as well. The Sharks lost their first 11 games and finished the season 17–58–5 with a league-worst 39 points. But their line of teal-and-black souvenirs became the hottest thing in sports, a must-buy for kids and yuppies all over North America. By season's end, *Advertising Age* included the Sharks in its "Marketing 100," an annual list of the stars of marketing.

IT'S HOW AL BUNDY STARTED

While it's not imperative that an individual in this field possess a comprehensive knowledge of sports, the director must have a complete understanding of the sportswear business and how it relates to athletics. Individuals interested in this area may wish to begin by working in a sporting goods or memorabilia store that specializes in athletic apparel.

This environment will prove to be a solid training ground for learning about the industry, both from the retailer's distribution perspective as well as from the manufacturer's supply side. You will also gain valuable insight into the consumer profile by working in a job at places like FootLocker, Athlete's Foot, Modell's, or The Sports Authority. The pay will probably be an hourly minimum wage, but think of it as building the foundation to a sky-high future.

Advancement prospects are usually determined by sales ability, and this is another reason to arm yourself with experience. Successful salespeople are part snake charmer, part snake oil pusher. Only by practicing your sales routine and developing good communications techniques can your pitch walk the tightrope that separates aggressive from overly pushy.

Another reason for gaining experience is the dreaded sales quotas. The more you can deal with the pressures of sales quotas, the better able you'll be to exceed these numbers. Individuals who develop lasting relationships with customers, suppliers, and manufacturer's representatives will increase their existing sales base and forge new accounts for future growth.

Educational requirements differ from person to person. Many companies require applicants to have earned a liberal arts college degree, but the area of emphasis can be as diverse as business management, sports administration, retail sales, marketing, promotions, public relations, finance, and accounting. The bottom line most prospective employers will look at is not good grades in the classroom; it's generating impressive sales results in the field.

CLOTHES MAKE THIS MAN

Peter Capolino is a businessman who capitalized on the popularity of licensed sportswear and began selling authentic baseball jerseys. Capolino, 52, the owner of Mitchell & Ness Sporting Goods in Philadelphia, creates faithful reproductions of classic jerseys that are, for all intents and purposes, the real thing. Sales for 1991 were predicted to be around $1.5 million due in large part to the nostalgia fans associate with baseball history.

Capolino had specialized in contemporary pro uniform shirts and historic baseball caps until one day in 1985. He was visiting a local manufacturing company that once produced amateur and college uniforms when he came across some bolts of long-discarded wool flannel. (Big league teams—having worn the heavy wool flannels through every summer—switched to synthetics in the late 1950s, then went to double-knits in the early 1970s.)

If contemporary baseball caps can sell, why not classic jerseys, thought Capolino. Collectors regularly shell out thousands of dollars for authentic uniforms, so wouldn't a serious fan pay $175 for a good reproduction? His first shirt was a copy of a genuine 1949 Roy Sievers jersey that a collector had brought in for repair—a vivid St. Louis Browns number 15 with orange-and-brown lettering.

After that, Capolino had a couple of other old-time shirts reproduced and they sold out quickly. Since his supply of fabric was limited, he tracked down a woolen mill in New Hampshire that had made uniforms for the big leagues. But that was before the advent of double-knits; the darn mill hadn't produced a uniform jersey in almost two decades. Fortunately, the mill hadn't lost its touch.

Capolino's clothing line, called The Cooperstown Collection, now boasts some 250 different models, ranging in price from $125 to $250, depending on the amount of detail in a team logo, number, and sleeve patch (call 215/592-6512 for a price guide). Capolino painstakingly leafs through piles of old sports journals—his library overflows with more than three-thousand publications dating back to the 1920s—looking for the right photos.

He spent months searching for a smiling Indian warrior emblem that had been worn on the sleeve of the 1957 Milwaukee Braves uniform. Warren Spahn's number 21—bearing the emblem and a bright tomahawk across the zippered front—is one of the biggest selling (and most expensive) shirts in the store. Another popular shirt, the brightly colored 1946 St. Louis Cardinals jersey worn by Stan Musial, is desired in part because that year the emblematic bat holding the two redbirds was black, not the customary gold.

That the period jerseys his tailors so carefully hand-stitch would become a fashion statement amuses Capolino, as do the frequent emotional outbursts from his customers.

"I have a friend, a stockbroker, who never mentioned baseball until he came in one day and saw a '51 Ted Williams," says Capolino. "He turned red and began to shake. He put on the shirt and said, 'I've got to have this. When I was nine, I got Ted Williams' autograph. I've had it in my wallet ever since.' To borrow that Notre Dame phrase, these shirts are waking up the echoes."

TIPSHEET

ⓘ Think about obtaining necessary experience at a sporting goods outlet or memorabilia store that specializes in athletic apparel.

- ◎ Target specific sportswear companies you wish to be associated with. When applying for a position, fashion an impressive cover letter to augment your resume.

- ◎ Before going in for an interview, go to the library and research all available information about the company and its merchandise. Your knowledge, drive, and conscientiousness will leave a lasting impression.

REAL-LIFE ADVICE

Stu Crystal,
director of marketing, Starter

Starter's marketing director, Stu Crystal, is responsible for strategic planning and implementation of marketing pro-grams for team services, sponsorship, endorsements, media, promotions, and league relations.

The New Haven, Connecticut–based company hired Crystal over eight years ago as the marketing/

personality sketch

Motivated; sales and marketing ability; good communications skills; personable.

merchandising manager. In this position, his duties included merchandising all aspects of Starter's line, including product development and direction, as well as marketing shows and co-op advertising.

Crystal received a bachelor of arts degree from the State University of New York at Stony Brook and his master of business administration from Northeastern University.

"The consumer will dictate the market, from the diehards, there game in and game out, to the fashion customer. The fan is asking for something that is authentic. That's why we're spending millions of dollars to be on the sideline, to be on the court, to get our logo synonymous with authenticity.

"How do we get growth? You can offer fresh, innovative products. It is a fashion market, even to the fan. They want this year's product, what's on the sideline this season.

"Leagues and teams can modify or change logos. The New York Jets— just by adding a little black accent—gave themselves a fresh look and drove their sales up dramatically.

"Every league is expanding. The [San Jose] Sharks, [Charlotte] Hornets, and [Anaheim] Mighty Ducks did their homework. They saw the consumer was looking for some fashion colors, some great aggressive logos, and that's a driving part of the business.

"Sometimes we forget we are marketing teams. Psychologists will tell you younger kids feel more comfortable wearing team apparel. As a team they're stronger, they have power, they belong."

Careers in the League Office 5

J erry Colangelo, the president and CEO of the NBA's Phoenix Suns, remembers the early days of his career in professional basketball. He was head scout and director of merchandising for the Chicago Bulls in the franchise's inaugural season.

"In 1966, there were nine NBA teams," he says. "A franchise cost $1.2 million. Our payroll was $180,000 for 12 players. Ticket prices were between two- and five-dollars a game, and national tele-vision income was $100,000 per team. Today, there are 30 teams. A franchise costs a mimimum of $100 million. Salaries are averaging over $1 million a player, and the national television income is about $7 million per team. Now that's real growth.

"Back then, the NBA was a real mom-and-pop operation," he continues. "The NBA offices in New York probably had about 25 people on staff. Now the league has over 350 positions."

The NBA's current success extends to the international marketplace as well. And the same is true of football, baseball, and hockey. With such a broad marketing reach, professional sports leagues have undergone enormous expansion and the potential for continued riches will surely increase the prospects for future growth.

Employment opportunities are available for professionals in league operations, business affairs, accounting, finance, tax and labor law, contract negotiation, marketing, communications, licensed merchandise, apparel, video production, and publishing—and that only suggests the scope of a league's organizational structure.

ADDRESS BOOK

Baseball

Major League Baseball
350 Park Avenue
New York, NY 10022

MINOR LEAGUES

American Association (AAA)
6801 Miami Avenue
Cincinnati, OH 45243
513/271-4800

International League (AAA)
55 South High Street
Dublin, OH 43017
614/791-9300

New York-Pennsylvania League (A)
1629 Oneida Street
Utica, NY 13501
315/733-8036

Pacific Coast League (AAA)
2345 South Alma School Road
Mesa, AZ 85210
602/838-2171

Texas Baseball League (AA)
2442 Facet Oak
San Antonio, TX 78323
210/545-5297

Basketball

Continental Basketball Association
701 Market Street
St. Louis, MO 63101
314/621-7222

National Basketball Association
645 Fifth Avenue
New York, NY 10022
212/407-8000

United States Basketball League
46 Quirk Road
Milford, CT 06460
203/877-9508

Bowling

American Bowling Congress
5301 South 76th Street
Greendale, WI 53129
414/421-6400

Ladies Pro Bowlers Tour
7171 Cherryvale Boulevard
Rockford, IL 61112
815/332-5756

Professional Bowlers Tour
1720 Merriman Road
Akron, OH 44334
216/836-5568

*Women's International
Bowling Congress*
5301 South 76th Street
Greendale, WI 53129
414/421-9000

Football

Canadian Football League
110 Eglinton Avenue West
Toronto, Ontario
Canada M4R 1A3

National Football League
410 Park Avenue
New York, NY 10022
212/758-1500

*World League of
American Football*
410 Park Avenue
New York, NY 10022
212/758-1500

Golf

*Ladies Professional
Golf Association*
2570 West International
Speedway Boulevard
Daytona Beach, FL 32114
904/254-8800

Professional Golfers Association
112 TPC Boulevard
Ponte Vedra, FL 32082
904/285-3700

United States Golf Association
P.O. Box 708
Far Hills, NJ 07931
908/234-2300

Hockey

National Hockey League
1251 Avenue of Americas
New York, NY 10020
212/789-2000

Western Hockey League
10333 Southport Road S.W.
Calgary, Alberta
Canada T2W 3X6

MINOR LEAGUES

American Hockey League
425 Union Street
West Springfield, MA 01089
413/781-2030

International Hockey League
1577 North Woodward Avenue
Bloomfield Hills, MI 48304
810/258-0580

Horse Racing

Thoroughbred Racing
Associations of America
420 Fair Hill Drive
Elkton, MD 21921
410/392-9200

*United States Trotting
Association*
750 Michigan Avenue
Columbus, OH 43215
614/224-2291

Motor Sports

Championship Auto
Racing Teams
755 West Big Beaver Road
Troy, MI 48084
810/362-8800

International Motor
Sports Association
3502 Henderson Boulevard
Tampa, FL 33609
813/877-4672

National Association for
Stock Car Auto Racing
1801 West International
Speedway Boulevard
Daytona Beach, FL 32120
904/253-0611

National Hot Rod Association
2035 East Financial Way
Glendora, CA 91741
818/914-4761

Soccer

American Professional
Soccer League
2 Village Road
Horsham, PA 19044
215/657-7440

Continental Indoor
Soccer League
16027 Ventura Boulevard
Encino, CA 91436
818/906-7627

Major League Soccer
2029 Century Park East
Los Angeles, CA 90036
310/772-2600

National Professional
Soccer League
229 Third Street N.W.
Canton, OH 44702
216/455-4625

Tennis

Association of Tennis
Professionals
200 ATP Tour Boulevard
Ponte Vedra Beach, FL 32082
904/285-8000

United States Tennis
Association
70 West Red Oak Lane
White Plains, NY 10604
914/696-7000

Women's Tennis Association
133 First Street N.E.
St. Petersburg, FL 33701
813/895-5000

Miscellaneous Sports Leagues

Association of Volleyball
Professionals
15260 Ventura Boulevard
Sherman Oaks, CA 91403
818/386-2486

Major Indoor Lacrosse
League
2310 West 75th Street
Prairie Village, KS 66208
913/384-8960

COMMISSIONER

The commissioner of a sports league or conference acts much in the same manner as a chairman of the board for a large corporation. The commissioner primarily serves in an advisory role, regulating the day-to-day activities of the league or conference and its member teams. Overall duties may vary depending on the size and structure of the league.

The commissioner of a minor league or small college conference may be responsible for overseeing all business ventures pursued by the league, as well as handling the marketing and public relations efforts of the league. The reach of this individual's jurisdiction may also extend to the areas of approving player contracts and trades (within the salary cap if applicable), doling out discipline, maintaining the integrity of officials, and ensuring the safety of arenas for fans and players.

While the commissioner of a major professional sports league will often delegate these duties to deputy commissioners, operations directors, and other top executives within the league office, the overall effectiveness and efficiency of the league or conference is the commissioner's responsibility. In this position, the individual's job is not only to keep the sport competitive, exciting, and fan-friendly, but also to attempt to maintain harmony between the league's players and owners.

THE WINNER...AND STILL COMMISSIONER

The commissioner is empowered to protect the integrity of the game through resolving disputes within the league and imposing disciplinary measures for conduct determinental to the league. The commissioner, however, reports to the owners, who must vote to approve or decline any measure or policy proposed by the commissioner.

The relationship between the commissioner and the owners can be strained. "No matter how much you stroke them," former National Football League commissioner Pete Rozelle once said of the owners, "it's never enough." The individual interests of the wealthy owners may often not be consistent with those of the league as a whole. To be sure, some owners are concerned only with their own bottom line, while others are more interested in the prosperity of the league as a whole. The successful commissioner will strike a delicate balance between all parties.

This is often easier said than done. Steve Kauffman, the former commissioner of the Continental Basketball Association, will readily attest that, on occasion, a commissioner confronted with tenuous circumstances be prepared to assume a defensive posture—literally. The problem began after Scranton had won the league championship in a bitter series over rival Allentown. During that off-season, the two teams were involved in a controversial player transaction that required the commissioner to intercede.

Kauffman attempted to mediate an arbitration hearing but was unsuccessful in his efforts to bring the warring factions to the bargaining table. When several certified letters to Scranton owner Art Packter went ignored, the commissioner issued a unilateral decision. Although Kauffman cannot recollect the exact details of the compensation award—"I think I penalized Scranton a player and a draft pick"—he would soon discover the unpopularity of his decision.

The next season opened with Scranton playing at Anchorage, a new team in the league. A major publicity event was scheduled to occur in the Anchorage airport once the Scranton team arrived. The local print media and television stations were waiting in the terminal, and the commissioner was in attendance to officiate the proceedings. "I was there to greet our championship team," says Kauffman.

"When the Scranton team came into the airport," Kauffman recalls, "Art Packter—who'd apparently been drinking the entire flight—he comes roaring out of the plane, charging me, and starts swinging at me. Two of the players immediately pulled him off of me, but all the reporters felt this was staged, as if we were professional wrestlers!"

IS THERE A LAWYER IN THE HOUSE?

Pugilistic prowess notwithstanding, the surest way into the commissioner's office is by first earning a law degree and then serving a sports league as general counsel. In this position, an individual will gain experience and knowledge in the important areas of player contracts, league financial reports, insurance statements, interpreting the league's salary cap and the right of first refusal, as well as other rules within the collective bargaining agreement.

When the National Basketball Association last needed a commissioner, in 1983, the owners promoted David Stern. A graduate of Rutgers University and Columbia (N.Y.) Law School, Stern was a tax lawyer by profession, who had shown great aptitude for making money.

He had joined the NBA in 1978 as the league's general counsel, with responsibilities in litigation, negotiations, and government relations. Two years later he expanded the league's marketing, broadcasting, and public relations activities in the newly created position of executive vice president for business and legal affairs.

Since becoming commissioner in 1983, Stern has presided over an unprecedented growth, prosperity, and internationalization of the league. The NBA thanked him in 1990 with a five-year deal worth $27.5 million.

When the National Football League last needed a commissioner, in 1989, the owners named Paul Tagliabue, the lawyer who was already serving the league for many years as an outside attorney. He succeeded Pete Rozelle, who retired after 30 years as commish.

A New Jersey native, Tagliabue was a high school honor student and an exceptional athlete. He was a state high jump champion and his basketball skills were much sought after by colleges. Tagliabue attended Georgetown University, where he was captain of the basketball team—he's the school's alltime leading rebounder— the senior class president, and a Rhodes Scholar finalist.

After graduating from Georgetown, he received a scholarship to attend New York University Law School, where he edited the law review and graduated with honors. Tagliabue began his career in 1965 as a law clerk in federal court in Washington, D.C. The following year he took a position with the U.S. Defense Department. He stayed until 1969, when he went to work at Covington & Burling, one of Washington's top law firms. He had risen to the post of senior partner when he became NFL comissioner.

When the National Hockey League last needed a commissioner, in 1993, the owners brought in Gary Bettman, the lawyer who had mastered the intricacies of the NBA salary cap. A graduate of Cornell University in 1975 and from New York University Law School in 1977, Bettman spent four years working for a corporate law firm. In 1981, at the tender age of 29, he joined the NBA as assistant general counsel.

He served in the NBA for twelve years, rising to the position of senior vice president and general counsel. In that function he worked closely with commissioner David Stern and served a main role in shaping NBA operations. Bettman, who is nearing the end of his five-year contract, can call upon a staff of 100 people, spread in offices in New York, Montreal, and Toronto.

THE BOY COMMISSIONER

Steve Kauffman's rise to prominence began as a sports agent, representing players from teams in the Eastern Basketball League, which later changed its name to the Continental Basketball Association. One of his clients was Jerry Baskerville, a Temple University graduate who'd had a cup of coffee in the NBA with the Philadelphia 76ers.

Upon his client's release from the Sixers, Kauffman began to search for ways in which Baskerville could continue his playing career. Europe was a possible consideration; however, Kauffman discovered a new vehicle closer to home: the Eastern League. Stan Novak, a family friend, who at the time was coaching in the league (he would later become director of scouting for the NBA's Detroit Pistons), began to refer more players Kauffman's way.

"I'd built up a substantial client base of Eastern League players," says Kauffman. "One day Stan Novak asked me, 'How would you like to be commissioner?' I looked at him like he was absolutely crazy. I thought he was kidding, but he was dead serious. I'm thinking, 'This is nuts. I have no idea how to be a commissioner. Is there someone I can call? Is there a book I can read on how to be a commissioner?'"

Kauffman stalled by asking to sleep on it before making a decision. It was the worst best night he never slept.

"I woke up during the night and realized opportunity was knocking; this is the big break. How could I not do it? At five o'clock in the morning I realized it's out of nowhere, but I've got to go for it. So I applied for the job, made my presentation, and was appointed commissioner. I was 27 years old. It's all because of one pro basketball client who'd played three weeks with the Sixers."

NO SNOW JOB

Kauffman's initial marching orders were to expand the league's marketing reach by improving its image. This would be a challenge. The blue-collar image of the Eastern Basketball League was well deserved. The league was comprised of teams that represented the coal-mining towns of Pennsylvania and the surrounding area where they were based.

"We wanted to change the image," says Kauffman, "without radically changing and forsaking the teams and cities that had been in the league all along."

In his second season as Eastern League commissioner, Kauffman received a phone call from a wealthy businessman in Anchorage. He and several other investors hoped to lure a team to their fair city and were willing to make financial guarantees to bring visiting teams to Alaska.

While the concept of a team from Anchorage playing in something called the Eastern League seemed ludicruous, Kauffman immediately saw the unlimited marketing possibilities that could be engineered by such an incongruous opportunity. "I decided to keep the name Eastern League," says Kauffman, "figuring maybe the press would pick it up."

Sure enough, *Sports Illustrated* dispatched a writer to Alaska, who subsequently filed a mocking report that was published in the national magazine. "It was just the push we needed," says Kauffman. "We then expanded around the country and renamed the league the Continental Basketball Association, which is now the top minor league in pro ball."

Kauffman, now 48, stepped down as CBA commissioner after the 1977–78 season to concentrate on his flourishing sports management group. He still follows the CBA standings in the newspaper.

SPOTLIGHT

Robert Ufer,
president and CEO, International Hockey League

Prior to the appointment of his current position, Bob Ufer had served 18 years as the International Hockey League's legal counsel. In his first season at the helm in 1994–95, league attendance increased by more than 67 percent. Under his leadership, the IHL has seen new franchises arrive in California, Florida, Utah, Michigan, and Canada.

"[Donald] Trump is our poster boy of what not to do," says Ufer, referring to the brash real estate tycoon who ran the fledgling United States Football League into the ground in the 1980s by throwing around million-dollar contracts. "The dominant pitfall is that you can buy a winner. That's not it. We've got to have group chemistry. We have to focus on making the whole pie bigger without bickering."

So when Ufer interviews potential owners who may be willing to plunk down $10 million for a franchise, he looks for more than money. "This is a partnership like a marriage," says Ufer. "We talk about their belief in the ideals and the mission of the league. We talk about their personal lives."

One of Ufer's first duties was to enhance the IHL's marketing and communications departments, as well as increasing the league's merchandising efforts. League sales of licensed merchandise has risen astronomically in his first three years as president, with sales surpassing $20 million in 1994–95.

Ufer is quick to credit several factors for the league's new-found popularity. The nontraditional fans, he contends, have been lured to the game by the insurgence of in-line skating. It also didn't hurt that major league baseball players went on strike and the National Hockey League locked out its players. "We were in the right place at the right time."

"We're not the minor league," he adds. "We're an alternative professional sports league. TV is not necessary to our equation. It's gravy."

Ufer attended Yale University where he played on the varsity hockey team for three years. He graduated in 1971 as Phi Beta Kappa, then attended Harvard Law School. After graduating in 1974, he joined the Detroit firm of Dickinson, Wright, Moon, Van Dusen & Freeman. It was while a partner at that firm that he was introduced to the IHL by John Ziegler, who would later become president of the National Hockey League.

"We're about entertainment," Ufer says of the IHL. "Someone once said to me, 'You can't control the game itself, but you can control the quality of the entertainment.' Anybody who misses that is missing the boat."

SUCCESS STORY

Alan Rothenberg,
chairman, major league soccer

A well-known litagator in Southern California, Alan Rothenberg joined Latham & Watkins in July 1990. Before coming to the firm's Los Angeles office, he had been a name partner at Manatt, Phelps, Rothenberg & Phillips for over 20 years. Marked by diversity, his practice has involved matters drawn from the banking, business, sports, and entertainment fields.

Rothenberg's love for sports, and soccer in particular, led him to serve as chairman of the 1994 World Cup organizing committee and president of the U.S. Soccer Federation. In the past, he has served in several prestigious positions within the soccer community, including commissioner for the L.A. Olympic Organizing Committee (1984), owner of the Los Angeles Aztecs of the North American Soccer League (1980–88), and member on the NASL board of directors (1977–80).

Rothenberg has also served two terms on the National Basketball Association Board of Governors (1971–79 and 1982–89), representing the Los Angeles Lakers and Los Angeles Clippers, respectively.

DIRECTOR OF OPERATIONS

The director of operations is the commissioner's top advisor on all sports-related matters. The individual is responsible for virtually every area that involves the playing of the game: player discipline, officiating, proposed rule changes, overseeing facilities, and international competition. He or she is also the main liaison between the league office and the general managers of each team.

A person in this position will oversee all details for getting a game on the field. Among other things, the operations director has ultimate authority on the hiring of officials, as well as the scheduling of games. The director of officiating and the director of scheduling report to the operations director.

The main function performed by this office is player discipline. Athletes must play within the rules, even when tempers flare and emotions became heated. Athletes perform under intense pressure; the slightest provocation may lead to fighting. Obviously, on-field violence must be discouraged. Fights tarnish the image of the sport and may bring harm to spectactors.

The director of operations is charged with the implementation and execution of procedures to limit violence among players. Rod Thorn, the NBA's senior vice president of operations, is jokingly known as the "vice president of violence." Players who stray from the NBA's increasingly straight and narrow path must deal with Thorn's punishments. Since he started reviewing video of NBA fights and flagrant fouls in 1986, Thorn has handed out more than $3 million in fines. And that doesn't include pay lost during suspensions.

A THORN IN THE SIDE

To be sure, basketball is a contact sport. But the state of the game has improved as a direct result of the not so subtle rule changes Thorn has endorsed over the years. He had much to do with the rule outlawing hand-checking above the foul line. He installed a flagrant-foul point system which results in a one-game suspension for every flagrant foul after the fifth in a season (the slate is wiped clean for the postseason).

He instituted a rule in which a player must be fined (at least $2,500 and as much as $20,000) and suspended for at least one game for leaving the bench during a fight, no matter what the extenuating circumstances. Additionally, a player must be ejected from the game and suspended for at least one game and fined (an amount determined by Thorn) for throwing a punch—even if it doesn't land—no matter how he was provoked.

"I used to believe nothing should happen if you threw a punch that didn't land," Thorn told *Sports Illustrated's* Jack McCallum. "But I came around to the opinion that that's the same as fighting because you intend it to land."

The most effective safety measure possible is the idea of players policing themselves. To this end, Thorn's zero-tolerance to retaliation is paying handsome dividends. Violent incidents are down to three from 11 in each of the previous two seasons, thanks largely to the ever-escalating fines levied by the NBA's lord of discipline. Thorn attributes this decline to the strong deterrents the NBA has in place. "A lot of times you'll see someone squaring off and a light goes on in his eyes," says Thorn. "Years ago there would've been punches. Now there's restraint."

THE JOB PATROL

Employment prospects are poor for individuals aspiring to be a director of operations. There are only a certain number of professional sports leagues that offer such jobs, and those people who are already in this position do not relinquish it easily.

Salaries for a director of operations can vary dramatically depending on the specific league one works for. Annual salaries can range from $50,000 to $200,000. An individual working in the major league baseball commissioner's office, for example, will earn a much higher salary than a person doing the same job in the low minor leagues. Variables for earnings may also include an individual's experience, prestige, and longevity in the position.

The operations director is one of the highest-ranking executives in sports. Prospects for promotion are limited at this level. However, individuals may advance their careers by becoming a league commissioner or deputy commissioner, league chief operating officer, or team owner.

While there is no formal educational requirement for this job, competition is fierce and only the most qualified candidates will be considered. A college degree in sports management or business administration is vital, as are courses in communications, law, marketing, and public relations. Experience in the sports industry, whether as a player or in team management, is also helpful.

SMOOTH OPERATOR

You might say Rod Thorn was born for the job of keeping the peace in basketball. Growing up in Princeton, West Virginia, his father was chief of police. An all-state hoops performer at Princeton High, Thorn attended West Virginia University on a basketball scholarship. Following in the large footsteps left by Hot Rod Hundley and Jerry West, Thorn dazzled the opposition with an unusual over-the-head, two-handed jump shot called the Thornderbolt.

Injuries nagged the slender, 6'4" Thorn throughout a solid but unspectacular eight-year NBA career in which the journeyman guard averaged 10.8 points for the Baltimore Bullets, Detroit Pistons, St. Louis Hawks, and Seattle SuperSonics. Thorn was recognized around the NBA as an intelligent player and a ferocious competitor, and it was logical that after his retirement in 1971 he stayed in the game.

Thorn served in a variety of roles, first as an assistant coach with the SuperSonics and the New York Nets of the old ABA, then as a head coach of the ABA Spirits of St. Louis, and finally as a general manager with the Chicago Bulls. In the Chicago war room on draft day in June of 1984, it was Thorn who ultimately decided to use the team's first-round pick, the third overall pick of the draft, to select a North Carolina Tarheel named Michael Jordan. Thorn was fired less than a year later, when Jerry Reinsdorf bought the Bulls and installed as general manager his own man, Jerry Krause.

Thorn took a job as a trader on the Chicago Board of Options Exchange. Shortly thereafter, NBA commissioner David Stern asked him to come to the league offices in New York to replace Scotty Sterling, who had become general manager of the Knicks. It didn't take Thorn very long to feel comfortable in his new position. Just 17 days after assuming his NBA post, Thorn handed down his first fines—a total of $6,500 for fighting to Seattle's Xavier McDaniel and Atlanta's Tree Rollins and Kevin Willis.

Over the years Thorn has expanded the operations job into the international arena, where he recently served on the selection committee that helped to decide the members of the 1996 U.S. Olympic basketball team. The picks were open for debate, but that's nothing new for Thorn, who is, or so it seems, always a lightning rod for controversy.

His handling of referees has drawn criticism by players who view the zebras as a robotic bunch that make calls almost by rote. And that's just fine by Thorn. "The more literal the calls, the better," he says. "Because of videotape, when everyone can review everything, there is little room for individualism."

TIPSHEET

Ⓘ A college degree in sports administration or business management is extremely helpful in this field.

Ⓘ An internship with a professional sports league or a college conference will help you gain hands-on experience as it relates to the inner-workings of a league office.

Ⓘ Try to gain an entry level position working for a person who already has a similar job. Learn the ropes and make it known you wish to move up the ladder. Volunteer for a heavier workload, earn the respect and trust of this person, and make contacts that will help you down the road.

SUCCESS STORY

Brian Burke,
director of operations, National Hockey League

On September 1, 1993, National Hockey League commissioner Gary Bettman named Burke senior vice president and director of operations. Burke is the commissioner's top advisor on all hockey related matters. He is responsible for player discipline, officiating, proposed rule changes, overseeing facilities, and international competition. He is also the main liaison with the NHL general managers. Before joining the NHL, Burke served as president and general manager of the Hartford Whalers from May 1992 to September 1993.

> ## personality sketch
>
> *Knowledge of sports; understanding of athletes; good communication skills; skills in crisis management; ability to think big-picture.*

In 1987 he joined the Vancouver Canucks as vice president and director of hockey operations, serving in that capacity for five years. Burke graduated from Providence College in Rhode Island, where he played hockey and was captain of the Friar team his senior year. He played one season for the Philadelphia Flyers' American Hockey League affiliate, the Maine Mariners.

Burke ended his playing career to attend Harvard Law School, graduating in 1981. He became associated with the Boston law firms of Palmer & Dodge and Hutchins & Wheeler, where he specialized in representing professional athletes. In addition to his duties with the NHL, Burke serves as a member of the board of directors for both the National Sports Law Institute and the Sports Lawyers' Association.

DIRECTOR OF COMMUNICATIONS

The director of communications serves as the chief information officer for the league. The individual in this position is primarily responsible for enhancing and maintaining the image of the game. He or she will report directly to the commissioner and work closely with various departments within the league operations.

The director of communications will be expected to assist the commissioner in formulating league positions on various issues such as league expansion, player discipline, substance abuse policy, and labor negotiations. The director of communications is required to provide the media with the official league response regarding any issue, or make accessible a person within the league office most appropriate to provide a response.

The communications department will also be responsible for producing and publishing a media directory of all sports writers and radio and television broadcasters who cover the sport. In addition, the department is in charge of handling the press operations at various league events like the All-Star Game, and championship events such as the World Series, Stanley Cup, and Super Bowl extravaganzas. At such mega-events it's commonplace to credential and deal with approximately 1,000 members of the media. While the bulk of these duties are performed by the communications staff and not by the director, the efficient servicing of the media is nonetheless his or her ultimate responsibility.

A career in corporate communications is fast paced and exciting. It's also stressful and deadline-oriented. The individual in this post will be highly visible and held extremely accountable.

"No day is the same," says Arthur Pincus, vice president of public relations for the National Hockey League. "The bulk of my time is spent on the telephone responding to various requests from the media, servicing the teams with information and support, and helping the teams with issues they may be facing."

THE COMMUNICATIONS COMMUNITY

A director of communications is supported by a staff of between eight and ten people. The entry-level position is the assistant communications managers, who perform much of the mundane tasks. Three or four assistants work the telephones to service the media and handle the fan mail. This may include answering correspondences and public queries or routing written requests to the proper department.

Two or three communications managers churn out press releases and issue statements regarding where the league stands on certain topics of the day. While the current environment is littered with terms relating to collective bargaining agreements and binding arbitration, communications managers need not be a paralegal, or even the next Scott Turow.

"We're not looking for Ernest Hemingways," says Rich Levin, executive director of public relations for major league baseball, "but for people who can put sentences together skillfully."

Two supervisors oversee the daily operation of the department. They serve to prioritize projects and funnel the flow of work, as well as guide the projects to completion and answer any questions the staff may have. The league also employs a chief statistician, sometimes called a director of information, who is responsible for accumulating statistics from each game and maintaining an updated seasonal database. Media requests often involve the compilation of statistics, so the individual in this position is a significant force in league communications as well as team public relations.

Salaries in the communications department may range from $25,000 for an assistant just starting out to upwards of $175,000 at the director's level. As employees rise up the corporate ladder, salaries may be determined by league policy as well as by the individual's burden of responsibility, background, and experience.

KEEP A STIFF UPPER LIP

The employment outlook for league communications officers is bleak. The communications department in a league office is a relatively small staff and job openings are few and far between.

"We don't go through the interview process very often," says Levin. "But when we do, if it's one of the junior positions, then we'd look for someone right out of college with a communications background and some writing skills. I'm particularly interested in writing skills and somebody who can get along with people. If it's the No. 2 position, I'd look for somebody more experienced, perhaps with a club, but certainly with considerable public relations knowledge."

Professional sports leagues require job applicants to have completed a four-year college education. Individuals seeking a position within the commissioner's communications department will be expected to have earned a degree in communications, public relations, or journalism. Other important areas of study include sports administration, English literature, and liberal arts.

Experience in corporate communications and an understanding of the media is vital to the success of a communications director. The individual in this position will be required to stand front and center whenever a controversial event or unsavory incident takes place. At the ensuing press conference, when the media sharpshooters take aim at the podium, it is the league's director of communications who is the stationary target in the crosshairs.

"To be honest," says baseball's Levin, "ever since the Pete Rose situation it seems like there's been one crisis after another. Crisis management is definitely something you learn to deal with."

The director of communications cannot ever utter the statement "No comment"—that's not an acceptable strategy. Further, he or she should not act merely as a buffer between the league and the media. No one ever believes a spokesperson who hammers out a singular, definitive message and the same droning philosophy day after day. Rather, the individual who advances in a communications career will be a proactive decision maker, readily accessible, and always knowledgable as to the facts.

TIPSHEET

- Learn as much as you can about the interaction of public relations and journalism. While in high school, work for a local newspaper as a writer covering community events and attend as many press conferences as you can.

- Attend a four-year college or university with a solid program in public relations, communications, or journalism. While working toward earning your degree, seek out internships within the field of corporate communications.

- In the early stages of your career, try to get a job with a professional sports team in the publicity or media relations area. This will give you a broad base of understanding as to how sports and the media are codependent.

- Once you've established yourself in the field of public relations, then try to make the lateral move into a league. This may not prove to be easy, so take any job within the league and be patient.

- Check the available employment opportunities listed weekly and, while you bide your time, forge relationships with people already working in the league's communications office. When a job is about to open up, these people will be the first to know. Hopefully, they will alert you, and you can sieze the day.

REAL-LIFE ADVICE

Arthur Pincus,
vice president of public relations, National Hockey League

Arthur Pincus brings nearly 25 years of journalism experience to his position as NHL chief information officer. At 19, he was working full-time as a copyboy for *The New York Times* at night while going to school during the day. He graduated in 1970 from the City College of New York with a degree in English.

He went from copyboy to clerk to copy editor and, in 1973, in

> ## personality sketch
>
> *Excellent communications skills; solid writing ability; good public speaker; supervisory; quick-thinker; troubleshooter.*

addition to his copy-editing duties, he also served as make-up editor and writer. In 1979 he was promoted to assistant sports editor in charge of the Sunday sports section. He was then named deputy sports editor with the additional responsibility of overseeing the Sports Monday section.

Pincus left the *Times* in 1987 to become executive editor of *Sports Inc.*, a weekly sports business magazine. When the start-up publication folded after 18 months, he began an independent consulting business before returning to the newspaper business. He joined *The Washington Post* as assistant sports editor and was promoted to sports editor, where he ran the day-to-day operation for almost three years. When Gary Bettmann became NHL commissioner in 1993, he appointed Pincus the vice president of public relations.

"The best college experience you can get is working for the sports information director. Relationships are everything. After you graduate and send out resumes, use whatever contacts you may have gotten while working in the SID's office. Work on a big game day or any big event where you can come into contact with the media. If your football team is playing the number one team in the nation and you've got six members of the national media coming in, make sure you meet those people.

"I am very lucky because I get to work in sports on a daily basis. It's what everybody loves, what everybody wants to do, and they all wonder how you were able to do it. I caught one break at the beginning on my own and then took advantage of the breaks that others helped me get after that. You never know where the opportunity is going to come from, so keep working. You've got to be outgoing, you must be respectful, you must not be a nuisance. There is a difference between being ambitious and being obnoxious; it's a real fine line that must be observed. If you get to speak to somebody who is in a position of some authority, treat that person with great respect and dignity at all times.

"Here's some key tips in getting a job. When writing a letter to someone, spell their name correctly. There's no embarassment in calling up and saying, 'I'm sending a letter to Mr. Pincus. How does he spell his last name and what's his title?' The last thing I want to see is my name spelled P-i-n-k-u-s. I will never hire someone who spells my name with a 'k.' It's not ego. It indicates a lack of attention to detail, a lack of respect for people, and an overall lack of intelligence. I'm not looking to hire geniuses, but street smarts is an important asset.

"When I'm interviewing someone, I want to know where they think they'll be ten years from now. And I always want to know what they read. You must read a newspaper. You must be familiar with popular culture and the political process. To maintain your connection with the world you have to be well read. If you become too focused on sports it will be a detriment to you. You have to understand what's going on around you. You have to have other interests besides sports. It's important, both psychologically and physically, to be able to get away from it. And you have to keep growing. The only way to grow is to be learning about new things."

SUCCESS STORY

Rich Levin,
executive director of public relations, major league baseball commissioner's office

Rich Levin has served the baseball commissioner for the past 12 years. Before coming to major league baseball, he was the assistant press secretary with the Los Angeles Olympic Organizing Committee from 1983 to 1985, where he worked closely with Peter Ueberroth. Levin has deep roots in the city of Los Angeles. He covered the Lakers for nine seasons as a sportswriter for the *Herald Examiner*. A graduate of UCLA with a degree in history, Levin played basketball for coach John Wooden and was a member of two national championship teams in 1964 and '65.

PROPERTIES

The properties division of a professional sports league acts as the licensing, marketing, and publishing arm of the league. This office produces books and magazines, trading cards and other collectibles, videos and CD-ROMs, electronic toys and games, sporting goods, youth products like lunch boxes and spiral-bound notebooks—and probably anything else you can think of—for worldwide distribution and sale.

The main function of the properties division, and far and away its biggest money maker, is the selling to manufacturers of the rights to reproduce team insignias and logos on licensed products. Properties is a relatively new revenue producer. The idea is to peddle the league imprimatur to various businesses who want an identification with the pro sport.

Logos are currently experiencing unprecedented popularity. The lust for emblems has turned licensed apparel into a fashion category all its own. Logos appeal to the Generation Xers who have grown up in a pre-packaged culture, and sports teams are on the cutting edge of this trend.

Driven by hot new team identities as much as won-loss records, sports licensing generates annual retail sales in excess of $12 billion. Is it any wonder pro teams can afford to pay their top players such exhorbitant salaries? In 1980 the NBA licensing department had $100,000 in total revenue. According to NBA Properties, which handles licensing arrangements with manufacturers, licensees in 1993 sold $2.8 billion worth of merchandise. You've come a long way, baby! Over at NFL Properties, sales of licensed merchandise in 1994 totaled $3 billion.

UNIFORM SUCCESS

It used to be that the sales of a teams' products were related to its success on the field. But according to Tom O'Grady, who heads the 12-person creative services department at NBA Properties, today's kids are much more fashion conscious. These sentiments are echoed by Alisa Klemm, senior correspondent at *Team Licensing Business*, a trade publication based in Scottsdale, Arizona.

"Teams design the logos and uniforms for consumer sales," she says. "They want to make sure what they unveil to the marketplace is definitely going to sell, to fans as well as the fashion-conscious because sports licensing has become such a fashion business. It's almost turning into what people want to wear every day."

Many established teams are going to new logos. The Houston Rockets, winners of two consecutive NBA championships, incorporated new team colors and a new logo for the 1995–96 season. Team and league executives insist that the change had nothing to do with greed and point out that the team had applied for the change two years earlier.

Perhaps the Rockets announcement was merely a case of bad timing—Houston, we have a public relations problem—coming as it did on the heels of two NHL and three other NBA teams declaring a change of logo. That had increased the number of baseball teams to 12 and basketball teams to 13 who had changed logos during the past five years.

IT'S NOT WHETHER YOU WIN OR LOSE, IT'S HOW YOU SELL THE GAME

Expansion franchises, which usually lose a majority of their games, are the hottest sellers these days. Right now, the hip teams include the Florida Panthers and the Anaheim Mighty Ducks in the National Hockey League. The Mighty Ducks derive popularity from their cartoonish logo that depicts a hockey-masked duck with two hockey sticks behind it, forming a whimsical takeoff on a skull and crossbones.

When the NBA's expansion franchise Toronto Raptors unveiled its new logo in 1994 (a snarling dinosaur decked out in hoops attire), licensed merchandise was readily available in 40 countries across five continents. Consumers all over the world quickly snapped up the basketball-dribbling beast. No less than one month later it was reported that $20 million in licensed products had been sold—and it was 18 months before the Raptors would set foot on a hardwood court!

The Raptors nickname is taken from a ferocious species of dinosaur seen in the blockbuster movie Jurassic Park. While it may seem like a calculated sports marketing ploy, the Raptors nickname was actually the winner of a Canadian contest in which 189 different names were considered for the final phase of voting.

"The field is very crowded," says William Nix, vice president of business affairs for NBA Properties. "Trying to come up with original imagery and descriptive terms is a real challenge for a new franchise."

Entries were reviewed and weeded out because they were deemed not applicable to basketball or ruled out due to legal and commercial considerations. Finally, and most crucially, the name's design potential was carefully considered. "We did not want anything cuddly looking," says the NBA's O'Grady. "Barney was our biggest concern."

From a marketing standpoint, the Toronto franchise is smiling wider than a Cheshire cat. "We wanted something that was different," says Tom Mayenknecht, communications director for the Raptors. "Something that was going to appeal to young and young-minded people that was competitive looking and animated without entirely losing a cute quality, and [one] that translated really well on television."

By the way, if you're wondering, bobcat was the runner-up.

PERSONAL PROPERTIES

These are the salad days for the properties divisions at the four major sports leagues. Individuals interested in a career in this field will be ecstatic to learn that employment opportunities are plentiful and the potential for growth unlimited.

The properties division at the NFL, for instance, staffs nearly 150 people, while the NBA has global offices in New York, Switzerland, Hong Kong, Australia, and Japan. Aspiring candidates may find employment opportunities in the areas of consumer products, creative services, finance, legal, marketing, and team services.

The "big four" sports offer internships in at least one of these areas. But not everyone can walk right into a job. Competition is fierce. Gordon Frank, a human resources consultant for the NBA, reports that the league each year receives nearly 4,000 job applications. To warrant serious consideration, applicants must indicate useful skills appropriate to a particular department.

A four-year college education is required for entry into this field, and an advanced degree in a specific area of expertise will be helpful for advancement. Good choices for majors include marketing, public relations, advertising, business administration, finance, accounting, and fine arts.

Salaries will be commensurate with experience. Generally, the pay scale is considered to be above average for middle-level managers ($50,000 to $75,000) because the properties department generates revenue. Top management is extremely well paid.

TIPSHEET

① Learn as much as you can about the field. Read *Team Licensing Business,* a trade publication based in Scottsdale, Arizona.

① Attend seminars and workshops to develop a network of contacts within the field.

① Try to earn an internship during college, or see about working a summer job in the marketing department with a minor league team.

① Breaking in will be difficult; resign yourself to that fact.

① A foot in the door is your best bet for advancement as many jobs just above entry level are assigned from within. Be prepared to answer telephones and perform other gopher duties. Check the job postings and pounce on any available opportunity to move up.

REAL-LIFE ADVICE

Sara Levinson,
president, NFL Properties

The National Football League named Sara Levinson as president of NFL Properties in September 1994. She was formerly president and business director of MTV Music Television.

She joined MTV in 1986 as executive vice president in charge of new business at MTV, Nickelodeon, and VH-1. She was promoted to executive vice president in charge of business operations at MTV in 1991 and to president/business director of MTV in 1993.

At MTV Levinson directed all business operations during a period of tremendous growth for the network. She is credited with being the architect of MTV's global expansion and was also responsible for extending MTV's core business into publishing, merchandising and licensing, new media, international syndication, and audio and video products.

A native of Portsmouth, Virginia, the 44-year-old Levinson graduated from Cornell University in 1972 and earned her master's in business administration from Cornell three years later. After graduation she worked for two years as an account executive at an advertising agency, then held a series of managerial jobs in the cable industry. That led to her appointment as advertising manager at Showtime, the TV cable network, before joining MTV.

"Many similiarities exist between MTV and the NFL. First and foremost are the passionate fans, fans who display a sense of ownership in the franchise. This passion has not gone unrecognized by corporate America. All of our business partners, benefit from their relationship with the NFL. The NFL also benefits. Most important, our fans benefit.

"The NFL has never been healthier. Any indicator you choose will reinforce the popularity of the game. So how do you stay healthy, stay number one? Anticipate the changes.

"The first step is gaining knowledge. We're undertaking a comprehensive survey of sports fans to determine exactly who our fans are and who our potential fans are. We must be closer to the fans to serve them better.

"At MTV we could slice and dice that audience and tell you anything about every segment. The challenge is greater at the NFL. The audience is broader and more complex. But with this research as a start, we'll be able to develop the programs that will appeal to the diehard fans, we'll be able to create new events that will increase the interest of the casual fan, and we'll be able to focus on ways to reach that soon-to-be fan.

"NFL Properties will [always look to] exploit the new technologies to enhance the game for fans. That may be working with NFL Enterprises to help broadcast same-day game highlights in all the NFL stadiums or implementing keypads in stadium seats to gauge the instantaneous fan reaction to events on the field. Or maybe allowing home viewers to choose their own camera angles while watching the game.

"How do we celebrate [the future]? By listening to our fans. But it's not just new fans in the U.S. It's bringing the game to fans around the world through the World League in Europe and American bowls and the hopes of additional leagues in Asia and Latin American in the new millennium. But most important, it's through change. The constant—we won't be afraid to change."

SUCCESS STORY

Rick Welts,
president, NBA Properties

Rick Welts, 42, has spent practically his whole life around pro basketball. He was a ball boy for the Seattle Supersonics and later returned to the team as an assistant trainer. While attending the University of Washington he moonlighted as a public relations assistant before becoming director of public relations. In 1979, after ten years with the Sonics, Welts left the club to join a sports marketing and promotion firm in Seattle.

He joined the NBA's league office in 1982 as director of national promotions for NBA Properties and later served as vice president of marketing. He was promoted to the NBA's vice president of communications in 1984 and four years later was appointed to his current post as president of NBA Properties.

ADDRESS BOOK

Major League Baseball
Properties
350 Park Avenue
New York, NY 10022
212/339-7800

National Basketball
Association Properties
645 Fifth Avenue
New York, NY 1022
212/407-8000

National Football
League Properties
410 Park Avenue
New York, NY 10022
212/758-1500

National Hockey
League Properties
1251 Avenue of the Americas
New York, NY 10020
212/789-2000

Team Licensing
Business Magazine
P.O. Box 5400
Scottsdale, Arizona 85261
602/483-0014

DESIGN DIRECTOR

Every professional sports league employs a designer, if not a team of designers, whose main duty is to create a visual identity for the sport and its member teams. The designer may be called upon to update a team's existing image or devise a new one.

The design director is responsible for defining "the look" and essence of everything from team uniforms and apparel to anniversary logos and stadium signage. To accomplish this, the design director meets with team executives to determine a logo and color scheme. When working with a team, the designer will function as part art director, offering style advice, and part club confidante, assessing whether a new logo, or "mark," can be reproduced on television and whether it can be silk-screened onto apparel. The design director can suggest and recommend, but the ultimate decision rests with the team's front-office executives.

Anne Occi, vice president of design services for Major League Baseball Enterprises, guided the redesign of the Seattle Mariners uniform prior to the 1993 season when the new owners wanted a new image. Occi (pronounced "OH-see") rejected a Poseidon-like figure that more resembled a label on a can of tuna fish than an insignia for a major league baseball team.

personality sketch

Skilled graphic designer; ability to execute creative concepts as well as communicate vision to others; artistic.

Occi suggested a striking nautical compass rose executed in forest green and deep blue "to make a connection to the colors of the Pacific northwest." Not surprisingly, Occi's color choices had coincided with her Pantone textile color swatches, the criteria based on psychographic research that indicates to fashion designers which colors are going to be hot. Stadium sales of Mariner merchandise jumped from $372,000 in the season prior to the redesign to well over $1 million during the first year after the transformation.

"Once you end up in the top 10 in sales," says Occi, "either you have a phenomenal club, a brand new ballpark, or colors that you know are hot in fashion. We knew going in that the combination of navy and green would be popular."

WINNING BY DESIGN

Sports licensing, once the concessionaire's territory, is now the valued domain of the sports business at all levels of retail distribution: from mass markets to upscale department stores, home shopping channels to Internet purchases. Sports merchandise sales exploded by more than 525 percent between 1987 and 1993. Combined sales of the four major professional sports leagues will amount to over $8 billion this year—and receipts are still growing.

Sports paraphernalia, particularly baseball caps and V-necked hockey jerseys, are fast becoming pop-culture artifacts as omnipresent as the Coca-Cola swirl (or is it the Nike swoosh?) Consumers, ever savvier, now demand the latest in styles, fabrics, and colors. Gone are the days when a kid from Chicago's Southside would wear his beloved White Sox cap until it frayed; that same kid today probably has a collection of caps from teams coast-to-coast and wears a different cap each day of the week.

"They're going to buy a hat not so much because it's their team of choice or the team in their backyard," says Tom O'Grady, creative services director at NBA Properties, "but rather because they've got a pair of purple shoelaces and they want a purple hat to match."

So whereas teams once picked their logos and colors and stuck with them for generations, now they are tinkering to pump up sales volume. Like many products, the design of sports merchandise is prone to a herd mentality, often resulting in a type of cross-pollination: the Florida Marlins' teal plays off the Charlotte Hornets' teal, which plays off the San Jose Sharks' teal.

Before teal, the big trend was black and silver, a color scheme aggressive in nature, with many psychological benefits for a sports team. Off the field, this fashion style received a tremendous boost from the music industry. When hip-hop artists and gansta-rappers appeared in music videos wearing the black and silver of the Oakland Raiders and Georgetown Hoyas, those teams experienced a huge surge in merchandise sales. Other teams—like the Los Angeles Kings and Chicago White Sox— were quick to follow suit.

"The reason to change is not to ring the cash register," says Occi, who points out that revenues generated from retail sales of licensed merchandise is shared equally among all baseball clubs. "A reason to change is a move from one city to another, a new ownership group, or a new stadium. In the case of the White Sox, they wanted to romance their past."

The interlocking Sox lettering from the "Go-Go Sox" of the 1950s was reinstated but changed from red, white, and blue to black, white, and silver. Spurred by the opening of the new Comiskey Park in 1991, sales of White Sox merchandise skyrocketed from No. 23 to No. 1 in the first season after the redesign.

BASEBALL'S DESIGNING WOMAN

Employment prospects are good for individuals who aspire to catch the career wave and ride to the top in this emerging and rapidly growing area of sports marketing. The four major professional sports leagues are just now beginning to take advantage (and control) of this retailing phenomenon. This bodes well for established design firms and recent graduates of art school now entering the job market.

Major league baseball's design department—which has counterparts in the NFL, NBA, and NHL—started in 1990 under Occi's direction. Since she arrived at her post, sales of licensed baseball merchandise for both the major and minor leagues have increased from $1.5 billion in 1990 to an estimated $2.7 billion in 1994. According to Karen Raugust, the editor of *The Licensing Letter*, major league baseball has finally realized that "people buy merchandise not for team loyalty but because they like the logo."

The consumers of these products may know nothing about the team at all. Even minor league merchandise has become a marketing juggernaut with as much gitty-up as a Roger Clemens fastball. Visit any local sporting goods store, and you'll no doubt find caps worn by any number of the 152 minor league teams now licensed by major league baseball. Another potential mother lode was created from a league that no longer exists. MLB Enterprises has introduced a full line of goods from the old Negro Leagues, with proceeds to benefit former players.

With all this work to be done, it's surprising to learn that Occi has a staff of just two designers. So obviously, job opportunities are not found within the league office. Occi relies on outside design firms to help execute her concepts—"We freelance 90 percent of the work to the outside," she says—and here is where the available positions are located: at independent design firms.

Acting on behalf of baseball in the role of creative director, Occi develops objective criteria for each project. She listens to and analyzes each team's needs and develops an understanding of the customers and markets to be served. Occi then selects a design firm that she feels will best fit the genre of what is being asked for.

"The designer never comes in contact with the ownership group," says Occi, 41. "That way, we can be the hard guy who can press for standards that the club may not know how to ask for or demand."

Occi functions as a liaison between the team and the outside design firm to ensure that both parties agree at all points in the design process. This ensures that the design firm will meet the league's objectives correctly and creatively. When the time comes for Occi to appear before the team's executive committee to make the league's final presentation, it will usually produce winning results.

Occi recently guided the redesign of the Chicago Cubs' uniform. This required subtle diplomacy. The franchise, understandably, didn't want to get away from their traditional bulls-eye logo. But Occi convinced the team to reconfigure the face of the cubbie bear, transforming the mangy old mammal into a lovable creature. Now, the logo, which is a patch stitched onto the left sleeve, "exudes the proper feeling," she says. "They had a face of a bear that looked more like a raccoon. We went with a utilization of shapes—a Japanese influence type of paper cut—to get the right look."

HUE'S ON FIRST?

The majority of design firms work with a diverse clientele, from professional sports leagues to major corporations, producing brand-building and corporate communications. In order to get that initial interview at a design firm, applicants will be expected to have earned a college degree in fine arts. This course of study provides valuable knowledge in graphic arts. Graphic arts is the key to creating brand identity; brand identity is what builds public awareness and consumer loyalty.

An employee of a design firm must approach a sports brand with the same philosophy as it would toothpaste or cereal. The most recognized logos, and thereby the most competitive, are inherently flexible and, instantly distinctive in all forms of brand applications. It's vital to the success of any logo—and particularly true for a sports insignia—that the symbol be able to move easily from embroidery on a jersey front to animation on the Jumbotron scoreboard.

"We want to create logos that are easy to read on the court and in all the brand extensions, giving the licensee more fodder to chew on," says Thomas Duane, a partner at SME Design Inc., a sports identity and marketing communications company.

Established designers with a passion for sports may wish to focus their efforts and energies on clients within the sports world. These individuals will have best served their interests by having also obtained an internship at a team, a league, or in the sports department of a newspaper, or radio and television station.

A thorough understanding of sports and a knowledge of a particular team's place in history will assist a designer when formulating a presentation. In her job at major league baseball, Occi walks a fine line trying to maintain the sport's traditional values while at the same time attempting to capture the lucrative youth market.

Since nostalgia is hot, Occi is helping many teams update their look while embracing the past. She convinced the Detroit Tigers to return to their Old English "D" logo and added a contemporary-looking jungle tiger that leaps through it with extended claws and snarling fangs. "One would never change a logo or a look to chase a fashion," says Occi, "because in six months that look or color could be out."

Indeed, Occi constantly worries about whether her designs will create an enduring legacy. Will these logos—like a sporting coat of arms—last a lifetime? The New York Yankees' pin-striped uniform and interlocking "NY" on the jersey front haven't changed since 1936. Will Occi's work for the Florida Marlins become the next sacred icon?

"I can track and trace and educate myself as to what trends will be hot in the coming year," says Occi. "But in baseball—particularly because of the traditional nature of the sport—it's important to create designs that are right for the times, and all times.

"The Marlins hit on a fashion wave," she adds. "But years later, after the popularity of teal has died, the team will still retain its graphic identity because the colors of Miami are turquoise and orange, and the fish itself goes through a coloration of that teal shade along with silver."

SORRY TO BRING THIS UP

Like peanuts and Cracker Jack™, fashion has long been an integral part of the game of baseball. The bold use of color began in 1876, when Alfred Spalding, the manager of the Chicago White Stockings, assigned different colored caps to each fielder—creating a tableau one writer likened to "a Dutch bed of tulips."

Since baseball's first professional league of 1871, teams have unveiled at least 3,000 different uniform styles, including some 50 incarnations for the Chicago White Sox alone. The franchise's creation of 1976 has to be the worst uniform in baseball history. The hot weather ensemble consisted of navy-blue Bermuda-length shorts, complemented with white nylon pullovers. After only three games, the players refused to wear them again.

At least the Pale Hose had the good sense to speak up. Bad taste permeated the Houston Astros uniforms from 1975 to 1986. Designed to conjure up futuristic images of the city's association with NASA and the first domed stadium, the red, yellow, and orange rainbows crossing the jersey front made players look, in *Sports Illustrated*'s words, like "a human popsicle." Another weird color combination was the brown, orange, and yellow San Diego Padres uniforms that first baseman Steve Garvey said made him "feel like a taco."

TIPSHEET

- ☺ Learn as much as possible about the field. Read *The Licensing Letter*, a trade publication based in New York.

- ☺ Attend seminars and workshops to develop a network of contacts within the field.

- ☺ Try to locate a college internship or summer apprenticeship with a design firm. Take any available job and learn about the business by asking questions and volunteering to help in any way you can.

SPOTLIGHT

SME Design Inc.

SME Design Inc. is a global leader in brand identity for the sports industry. Since its inception in 1988, the company has earned distinction as the only firm to have designed expansion team identities for all four major professional sports leagues, as well as assisting over thirty universities with their athletic identities.

Sean Michael Edwards Design (the middle names of the three original partners) developed the logo and uniform for the National Hockey League expansion Florida Panthers. In April 1993, after team owner Wayne Huizenga and president Bill Torrey settled on the name Panthers, it was decided that a logo and color scheme should be distinctive from the other South Florida teams: the aqua-blue commonly associated with Miami's Dolphins, Marlins, Heat, and the University of Miami Hurricanes.

Torrey gathered some pictures of panthers—Florida's state animal and an endangered species—that portrayed the presence he wanted the team to have ("aggressive, smart, challenging, sleek") to NHL Enterprises, the league's marketing and merchandising arm, for guidance.

Fred Scalera, general manager for retaling and licensing, pointed the Panthers toward SME Design. The firm was started by Tom Duane and Ed O'Hara, who had met at a computer convention. Their first sports job was designing a 100th anniversary patch for the St. Louis Cardinals.

The company, less than a decade old, now has dozens of clients in all four major professional sports leagues; they have redesigned uniforms and event and anniversary logos for the Washington Capitals, Atlanta Hawks, Jacksonville Jaguars, St. John's Red Storm, the NBA Finals, and the Tampa Bay Devil Rays, just to name a few. The company earned an estimated $2 million in sales in 1992 and has been growing ever since.

After meeting with Panthers executives, Duane and O'Hara researched hundreds of images of big cats in coffee-table and history books and sketched slinking panthers, ones with ripping claws, snarling panthers and panthers with flames behind them to present them on storyboards to Panthers executives.

The result was a striking logo of a pouncing panther, claws extended, for the jersey; a secondary logo for the Panthers shoulder patch (a hockey stick crossed with a palm tree against a sunset); and an inaugural logo, dominated by the team name.

After agreeing on logos, "We talked with Bill, Wayne, Mrs. Huizenga, GM Bobby Clarke, about colors," said Duane, a Pratt graduate who was director of special projects at Polo/Ralph Lauren, where he introduced computer technology into the design process, before helping found SME. "We looked at the top 10 selling color combinations in each of the pro leagues. There were all kinds of suggestions about black and teal and purple and lime green, which Bill hated. And we felt that trend is dying."

The final mix was a "rich navy blue, lipstick red, and gold combination with the in-your-face panther dominating the white [home] and red [away] jerseys," said O'Hara, who guides the SME Design team. The jersey's unusual angled stripes "are designed to be parallel to the ice when a player is holding his stick, to give the appearance of speed," says O'Hara.

Aesthetics aside, the bottom line is sales, and Panthers merchandise got out of the starting gate from the drop of the puck. The NHL expansion team broke the league record by selling $750,000 worth of product on opening night. In addition, in 1995, the Panthers jersey was the number one seller, beating out the Disney-owned Mighty Ducks of Anaheim.

SUCCESS STORY

Anne Occi,
vice president/design services, MLB Enterprises

Hired in 1990 by major league baseball for the newly created position of creative director, Anne Occi spends her time advising ball clubs that want a makeover for their uniforms and logos. She came to baseball from Adidas, the sports equipment and apparel company, where she worked as the director of marketing and communications. Prior to joining Adidas, she spent seven years in advertising as an assistant art director. Occi earned a bachelor of fine arts in illustration and design with a minor in advertising from Moore College of Art in Philadelphia.

ADDRESS BOOK

The Licensing Letter
160 Mercer Street
New York, NY 10012
212/941-0099

*Major League Baseball
Properties*
350 Park Avenue
New York, NY 10022
212/339-7800

*National Basketball
Association Properties*
645 Fifth Avenue
New York, NY 1022
212/407-8000

*National Football League
Properties*
410 Park Avenue
New York, NY 10022
212/758-1500

*National Hockey League
Properties*
1251 Avenue of the Americas
New York, NY 10020
212/789-2000

SME Design Inc.
28 West 25th Street
New York, NY 10010
212/924-5700

DIRECTOR OF PUBLICATIONS

The director of publications is in charge of producing all event programs for the sports league. These include All-Star Game programs, divisional playoff programs, league championship programs, as well as commemorative books and special anniversary issues as needed.

The individual in this position acts as an editor-in-chief. The main function performed by the director of publications is to create an editorial vision for the program and then implement its execution. To accomplish this goal, the director's primary responsibility is the development of story ideas.

Once the story ideas have been formulated, the director of publications will recruit writers to carry out the assignment. To be successful, the director will possess an uncanny ability to select a writer with unique skills apropos to the assignment. To this end, the director is expected to possess a large network of writers from whom to tap into.

The majority of writers are hired as independent contractors on a freelance basis. Therefore, the publications director will be required to negotiate a deal with each writer and execute a letter of agreement. In most cases, the director's spending is limited by an editorial budget set forth by the sports league. Proper advance planning by the director is vital to controlling editorial expenses.

When the writer accepts the assignment, the director will then request that the writer provide an outline. The main purpose served by the outline is to help the art director decide how best to illustrate the story. Articles may be complemented with original artwork or photography. Whatever the decision, an artist must be hired to create the illustration or a photographer dispatched to the scene. In some cases stock photos may be used. This too requires adequate lead time in order to research the photos.

ALL THE NEWS THAT FITS, WE PRINT

A writer may submit the finished story in raw manuscript form, on a computer disk, or via electronic mail. (This should be decided at the initial contact when discussing the assignment.) The publications director now begins the editing process. Since articles are usually written longer than needed, the editing process entails cutting the story to fit the alloted space.

"Editing is a matter of paring off what you don't want," says Gary Perkinson, the editor of Major League Baseball Enterprises. "Start with the least important sentences and keep whittling away in cycles. It's like giving a haircut; trim a little here, trim a little there."

Fitting text within an alloted space is a function the director of publications performs in conjunction with the art director. But the allocated space is predetermined by the advertising sales staff. Early in the process the art director has devised a mock-up, or map, of the book. This is done simply by drawing boxes to represent each page spread. It works like a storyboard for the publication. In certain boxes you drop in the advertisements—some ads are presold with special requests that must be met, like farther forward in the book or next to a particular piece of editorial—and other boxes are delegated as copy. The storyboard is ever-changing as advertisements come in or drop out.

The edited text is then transferred to Quark Express, a popular desktop computer publishing program. The art director flows the text into the allotted space. At this point stories may still need tweaking, as facts change or featured players get injured. The director of publications will now write headlines, decks, also known as subheads (sentences under the headlines), captions, pull quotes, also known as blow-outs (a sentence from the text printed in enlarged type), and any other extemporaneous edit to appear on the page. The art director will decide on type styles, fonts, photo placement, and color coordination.

The completed layout is then shipped to a prepress plant, where finished page proofs are created. The page proofs display the stories in basically the same form as you'll see in the magazine. The director of publications will then give each story another read. No heavy changes should be made this late in the game, but typographical errors and sentence widows (an incomplete line of type) invariably need to be corrected before the magazine goes to the printing plant.

WORK ON OUR TEAM

Publication jobs within a league office are seldom available. The people currently in these positions have worked hard to get there and, once they've arrived, they rarely leave. To make matters worse, there are only a few positions to begin with as staffs are small. The publications staff of Major League Baseball Enterprises, for instance, is comprised of six people: vice president of publishing, manager of publishing, editor, art director, production coordinator, and assistant editor.

The vice president and manager of publishing spend the majority of their time in an administrative capacity, dealing with budgets, circulation, distribution, contracts, and other logistics and legalities. The production coordinator acts as a liaison between the editorial staff and the advertising sales staff, as well as between the preproduction house and printing plant. He or she will also act as a traffic manager, logging incoming and out-going materials.

Earnings vary depending on the individual's experience, aptitude, and longevity in the job. Salaries range from $25,000 a year for entry-level personnel to $150,000 in upper management. Individuals at the associate levels most frequently increase their wages by taking on added responsib-lities within the structure of the department or by contributing to the publication in other ways, such as writing articles or taking photographs.

The ability to write well is necessary to pursue a position in this field. Candidates who asprire to become a director of publications should have a strong journalism background. While a degree specific to journalism is not always a requirement, a proven track record as a managing editor is vital. For college-bound individuals who wish to major in communica-tions, English literature, or any of the liberal arts, it's strongly recom-mended that they get involved with the school newspaper and obtain an internship at a local paper or magazine.

Opportunities for advancement are poor within a sports league's publica-tions department. As previously stated, individuals in these positions rarely leave, and, frankly, there's not many avenues available for growth. An assis-tant editor may go on to work for a team in media relations; a production coordinator may jump to a magazine as director of editorial operations; an art director may become creative director at an advertising agency.

By and large, these people love the sport they work for and wouldn't dream of going elsewhere. Nor would they enjoy the pressure. Moving from director of publications at a sports league to editor-in-chief of a weekly consumer magazine is analogous to a director of feature films switching gears and becoming a director of a weekly television show. The change of pace notwithstanding, individuals in the league office are not accustomed to creating controversy, the fuel that flames the media fire.

Creating an event program is truly a team effort. The director of pub-lications and the art director need to communicate their vision to one another and trust each other to successfully execute the plan. The editor-in-chief and assistant editor must perform tasks in tandem, coordinating their efforts to work in the most efficient manner possible. And the pro-duction coordinator should be kept appraised of all developments to maintain an orderly flow of projects and assure an uninterrupted workload for members of the department.

"You have to allow talented people the freedom to do their jobs," says Perkinson. "That's why they were hired in the first place."

TIPSHEET

- Ⓤ Experience in journalism is vital. Begin working for a school newspaper as soon as possible. Get an internship at any publication and volunteer for a vast array of duties.

- Ⓤ Put your best writing samples together in a portfolio. Prospective employers will want to read these clips to gain a sense of your ability.

- Ⓤ Develop a network of contacts among other writers. Jobs are often bandied about within the same circle of friends. When one person cannot accept a job, he or she will often recommend that a friend be hired instead.

- Ⓤ Competent writers become good editors. After you've established your writing career, look to move into editing. Gain experience in copy editing and proofreading, and learn the proper language and markings to carry out the task.

- Ⓤ Obtain an editorship anywhere you can, even if it's not a sports publication. Successful editors can translate their skills to any subject.

REAL-LIFE ADVICE

Gary Perkinson,
editor, Major League Baseball Enterprises

For the past year Gary Perkinson has been the man in charge of producing all event programs for major league baseball. Prior to his current position, he served for three years as managing editor of *Senior Golfer* magazine. Before that he worked for *Golf Illustrated*, coming aboard in 1989 as associate editor and rising to the position of editor-in-chief for the magazine's regional publication, *Fairways and Greens*.

personality sketch

Journalistic sensibility; sports lover; supervisory; skilled editor; ability to handle simul-taneous projects; communicative; detail-oriented.

Perkinson graduated from Fordham University in 1983 with a bachelor of arts in English and earned his master's two years later. After working as a legal proofreader and a crossword puzzle editor, he landed at *The*

Discount Merchandiser, a retail trade magazine, as an associate editor and writer.

"My first magazine job was at a trade publication called *The Discount Merchandiser*. I was covering Wal-Mart and KMart. As boring as the subject matter was—and it was; I mean, who wants to write about super-markets?—it was a great opportunity. It was my first chance to put together a portfolio. And being on staff I was able to get lots of clips quickly.

"To anybody getting out of college who wants to write, I highly recommend joining a trade magazine. Everybody wants to write for a consumer magazine, and that's fine, that's what you probably should aim for. But there are so many trade magazines around; poeple don't know this, but they pay pretty well. It's a great training ground; you learn how to interview. A writer needs to have interviewing skills to get the right information. I'm basically a shy person and I don't like being nosey and bothering people, but I needed to learn proper interviewing skills and I did eventually.

"All along I wanted to work in sports, but I'd never done anything about it. I'd be just as happy working on a music magazine, but I love sports. I sent out tons of cold letters to editors of consumer sports magazines. I kept doing it. It's a tedious process, but if you get a system going you can do it easier. I kept getting form letters back: No thanks, we'll keep your resume on file.

"Finally I got one letter back from the editor of *Golf Illustrated*. He didn't have any positions, but he was nice enough to sit down and talk to me. I gave him some clips. As it turns out, eight months later he did have an opening and he called me back in. I got the job of associate editor. That was my dream come true.

"As far as getting a job, it sounds cliche, but if you want something bad enough you can get it. You have to be persistent with people and have no shame. Don't make a jerk out of yourself; be polite and friendly and not too overbearing, but you've got to keep writing letters. Nobody out there knows you. If you send them a letter, even if they reject you, you're one step closer. Send clever, semihumorous, friendly letters to editors.

"Be honest with them. Tell them you have no experience, but you'd love to work there. Ask if they can help you. Most people will respond to that. Don't bother them, but be persistent. And be persistent with yourself. You will get rejected left and right. It's like actors who audition for parts and get turned down. But if you do it long enough, the law of averages say you're going to be successful at some point. It's a matter of being persistent and forgetting all the insults.

SUCCESS STORY

Gregg Mazzola,
director of publications, New York Yankees

During his decade-long tenure with the New York Yankees, Gregg Mazzola has shaped the editorial policy of the team's official publications, which include a monthly magazine, game-day scorecard, as well as the annual yearbook and media guide.

After graduating from the University of Dayton with a degree in journalism in 1983, Mazzola remained at school as an academic recruiter for the university. He then held various sales positions before enrolling at Northeastern to pursue a master's in journalism. As part of his work-study program, Mazzola was a newspaper writer in the sports department of *The Patriot-Ledger* in Boston.

In 1988, nearing the end of the master's program, Mazzola received an employment tip from a fellow Dayton alumnus that the Yankees were conducting interviews to fill the position of assistant director of publications. He got the job and held the position for eight years. In November 1995, Mazzola was promoted to his current post as director of publications, where he also functions as the publisher of *Yankees Magazine*.

Careers in the Sports Media

6

We watch all the games on live broadcast and the taped highlight shows that dissect the action. The next day we call the all-sports radio shows to vivisect the participants. Come evening we read all about it in newspapers and magazines. The sports media is the self-perpetuating game within the game.

Sports is the only industry capable of supporting its own national cable network. In addition to ESPN, there are numerous regional cable networks devoted to providing sports programming. The current technology brings the sports world into the living rooms of just about every wired sports enthusiast in the nation, and offers viewers a vast array of programming options. Growth is particularly strong for the regional sports networks. In the five years from 1987 to 1991, the number of regional subscribers grew at an unprecedented rate of 216 percent, from 11.6 million to 36.6 million viewers.

The broadcast industry is a multi-dimensional field. The on-air talent we all see and hear comprise but a small fraction of the personnel necessary to broadcast sporting events. Television staffs are comprised of people with diverse backgrounds and a myriad of career interests. Aside from the on-air talent, the production staff, directors, promotions directors, and commercial advertising sales representatives all play an important role in the station's success. Job opportunities in television production are extremely competitive, so it's imperative for applicants to obtain grass roots experience at small local stations.

As the television industry has focused the definition of its broadcasting, so too has the radio and print media expanded its sports coverage to offer listeners and readers a wider array of options. As television sports programming reaches a more targeted audience, the radio and print media is striving to service this new fan base with specialized products devoted to regional market share. Most every major city now has a round-the-clock all-sports radio station. This growing trend has created the need to employ a full staff of broadcast professionals necessary to produce a radio show, such as talk show host, production staff, broadcast engineers, and sports anchors.

Newspapers and magazines are in the midst of a transitional phase as well. Specialty publications translate into new and exciting career opportunities that are available for qualified individuals. As in television and radio, most publishing professionals must begin on a local level, obtaining experience in all aspects of the print media environment.

SPORTS ANNOUNCER

The job of the sports announcer is to report the game live on the air to television and radio audiences. The sports announcer is a journalist of the unrehearsed spoken word. Anyone who has heard New York Giants broadcaster Russ Hodges' spontaneous description of Bobby Thomson's home run in the 1951 National League playoff ("The Giants win the pennant! The Giants win the pennant! The Giants win the pennant!") knows how brilliant and dramatic such treatment can be, in the right hands (or mouth).

There are two types of sports announcers: the play-by-play announcer and the color commentator. As the term indicates, the play-by-play announcer reports the game action as it happens. Baseball announcers, for instance, document the result of each pitch, and keep the listeners informed as to the count, the number of outs, and the score. The color commentator provides additional insights on what has already occured. On television, the color commentator also narrates the action as it is being replayed in slow motion.

The announcers' responsiblities have changed with the times. During radio days, the announcer was an objective reporter. Red Barber, who was the folksy voice of the Cincinnati Reds, Brooklyn Dodgers, and New York

Yankees from 1934 to 1966, set the standard for baseball radio broadcasters.

He spent hours before the game talking to players and coaches and absorbing baseball strategy to better convey the subtleties of the game to his listeners. "I described the game in the best way I knew how without partiality," he once said. "I think the listeners appreciated that."

In 1966, while doing television play-by-play for the CBS-owned Yankees, Barber was fired for telling his audience that only 413 people were present at a late-season game. While the firing seems preposterous by today's standards, keep in mind that it pre-dated the Howard Cosell style of controversial TV announcers who "tell it like it is."

TESTING: ONE, TWO, THREE

While there is no formal educational requirement for becoming a sports announcer, many stations currently prefer their announcers to have college degrees. Others only require that the individuals have experience and an established audience.

Those attending college should enroll in courses in radio and television broadcasting, journalism, and communications. Colleges also afford valuable opportunities such as internships and jobs on the school's radio and TV stations. There are also trade schools located around the country offering programs in broadcasting.

Bob Costas of NBC logs more air time on more sports than perhaps any other announcer currently working. Viewers have enjoyed his baseball work on NBC's *Game of the Week*, his football work on *NFL Live*, his basketball work on *NBA Showtime*, his radio work on *Costas Coast to Coast*, and his TV talk-show work on *Later with Bob Costas*.

Costas played baseball at Commack (N.Y.) High School South and while at home practiced announcing games by turning down the television volume and doing the play-by-play. Later he attended Syracuse University, majoring in broadcast journalism and covering Orangemen football and basketball games.

In 1974, Costas left Syracuse to take a job doing play-by-play for the St. Louis Spirits of the now defunct American Basketball Association. (He had fiddled with the bass on his audition tape to make himself sound older).

In 1980 he was hired by NBC to do baseball play-by-play on the back-up *Game of the Week*, even though, much to NBC's surprise, he had done a grand total of four baseball games in his life, two of which were minor league games. But Costas was up to the task. In 1984 he was made host of the NFL pre- and post-game shows, even though he had little studio experience.

FROM SHEEPSKIN TO PIGSKIN

Most radio and TV stations prefer that announcers have broadcasting experience. This may be acquired by working at college stations, or at small markets that broadcast minor league games.

Sports announcers must have a clear speaking voice. Successful ones possess good communications skills and excellent descriptive powers. The ability to analyze and interpret events as they occur is necessary, as is a tireless work ethic. Also important is an understanding and love of sports, and the flexibility to comment on several different sports during one broadcast.

Costas sat in the anchor chair during the 1992 Summer Olympic Games in Barcelona, Spain. NBC had 161 hours of Olympic coverage, about 80 of which were anchored by Costas. His typical Barcelona schedule consisted of daily 12-hour shifts, from noon to midnight with just a one-hour break.

As daunting as that sounds, it's nothing unusual for Costas. On Sunday, May 17, 1992 he anchored an NBA playoff doubleheader from 1 p.m. to 7 p.m.—traveling back and forth between Rockefeller Center and Secaucus, N.J., for the NBA draft lottery—and did his live radio show from 9 to 11 p.m.

Only someone who is genuinely excited about sports could keep up this pace. Costas, who carries around a Mickey Mantle baseball card in his wallet, knows as much about Tamas Darnyi (the Hungarian swimmer) as he does about Frank Thomas (the White Sox first baseman), and that's saying something.

He once left a $3.31 tip at Stan Musial's restaurant in homage to Stan The Man's .331 lifetime batting average. And in May 1986, in the ultimate gesture of sports addiction, a newborn baby was dubbed Keith Michael Kirby Costas. The second middle name fulfilled a promise Costas had made to name his child after Kirby Puckett if the Minnesota Twins outfielder had a .350 batting average by the time of the birth.

TALKING FOR DOLLARS

Earnings for sports announcers vary greatly and are dependent on a number of factors. These factors include the size, popularity, prestige, and location of the station as well as the experience, reputation, and popularity of the announcer. The announcer's status will also play a role in earnings. An announcer who does television play-by-play will earn more than an anouncer who does radio color commentary. Annual earnings range from $20,000 to $500,000 or more. Those with limited experience working in smaller markets will have earnings on the lower end of the scale. To augment earnings, many sports announcers do voice-overs for commercials.

THE OLD BOYS NETWORK

Sadly, female sportscasters have not come a long way, baby. Women hold less than 20 percent of the on-camera sports jobs at ABC, CBS, NBC, and ESPN, and even this figure is misleading since most female announcers turn up only once every Olympiad to comment on events in which they competed.

Nationwide, there are fewer than 50 female sportscasters at the 630 network-affiliates. Mary Carillo (CBS, ESPN) is the only women who regularly comments on a male sport (she covers both men's and women's tennis) at the championship level.

Donna de Varona (ABC) was the first woman to appear consistently on a network's sports telecasts, having debuted as a swimming expert in 1965. Other high-profile women in sports broadcasting include Robin Roberts (ESPN), Hannah Storm (NBC), and Lesley Visser (ABC), a veteran sportswriter of 14 years with *The Boston Globe*.

A VOICE FOR ALL SEASONS

Sports announcers advance their careers by obtaining experience, developing a unique and personal reporting style, and building a loyal following. Those who accomplish this can advance to positions at larger and more prestigious stations. The most celebrated announcers remain with one team for almost their entire career.

Los Angeles Dodger broadcaster Vin Scully has been the voice of the Dodgers since 1950, when the team was still in Brooklyn. Over the last 46 years, he has described many of baseball's most thrilling moments, including Don Larsen's perfect game in the 1956 World Series and Kirk Gibson's memorable game-winning homer in the 1988 Fall Classic.

Scully's broadcasting career began while attending Fordham University, where he covered the Rams' football and basketball games for WFUV, the student radio station. Scully also wore the baseball uniform of the Maroon and White, lettering two seasons as a good field, no-hit rightfielder. He graduated in 1949 with a degree in speech after a two-year interruption in the U.S. Navy.

A year after receiving his diploma, Red Barber invited Scully to join him in the Dodgers' announcing booth (the catbird's seat). Five years later, Scully became the Number 1 man when Walter O'Malley, the miserly owner, fired Barber for requesting a raise. When the team moved to Los Angeles in 1957, Scully also went west, and his popularity rose.

Major league baseball had just arrived in Southern California and the transistor radio was new on the market. Since the region was not familar with all the players, fans carried radios with them to listen to Scully's description of the game they were watching. During a game in 1960, Scully convinced his stadium audience to serenade umpire Frank Secory with a rendition of "Happy Birthday."

A HISTORY LESSON

On August 5, 1921, sports announcing made its debut on radio. The game at Forbes Field in Pittsburgh had no impact in the standings of the National League. The first-place Pirates beat the last-place Philadelphia Phillies, 8-5. But at that game, Harold Arlin made history.

Sitting at field level behind home plate, Arlin, a 26-year-old Westinghouse engineer, described the action, pitch by pitch, into a converted telephone. His play-by-play descriptions were carried over a radio signal transmitted by station KDKA in Pittsburgh, becoming the first-ever broadcast of a baseball game.

"Sometimes the transmitter worked and sometimes it didn't. Sometimes the crowd noise would drown us out and sometimes it wouldn't," said Arlin about that first game. "We didn't know what the reaction would be, whether we'd be talking into a total vacuum or whether somebody would actually hear us."

People were listening, and they liked what they heard. In an era when a ball game was as distant for most fans as tomorrow's newspaper, Arlin's play-by-play demonstrated to the public that baseball could be brought right into the American living room with immediacy and intimacy. Baseball's message was ideal for the medium of radio. The game's popularity increased and, concurrently, sales of radios boomed.

TIPSHEET

- Practice announcing games by turning down the television volume and doing the play-by-play.
- Tape record yourself and critique the effort.

- ⓤ Listen to and learn from established announcers, but create your own on-air identity.

- ⓤ Gain necessary experience, even at the lowest level.

- ⓤ Prepare a demo tape and send it to prospective employers.

REAL-LIFE ADVICE

Warner Fusselle,
play-by-play announcer

As the voice of Major League Baseball Productions since 1977, Warner Fusselle is recognized wherever he speaks. His narration can be heard on "This Week In Baseball" and numerous ESPN programs produced by Phoenix Communications, Inc. in South Hackensack, New Jersey.

Fusselle has vast experience doing play-by-play, both on radio and on television, and the teams he's covered, both minor and major league, is a diverse lot. Since 1969, he's done play-by-play for the Spartanburg (S.C.) Phillies, the ABA's Virginia Squires, the Richmond (Va.) Braves, and the Baltimore Orioles. He was most recently heard on WABC Radio as the voice of the Seton Hall (N.J.) Pirates college basketball team.

A graduate of Wake Forest (N.C.) University with a bachelor of arts in history, Fusselle then attended the Career Academy School of Broadcasting in Hollywood, California, where he graduated in 1969 as class valedictorian.

"You can practice as a child and work hard to become a good announcer. But that doesn't mean you'll ever get any job, anywhere, doing anything, for any amount of money. It has nothing to do with ability, nothing to do with talent; that's the problem. It's all about timing and luck.

"I was the valedictorian at broadcast school in Hollywood, California. I got a library book that listed addresses of every radio station in the

> **personality sketch**
>
> *Good communications skills; understanding of sports; ability to analyze and interpret events; experience broadcasting for radio or television; clear speaking voice.*

country. I had just two requirements. I wanted to work at a small 1,000-watt radio station in any one of 12 south-eastern states. I found 100 stations that fit the bill.

"In my letters to those 100 stations I enclosed a stamped, self-addressed, pre-printed postcard. On the back were three categories with a box that could be checked off. One category was marked, 'Send tape and resume.' Another category said, 'No current openings, send resume.' The last category said, 'Not interested.'

"Well, this was the first rude awakening of my early adulthood. I thought 100 postcards would come back. I'd made it so easy. But only 30 came back. I couldn't believe that 70 percent of the people didn't even care enough to have the courtesy to check the box labeled 'Not interested' and place it in a mailbox. That was a real wake-up call.

"Now of the 30 I got back, 8 had checked the box 'Send tape and resume,' which I did. Of those eight stations, one called me back and asked if I'd be interested in a news position. Well, I hate news, can't stand it, but I took the job anyway. I went to WSTP in Salisbury, North Carolina. The whole process taught me a very valuable lesson. When you're trying to land that initial job, it only takes one. You can be turned down 99 times out of 100. All you need is one job, and you're on your way.

"From there I got a job in Spartanburg, South Carolina where I did 130 games a year for the Spartanburg Phillies Class A baseball team. I did another 20 to 25 high school football and small college football games a year, and I did girl's high school basketball.

"If you want to be a play-by-play announcer, you need to go somewhere, anywhere, to get as much experience as possible doing play-by-play. You should be willing to go anywhere to let people see you. Walk into a radio station unannounced and say, 'Hi, I'm Warner Fusselle. I'd like to apply for a job. Do you have any employment forms? Have you heard of any openings in the area?' Go there to make a good impression. Nobody's going to say 'Oh yes, somebody quit this morning, you can start tomorrow.' But in a few months a position may very well open up, or they might let you know of a station nearby that does have an opening.

"The most important thing is to go somewhere and do as much play-by-play as you can. Don't worry about where the job is, or how much money the job pays. For years the only money I spent was for gasoline and food. You're young, how much money do you need anyway? Go have a great experience and have some fun. Just get as much experience as possible. Then you'll be able to hone your craft and, if you apply yourself, you'll be good."

SPOTLIGHT

Bill Stern,
sports announcer, NBC Radio

A popular sports announcer from the early days of radio was Bill Stern of NBC. Stern died in 1971, some two decades after he dominated the nation's airwaves, becoming as famous in his day as Howard Cosell would later become in his.

The stage manager of Radio City Music Hall as a young man, Stern switched to sports broadcasting and became an NBC Radio celebrity between 1939 and 1952. He announced the first live TV sports event (a baseball game between Columbia and Princeton in 1939), he called hundreds of major football games and fights on radio, and his voice was heard on countless movie newsreels.

For all his success, the proud, melodramatic Stern sometimes was the butt of jokes. Misidentifying the ball carrier once during an Army football game, he invented an open-field lateral from one player to another so he wouldn't have to admit his mistake. Years later, the famous race track announcer Clem McCarthy cautioned Stern about calling thoroughbred races. "Remember, Bill," he said, "you can't lateral a horse."

Stern's career declined as television gained in popularity, mainly because he never learned that in TV the pictures had to do most of the talking.

SUCCESS STORY THEN ...

Howard Cosell,
sports announcer, ABC

Howard Cosell gave up a promising law career in the 1950s to go into broadcasting. He became the most unforgettable television sports announcer ever.

Cosell was a trailblazer in that he introduced sports journalism to television. Upon arriving on the national scene in the late 1960s, Cosell championed Muhammad Ali's fight against the draft, and was among the first to recognize Ali by his Muslim name. In the 1970s he brought entertainment to prime-time on ABC's Monday Night Football.

By the time his career ended in the mid-1980s, Cosell had become one of the most influential figures in sports.

...AND NOW

Joe Buck,
play-by-play announcer, The Fox Network

His father, Jack Buck, 72, has called the radio or television play-by-play of 14 World Series. Joe Buck, 27, got his first crack at a Fall Classic in 1996 and made a positive impression.

In three years at Fox, he has called National Football League regular season games and, in 1996, when Fox bought the rights to baseball, he added the national pastime to his network commitment. Now, as Fox's Number one baseball announcer, he has displayed a style that was nurtured by being raised in the sport and by working with his father on St. Louis Cardinals broadcasts since 1991.

Upon graduating from Indiana University, the young Buck announced games for the Louisville Redbirds, the Cardinals' Triple A farm team. "I sent my tape to Anheuser-Busch," he said of the former owner of the Cardinals, "and they saw the novelty of my being Jack Buck's kid."

In his job with the Cardinals, Buck shares three innings on the radio with his father and does the other six innings on television. "Dad is not afraid to put me on the spot," he says.

ADDRESS BOOK

American Sportscasters Association
5 Beekman Street
New York, NY 10038
212/227-8080

National Association of Broadcasters
1771 "N" Street N.W.
Washington, D.C. 20036
202/429-5300

National Sportscasters and Sportswriters Association
Box 559
Salisbury, NC 28144
703/633-4275

Phoenix Communications, Inc.
3 Empire Boulevard
South Hackensack, NJ 07606
201/807-0888

SPORTS NEWS BROADCASTER

A sports news broadcaster is responsible for reporting the sports news on television or radio. The individual in this position usually performs live on the air. While the television sportscaster will appear during the sports segment of an evening newscast, the radio counterpart will update the sports news at regularly scheduled intervals during the four-hour shift. Common to individuals working in both mediums is a love of sports.

Whereas news reporters may seek to break stories, by and large, the sports news broadcaster is limited to covering the events of the day. This may be accomplished by obtaining information from a variety of sources, the most popular and reliable being the Associated Press wire service and SportsTicker. These organizations employ staff and free-lance personnel to attend sporting events and report up-to-the-minute results.

The sports news broadcaster—also called sports anchor, sports reporter, or sportscaster—will be expected to act as gatekeeper of the news, monitoring events and filtering out what isn't important to the audience. "My job is to tell you what I think you need to know," says John Minko, radio sports anchor for WFAN in New York. "And because I have a very limited time span, I'd better do it pretty quick."

Sports news broadcasting goes deeper than a mere recitation of scores. The individual in this position must prepare for the broadcast well in advance of going on the air. He or she should be an avid fan who is knowledgable about all sports. Respect and credibility are a broadcaster's most valuable assets; the listening audience can detect immediately when an imposter is in their midst.

Two jokes related to this topic come to mind. During George Carlin's humorous hippy-dippy newscast, the sports reporter gives the partial scores as 5, 2, and 9. And the late comedian Myron Cohen told a story of his wife informing him that the score is 86-78. When Myron asks who is winning, she replies, 86.

HAPPY DAYS

Prospects for employment are better than ever for individuals who aspire to become sports news broadcasters. The United States has almost 5,000 AM radio stations, over 6,500 FM stations, and over 1,500 television stations. Add to that the growing number of cable systems—over 11,000 according to the National Cable Television Association—and the outlook for the future is rosy.

Grass roots experience is imperative when pursuing a career in this field. The majority of colleges and universities throughout the country prepare candidates for the real world of broadcasting by offering a comprehensive course load related to the industry. The top-notch schools provide hands-on experience in on-campus facilities, and many boast state-of-the-art technology.

In addition to obtaining the required educational degree, i.e., broadcasting, radio, television, or journalism, it's important to take advantage of the university broadcasting facilities. "Announcing sports is just like playing sports," says Minko. "The only way you're going to get better is by doing it."

Students should volunteer for radio or television shifts as often as possible. For it's in this training venue that aspiring broadcasters can learn the ropes and not suffer humiliation from the inevitable mistakes of youth. "Our college motto was, 'We learn at the listener's expense,' " says Minko, a Butler University alumnus.

A significant benefit of working on the campus radio and television station is the opportunity to create a versatile demo-tape to share with prospective employers. Send this tape to the news director at stations you've targeted as having possible openings. Keep the tape relatively short (under ten minutes should suffice), and include several segments of material that best indicate your ability to handle various aspects of broadcasting.

RATINGS BATTLE

It's impossible to pinpoint exact salaries for sports news broadcasters. Earnings vary greatly depending upon several factors, the most obvious being an individual's experience, reputation, and longevity with the station. Other variables include the station's prestige and the size of its market share.

To be sure, television pays better than radio. According to a survey conducted in 1993 by the National Association of Broadcasters, the average pay for a radio sports reporter was $25,000, compared to $45,000 for a TV sports reporter. Bear in mind this is average salary, but the pay-scale discrepancy is still worthy of a closer look.

Both radio and television sports news broadcasters will be expected to write their own script. The script must be penned to fit an exact length of time predetermined by the item's importance in relation to the time alloted to the overall sports segment. In the old days, individuals knew that 16 typewritten lines equal 1 minute. Today, a special news writing computer system tracks how much time you've written.

Since television is a visual medium, the TV sportscaster must write the script to reflect the pictures. The majority of TV sports anchors utilize the skills of a talented highlights coordinator to produce the video package for the broadcast. This involves editing tape to create a brief explanation of the game in pictures. The anchor's words augment the video.

HEARD BUT NOT SEEN

The radio sports news broadcaster, by contrast, relies solely on his or her words to communicate ideas to an audience. The individual may play audio sections, called sound bites, from a press conference or locker room interview to provide added insight and bring an authoritative perspective to the report. These sound bites are usually gathered by other members of the production staff, who supply them to the station for use during the broadcast.

Perhaps the single greatest distinction between on-air talent on radio and television is what you see. Make no mistake; TV broadcasters are entertainers. They wear makeup, expensive suits, and have their hair styled. An integral part of a TV reporter's job is to be on-the-scene, rubbing elbows with the superstars. Simply put, that's why they're called TV personalities.

A radio sports reporter can wear jeans and a T-shirt to work; men needn't even shave! The quality of the job is all the audience cares about. Radio stresses substance over style. Radio's main function is a bare-bones approach to information. "As a radio sports anchor," says Minko, "I'm there to communicate, not to entertain."

TIPSHEET

- Hands-on experience is imperative to a career in broadcasting. Work on the campus radio or television station from day one.

- Volunteer to work at a local station or affiliate and try to get an internship at a small station. Don't worry if the opening isn't in sports; it's the experience you need.

- Create a well-edited demo tape and send it to news directors at stations around the country.

- Good writing skills can be a help when trying to land a job. Many broadcast professionals came from print journalism. An applicant who has written for the college newspaper may have an advantage when interviewing with a former writer.

REAL-LIFE ADVICE

John Minko,
radio sports anchor, WFAN

On July 1, 1987, New York's first all-sports radio station, WFAN, took to the airwaves. And John Minko was there, having been hired for the midnight shift on weekends. Ten years later, Minko is now in prime time, working as the sports anchor for the "Mike and the Mad Dog" program.

Prior to joining WFAN, Minko was the afternoon sports anchor for eight years at WIRE (1430 AM), a country music station in Indianapolis. During his last two years at WIRE, the station broadcast the NBA's Indiana Pacers, and Minko handled the halftime show as well as pre- and post-game duties.

> **personality sketch**
>
> *Excellent communicator; knowledge of sports; good writing ability; personable; clear speaking voice.*

Minko graduated from Butler University in Indianapolis in 1975 with a degree in radio and television.

"First, you need to be a sports fan. That may sound simple, but in this job you watch a good amount of sports on television. Your job is not over when your shift is over. You have to be aware of what's going on in the sports world and have a working knowledge of it all.

"You should sit down and literally say to yourself, 'five years from now, what do I want to be doing? What position do I want?' If you cannot answer that question, then you've got a problem. Once you come to a definitive answer on that question, then you figure out how you're going to reach that goal. Physically write it down.

"If you're in college, hopefully, you're going to a school that has a radio and television station. If not, you might be thinking about transferring. One of the reasons I chose to attend Butler was because the school has a full-scale, 37,000-watt FM radio station. I practically lived at the radio station for four years.

"When you're in college, you should be at that station constantly and trying to get as many shifts as you can. Radio and television, unlike other college courses, can't be learned from a book. The only way you learn is by doing. If you go to a solid school with a sound program—one that has a good track record for placing people in jobs—your friends become your contacts.

"In terms of style, you've got to be yourself. Listening to others and imitating them, well, once you try to be somebody you're not, then you're getting into trouble. It takes years to develop a style that's your own because you develop your personality on the air. Your voice does not mature until you reach your mid 30s. Listening to yourself is the toughest thing you can do. That's why you have to be yourself and not use any phony voice. You have to develop your style, you don't invent it.

"Some people may write a story and then figure out how to incorporate a sound bite into the script. My philosophy is the opposite. If I have a good sound bite, then that's the story. Whether it's a comment from an athlete or a coach, their words are better than mine.

"I come on the air every 20 minutes and tell you what's going on. I put it in as brief a structure as I can. I don't go into many details or analysis. You have to communicate, you have to talk to the people. You don't want to read."

SUCCESS STORY

Iain Page,
sports anchor, ESPNEWS

Iain Page joined ESPNEWS, ESPN's 24-hour sports news network, as anchor for the November 1, 1996 launch. He had been at NewSport, a 24-hour sports news and information network, since February 1996. Prior to that, he worked as a sports anchor for the regional cable news network, News 12, in Yonkers, New York. Page began his broadcasting career in 1994 at WAPT-TV in Jackson, Mississippi as a weekend sports anchor.

He graduated from Boston University in 1985 with a degree in political science. In 1988, he received his law degree from George Washington University. Initially pursuing a career as a lawyer, Page worked at a law firm in Boston from 1988 to 1990. Following that, he worked for four years as a lawyer for the Securities and Exchange Commission in Washington, D.C., before entering the broadcasting field.

ADDRESS BOOK

American Federation of Radio and Television Artists
260 Madison Avenue
New York, NY 10016
212/532-0800

American Sportscasters Association
5 Beekman Street
New York, NY 10038
212/227-8080

continues

National Association of
Broadcast Employees and
Technicians
7101 Wisconsin Avenue
Bethesda, MD 20814
301/657-8420

National Association
of Broadcasters
1771 N Street N.W.
Washington, DC 20036
202/429-5300

National Cable Television
Association
1724 Massachusetts Avenue
N.W.
Washington, DC 20036
202/775-3550

National Sportscasters and
Sportswriters Association
Box 559
Salisbury, NC 28144
703/633-4275

NETWORK TELEVISION

ABC Sports
47 West 66th Street
New York, NY 10023
212/456-7777

CBS Sports
51 West 52nd Street
New York, NY 10019
212/975-4321

ESPN
ESPN Plaza
Bristol, CT 06010
860/585-2000

Fox Sports
1211 Sixth Avenue
New York, NY 10036
212/452-5555

NBC Sports
30 Rockefeller Plaza
New York, NY 10112
212/664-4444

Turner Sports
One CNN Center
Atlanta, GA 30303
404/827-1735

CABLE TELEVISION

Home Team Sports
7700 Wisconsin Avenue
Bethesda, MD 20814
301/718-3200

Madison Square
Garden Network
Two Penn Plaza
New York, NY 10121
212/465-6000

New England Sports Network
70 Brookline Avenue
Boston, MA 02215
617/536-9233

Prime Sports Network
44 Cook Street
Denver, CO 80206
303/355-7777

Prime Ticket
10000 Santa Monica Boulevard
Los Angeles, CA 90067
310/556-7500

SportsChannel America
3 Crossways Park West
Woodbury, NY 11797
516/921-3764

SportSouth Network
One CNN Center
Atlanta, GA 30374
404/827-4100

Sunshine Network
390 North Orange Avenue
Orlando, FL 32801
407/648-1150

TELEVISION DIRECTOR

The director of a televised sporting event is expected to bring the game to life through the eye of the camera lens. The individual must be a vivid storyteller, deciding which players and what game action should be seen on camera at each moment.

The director is in charge of coordinating every facet of the broadcast, and also provides input

personality sketch

Vivid storyteller; detail-oriented; able to handle pressure; supervisory; experience working in all aspects of television production.

with all creative and technical aspects of the production. He or she oversees and guides rehearsals as well as the actual shooting of the game.

Developing a plan of camera angles is essential to the success of television directing. As part of the job, the individual is required to determine the number of cameras needed and where in the stadium or arena the cameras will be placed. The goal is to attain the most effective camera shots possible.

In a baseball game, for example, as live action progresses, the director must convey his or her personal interpretation of the game to the audience. This is accomplished by ordering the proper sequence of shots to show the ball being hit for a single, fielded and thrown by an outfielder, and caught by an infielder. The result will provide viewers with a seamless visual narration.

Directing a live, televised sporting event is a laborous, yet ultimately, rewarding job. The director works long, tedious hours in an attempt to present a production of the highest quality. Creatively talented, innovative directors can put their personalized stamp on a thrilling moment and turn it into sports history.

For 42 years, NBC's baseball telecasts bore the signature of Harry Coyle. Coyle was a director who pioneered the on-air look of televised baseball games over a career that spanned five decades. His most memorable shot was the dramatic, lingering view from a camera inside Fenway Park's left-centerfield scoreboard showing Carlton Fisk of the Boston Red Sox waving his game-winning home run fair in Game 6 of the 1975 World Series.

CAREER DIRECTION

Because of the competitive nature of the business, most employers require television directors to earn at least a bachelor's degree. While a college degree will not insure a career as a television director, it is helpful for a number of reasons. A college education is useful for the credibility it lends and the education, experience, and opportunities it affords.

Good majors include broadcasting, communications, and journalism. Courses and seminars in television and related subjects will be helpful in honing skills. Those who do not pursue college often obtain training by working with and watching other directors on the job and by participating in internships.

While the greatest number of employment opportunities are at the large networks with contracts to broadcast more than one sport, it is easier to break into the field at a small market television affiliate. Individuals may work on staff or freelance. Directors may be assigned to a variety of sports or may specialize in a specific sport.

Earnings for directors vary greatly, but can range from approximately $25,000 to $150,000. Variables include the experience, expertise, and reputation of the director. Earnings are also dependent on the prestige and market size of the TV station. Directors just starting out in a small market, or those working on the minor league level, will earn less than their counterparts at large networks and in major league cities.

TAKE TWO: CAREER ADVANCEMENT

There are a number of paths for career advancement for television directors, depending on the chosen method. Some directors learn their craft from the bottom up at a small market station, where they are given the luxury of on-the-job training. Others begin their career as a producer or technical director, while training for the director's position.

Directors can also advance their careers by working for more prestigious stations with exclusive broadcasting rights to a variety of sports. Most in this field aspire to direct the championship sporting events. Coyle directed 36 World Series and 27 All-Star Games, as well as 27 Rose Bowls and 12 United States Open golf championships.

THE MASTER STORYTELLER

Coyle, who was born in Ridgewood, New Jersey, and raised in Paterson, attended William Paterson College for two years. He then served as a fighter pilot in the Air Force. He joined the Dumont Network in 1947 and directed part-time at NBC before joining the network full-time in 1955. He retired in 1989 and died in 1996 at age 74.

Coyle is an excellent example of a director setting the standard, and then adapting it to new technologies. He bridged the eras from the late 1940s, when games were broadcast in black and white using 3 cameras, to the late 1980s, when slow motion, instant replays and 14 cameras were commonplace.

Coyle introduced the use of hand-held cameras, close-ups, player reactions, and smooth cutting from shot to shot. He also introduced a center-field camera 40 years ago to let viewers follow the path of a pitch from behind the pitcher and into the catcher's mitt. It is standard now, but represented a quantum leap from the traditional view from high above home plate that focused on the infield. He got the idea from watching an umpire call a softball game from behind the pitcher.

ON THE AIR

Directors who become successful have the unique ability to bring into the living rooms of their viewers the sights and sounds of the game. These individuals have discovered a dramatic method of conveying to an audience their unqiue interpretation of the game.

When directing baseball, Coyle's style was mellow, not melodramatic. He respected the game's geometry, and enjoyed it's pace. The nuances of the game were not taken for granted during his telecasts.

He didn't just follow the ball; he possessed a storyteller's uncanny sense of timing. And he was the first director to personalize the players: Getting the batter in close-up as he takes strike three; capturing the look on a pitcher's face as he wipes his brow; then cutting away from a close-up in time for the pitch.

In 1988, when Coyle was 66, he directed his 36th and last World Series. In Game 1, the Dodgers' Kirk Gibson, on two gimpy legs, hit a pinch-hit home run off Oakland's Dennis Eckersley in the bottom of the ninth for a 5-4 victory. "We told Harry that Gibson was hitting off a tee under the stands and he just started building the tension," said John Filippelli, who produced the game, which was called by Vin Scully.

As Richard Samdomir of *The New York Times* explained, Coyle directed the drama with such subtelty as to be almost coy. He shifted seamlessly between tight close-ups of Gibson and Eckersley, cutting to the center-field camera for every pitch, then more close-ups of the dugouts and managers.

He created a montage of 57 shots—calling for only two replays—before the climatic hit. And, then, during Gibson's fist-pumping home run trot, Coyle followed the hero with one camera shot, from second base to home.

"Harry's genius was setting that up from the second inning on," said Michael Weisman, then the executive producer of NBC Sports. "Every time Scully made a reference to Gibson being out, he'd pan the dugout looking for Gibson; sometimes he was there, sometimes he wasn't. If he hadn't set it up so well, it would have just been, 'Oh, there's Gibson.'"

TIPSHEET

- Internships and apprenticeships are extremely useful in breaking into this competitive field. Speak with a college advisor to locate where such programs are available.

- Approach small television and cable stations in local markets to offer your services. Smaller-market stations are better able to provide a training ground for inexperienced prospects.

- Secure any television job available to get your foot in the door. Work hard, volunteer your time, get noticed, and climb the ladder as others leave for better positions elsewhere.

- Contacts and networking are helpful in succeeding in this field. Meet important people by attending seminars and trade workshops. Enroll in as many courses as you can find in television directing. Ask questions and learn by watching.

- After you obtain experience, send your resume and highlight tape to other stations.

ADDRESS BOOK

Directors Guild of America
7920 Sunset Boulevard
Hollywood, CA 90046
213/289-2000

TELEVISION PRODUCTION ASSISTANT

The screening area at ESPN looks like the television showroom at a department store. Twenty color sets are tuned-in to a different sporting event; each set is hooked-up to a state-of-the-art video recorder. Perched in front of each TV is a temporary production assistant. Each has one goal: to be selected for a permanent position.

"The production assistant is our entry-level job," says Al Jaffe, a vice president of production recruitment at ESPN. "But it's the beginning of a career path toward producing."

Located in Bristol, Connecticut, ESPN is a 24-hour sports cable television network. In addition to broadcasting live remotes from professional and collegiate sports games, ESPN produces an assortment of sports highlights shows, including its flagship, SportsCenter, as well as blooper tapes that are sold in video stores. At ESPN, every frame of footage must be viewed as events are happening, and to be a production assistant is to watch lots of sports—eight hours a day and as many as six days a week.

THE REEL DEAL

Sounds like a dream job, right? Put up your feet, crack open a soda, and get paid to watch the Celtics play the Bulls. The starting salary is $300 a week plus overtime. But before you hitch a ride through New Haven, get real. ESPN has 92 production assistants on staff, including a slew of temporary PAs in a seven-month program with no benefits—and no guarantee beyond the seven months.

Most temporary PAs are recent college graduates who aspire to produce, write, or direct one of the company's sports shows. When they watch a broadcast, clipboard in hand, they keep track of the action with a unique shorthand that allows a producer to put together a highlight package by simply scanning the view sheets and selecting the most appropriate snippets.

Experienced PAs at ESPN do more than log every play; they are entrusted with making decisions based on which highlights will be used to represent that game on SportsCenter. They also oversee the editing with the tape editor, as well as write the shot-sheet that becomes the basis for the narration voice-over.

LET'S GO TO THE VIDEO TAPE

The production assistant must be knowledgable about sports in order to determine the plot lines of a game and how it can best be presented on television. Was it a pitcher's duel, or a defensive struggle? Was the game decided in the last minute, or was it a blowout? Even if nothing spectacular happens on the field, the production assistant can inject humor. Because the feeds are usually direct from the satellite, the broadcasts that PAs normally see don't break for commercials, and it's during this time that much of what's funny and unexpected occurs.

"Highlights need to have a creative theme and be distinctive," says Jaffe. "We're looking to hire people who can go beyond the generic, chronological highlight package and display flair and style."

Jaffe says he gets about 100 resumes a month—just for the temporary PA position. He expects applicants to have earned a college degree in television, radio, broadcasting, journalism, mass communications, theater, film, or a related field. Most of all, he says, the candidate must demonstrate a serious interest in sports broadcasting; experience on the campus station, and an internship at a local network affiliate will increase your odds for obtaining an interview.

BIG BROTHER IS WATCHING

Individuals who make the grade are primarily assigned to two areas: the screening area and the newsroom. Candidates will get a chance to work in both areas during their seven-month tryout period. The newsroom duties include filing wire service copy; helping directors with pre-production tasks, such as coordinating graphics; answering telephones on the assignment desk; updating the library archives; and performing maintenance on the newsroom computer system.

The job of temporary production assistant is a stepping stone to further advancement. The PAs who distinguish themselves during the audition period will be retained on a permanent basis. Production assistants may be promoted to associate producer, feature producer, highlight supervisor, producer, coordinating producer, and senior coordinating producer.

"Seven months is what you make of it," says Jaffe. "When we decide who stays and who doesn't, we're projecting people's future. What we're really doing is determining the next generation of ESPN producers."

TIPSHEET

- Demonstrate a serious interest in television by working in the sports department at a local station.

- Apply to colleges that offer a degree in television. Take any related courses, enroll in seminars, attend trade shows, and read the trade magazines.

- Get as many internships as you possibly can. Internships are helpful for breaking into this competitive field, making contacts, and gaining experience; you'll become more marketable.

REAL-LIFE ADVICE

Al Jaffe,
vice president/production recruitment and talent negotiations, ESPN

Drawing on over 25 years of television experience, Al Jaffe is the point man for all on-air and off-air positions at ESPN, the Connecticut-based 24-hour cable sports television network. He is responsible for recruiting and evaluating all production personnel, as well as assessing commentators and negotiating contracts. Jaffe was previously the news director at ESPN and also served as manager of talent and production recruitment prior to being promoted to his current position.

> **personality sketch**
>
> *Eager team player; knowledgable about sports and broadcasting; creative; aggressive but willing to pay your dues.*

"We're looking for smart people. People who know sports, have a journalism background, a television production background, as well as an overall sense of creativity. People who are strong in those four areas will generally succeed and flourish.

"People applying here need to have a demonstrated interest in sports television. When a resume hits my desk, I'm looking to see what kind of internship they've had. If somebody went to Syracuse, for instance, and interned at the local ABC affiliate in the sports department, that means a lot to me. That shows this person is serious about a career.

"When they come in for an interview, we ask them sports questions—not trivia—but questions about the current sports scene to get a feel for their sports knowledge. Most questions have no right or wrong answers, it's their opinions we're interested in. Mainly we ask about the four major sports—baseball, basketball, football, and hockey—college and professional, on a national level. We find the good candidates know the stuff cold. We're not looking for people to memorize the rosters of every team, but they need to know about the major players and issues of sports.

"Once you've decided on a career in sports television, your first fundamental decision has to be, 'Do I want on-air or off-air?' Once you decide that, you can proceed. When a person comes on as a temp PA, we can usually tell after a few weeks who the superstars are. The PA's job is to tell a story in microcosm. They're like a reporter at the game; they need to figure out the lead for the story. The smart people stand out.

"We don't like to put people into that [PA] job who really want to be on the air. If you want to be on-air, you need to be honest with yourself. Are you really good enough? The on-air jobs generally pay more and are more glamorous, but you have to assess your talent and evaluate yourself critically. It's tough to be honest and admit that you don't have the stuff to make it beyond a small market.

"You have to compare yourself to the people you see on the air. Your best bet is to go be on the air somewhere in a smaller market and work your way up. Can you make it to ESPN? If you truly believe that you can, you should go for it. If not, look at the off-air, behind-the-scenes jobs. There are very few on-air jobs; there are many more off-air jobs."

SUCCESS STORY

Mark Gross,
coordinating producer, ESPN

In his current position as coordinating producer at ESPN, Mark Gross oversees the content, budget, and personnel for such shows as SportsCenter, NFL PrimeTime, and NFL PrimeMonday. During the summer of 1996, he also served as coordinating producer for SportsCenter's coverage of the Olympic Games from Atlanta.

Gross began his career at ESPN in 1988 as a temporary production assistant and was hired full-time soon after. In 1990, he was named associate producer for SportsCenter and College GameDay, a post he held until late 1992, when he became a highlights supervisor.

In July 1993, Gross was promoted to SportsCenter producer with responsibilities in content development and telecast presentation. On October 1, 1993 he was the producer of the first-ever broadcast of ESPN2's SportsNight. One year later he was promoted to his current post.

Gross has amassed over ten years experience in television production. During high school he worked on weekends at the local network affiliate, and during college he obtained three different internships. Gross graduated from Ithaca College in 1988 with a bachelor of science degree majoring in television and radio, and a minor in history.

ADDRESS BOOK

ESPN
ESPN Plaza
Bristol, CT 06010
860/585-2000

International Radio and Television Society Foundation
420 Lexington Avenue
New York, NY 10170
212/867-6650

National Association of Broadcast Employees and Technicians
7101 Wisconsin Avenue
Bethesda, MD 20814
301/657-8420

National Association of Broadcasters
1771 N Streeet, N.W.
Washington, DC 20036
202/429-5498

RADIO TALK SHOW HOST

In an effort to attract new audiences, many radio stations throughout the country are adding additional sports talk shows to their programming or turning to an all-sports format. The radio personalities leading the conversation during these shows are called the sports talk show hosts.

This person may be expected to host a daily show or may host shows only on specific days of the week. Shows can run one hour to full four-hour shifts. The host may work alone or with a co-host, and usually performs live. Individuals in this job also may be expected to make public appearances on behalf of the station.

Responsibilities vary depending on the specific show and its format. The host's main duties include introducing and interviewing guests, discussing subjects relevant to the specific show, and keeping the show moving in an entertaining manner.

Most stations incorporate a call-in format, in which the host takes phone calls from the listening audience. Callers may comment on the subject at hand or ask related questions. Successful talk show hosts have the ability to keep the show dynamic by bantering back and forth with guests and callers.

In order to perform the job effectively, the host must be knowledgable about all sports and the people who play them. The host must watch games, read newspapers and magazines, and talk to informed contacts.

The host may also be required to do research prior to an interview in order to fully understand the subject being discussed. Some hosts will do research on their own, while others may have assistants who handle this task and then report the facts to them.

A radio talk show host should have a unique speaking voice and the ability to speak on many topics. The host must have a license from the Federal Communications Commission. The license can be obtained by submitting an application, as well as a letter written by an employer stating that the applicant has a job in the broadcasting field.

RAREFIED AIR

The sports radio phenomena has evolved during the past decade. In the early 1980s, aspiring broadcasters wanted to be on television like Marv Albert or Bob Costas. Today, however, there's a whole new generation of youngsters who grew up listening to sports radio. These kids want to host their own talk show. This idea didn't exist ten years ago, and the result is keen competition.

Most careers begin behind the microphone, in the control room or as an assistant to the producer. From the control room, aspiring talent may assist the engineer by working sound controls or putting cassettes in tape decks. In a production capacity, individuals may be responsible for booking guests or writing promos.

The select few who are lucky enough to get on the air usually begin at the most mundane levels. A traffic reporter, for instance, may move up the ladder and get to cover sporting events and give live, periodic updates, then get promoted to reading the sports news. Only after gaining name recognition and credibility as a sports reporter will the individual be in a position to host his or her own show.

Sports radio talk show hosts will find employment with stations located in cities throughout the country. But it's difficult to obtain initial employment in major markets located in large metropolitan areas. It's usually easier to find positions in small markets because the turnover is so great. Most people seek jobs in these markets to acquire experience in all facets of radio. After experience is obtained, they move on to larger markets and more prestigious stations.

Sports radio can be found all around the dial. When WFAN began broadcasting in New York City in July 1987, it was the first all-sports station in the United States. In 1990 there were still only a handful of all-sports radio stations. By 1994 there were 78. Today there are 157, although, says Robert Unmacht, editor and publisher of the radio newsletter The *M Street Journal,* "In the last six months growth has slowed down considerably."

Radio hosts advance their careers by obtaining experience, developing a unique personality, and building a loyal following. Those who accomplish this can advance to positions at larger and more prestigious stations. The most popular hosts will expand their audience through national syndication. Other methods of career advancement include becoming the program director of a station.

TALK THAT AIN'T CHEAP

A formal education is not a prerequisite to becoming a sports radio talk show host. Many stations, of course, prefer their hosts to have college degrees. Others only require that individuals have experience and the ability to capture an audience's attention.

Those attending college should consider a course load in communications and broadcasting. Colleges also afford opportunities including internships and jobs on college radio stations. There are also vocational technical schools and trade schools located around the country offering programs in radio broadcasting.

Earnings vary greatly, depending on the size, prestige, popularity, and location of the station as well as the experience, reputation, and popularity of the individual. Annual earnings range from $15,000 to $150,000 or more. Those with less experience at small markets will earn wages on the lower end of the scale.

Many radio personalities augment their income with personal appearances and voice-overs for commercials. Those who increase their exposure and popularity will be in greater demand and will be able to negotiate increased earnings.

TIPSHEET

- Join your school's radio club and volunteer for any school-related activities that will give you experience speaking in front of an audience. Some activities may include becoming the public address announcer for sporting events, or acting as emcee for assemblies.

- Try to secure an internship at a local station. Knowledge of all aspects of radio will be helpful when trying to land that first job.

- Convince your friends to be guests on your own talk show. Sit around a tape recorder and you play the host. Listen to the tape, critique yourself, and keep practicing to improve.

- Send your homemade demo tape to a local station, accompanied by a good cover letter. To help ensure you get a reply, find out the name of the program director before mailing it.

REAL-LIFE ADVICE

Jim Rome,
sports talk show host

The Jim Rome Show is a syndicated sports talk show that is heard weekdays from 9 a.m. to 1 p.m. (PST) on 37 stations nationwide. Rome, who graduated from the University of California at Santa Barbara in 1986 with a communications degree, completed an incredible seven—7!—radio internships. After more than three years at KTMS in Santa Barbara, he was hired at XTRA in December 1990.

personality sketch

Unique speaking voice; good communication skills; ability to ad-lib and think quickly; knowledgable about sports; personable.

"I was lucky in that I started in a town that not only had a reputable university, but it was in a small radio market. [Santa Barbara is market number 174.] So I was able to get a good education and actually get on the air at a commercial station before I graduated.

"The UC system preaches all theory in communications. There was no radio and television. I took classes like non-verbal communication. I never learned one thing in four years in the classroom that I could apply to my trade. That's why I did seven internships in three years.

"To anyone who wants this line of work, I would ask: This business is so competitive, what makes you different? What makes you better? Why should somebody hire you over 10 million other people? What do you bring to the table?

"I used to think about those questions all the time. I'd look at myself in the mirror and wonder why I deserved to make it more than every other kid on campus. Then one day it came to me. The only thing I had that distinguished me from other people was I wanted it worse. "I was hungrier and I was driven. I didn't care how many 'Noes' I heard until I got to the big 'Yes.'

"What really helped me was a change in attitude. Whenever I'd watch TV or listen to the radio, I'd say to myself, I know I'm better than that guy; he's got a terrible voice and no talent. I'd sit around with my buddies who also wanted to get into the business, and we'd pump each other up by talking about how bad everybody else was.

"Then it hit me. It doesn't matter how much talent you think you have, they have the job and you don't. There's something to be said for someone who has enough talent to work their way into the position. So give them some respect, stop complaining, and figure out a way you're going to get a job. As soon as I came to grips with that idea, I was much better off.

"Another thing I tell people is to develop yourself off the air before you develop yourself on the air. You have to fight the fight off the air before you even get near the field of play. You don't want to be reckless or irresponsible, but you need to be able to take some chances.

"While working in Santa Barbara at KTMS I had just one dream in life. That was to work for XTRA 690 AM. I wanted it so badly it kept me up at nights. So I started firing off resumes and making phone calls. Every time I called somebody and didn't get a return call, I'd call somebody else at the station. I went from general manager to program director to sports anchor and I kept sending resumes. This literally went on for about a year and half. I couldn't get a break.

"Finally, I got a call. They said, 'Look Jim, we know who you are. A guy here is taking a week off. Come down to the station and audition as his vacation relief. If you get it, great. If not, leave us alone.'

"Now I had a week of vacation coming to me. So I went to KTMS and told them about the opportunity. I wanted to be honest with them because XTRA has a strong enough signal that it can be heard in Santa Barbara. I didn't want to get caught in a lie, and then not get the job. They told me no, that I absolutely could not go.

"I was scared. I wasn't making a lot of money, I wasn't real confident, and I didn't have any leverage. But I had to make a decision. Was I going to risk it all for this chance? I'd sent them resumes for a year-and-a-half; I had to make a run at it. My station told me that if I didn't get the job, I might not be welcome back. I told them fire me if you've got to, I'm going. Luckily, I got the gig." [Author's Note: After conducting this interview an ironic situation developed. KTMS ultimately became an affiliate of the Premiere Radio Network, which carries Rome's show. KTMS dropped the show, citing as the reason a change in format.]

SPOTLIGHT

The Fabulous Sports Babe,
sports talk show host

In the male-dominated world of sports talk radio, The Fabulous Sports Babe has become the hottest new voice on the air. When ESPN Radio launched her on the Fourth of July in 1994 from their studio in Bristol, Connecticut, less than 30 stations had signed on. But today, 215 stations broadcast The Babe's show, the only nationally syndicated radio sports show hosted by a woman.

The Babe's real name is Nanci Donnellan. She was determined to become a sportscaster, but after attending several colleges, found on-air sports jobs for women hard to come by. She landed her first full-time radio job in 1977, paying her dues doing traffic and weather reports.

"I've learned in radio that there is a certain percentage of people who believe they can do a better job than you," says Donnellan. "When that format is sports talk, the percentage is even greater. When you're a woman doing sports talk, the percentage is enormous."

Bucking the odds, she began working as a radio sportscaster in Tampa, Florida. Confined to her bed because of a back injury from playing golf in 1989, Donnellan started her show by saying "Come spend the afternoon in bed with a fabulous sports babe." And the name stuck.

Soon after, Seattle radio station KJR gave her an opportunity to host her own call-in radio show. Ratings jumped by 900 percent in her time slot over a three-year period. Donnellan soon caught the ear of ESPN, which had several female sportscasters on television, but none on radio.

"I'm not kidding myself," says Donnellan. "I'm lucky to be in the right place at the right time."

The Fabulous Sports Babe's call-in program airs on the ESPN radio network weekdays between 10 a.m. and 2 p.m. In between commentary and interviews, she jams in about 200 calls a day. Surveys show upwards of 200,000 callers try to reach her monthly. (Industry experts report that only 1 to 2 percent of a sports talk show's listeners call in.)

The Babe's success enabled ESPN radio to grow from part-time to seven-day-a-week syndication, says Mark Mason, the network's radio general manager.

"I don't profess to know everything," Donnellan says. "I never put myself out there as an expert. I just have access. I'm not afraid to ask someone in Detroit what's going on there. They know. I'm just here to provide the forum and a little entertainment. I say what you'd hear in the bleachers."

ADDRESS BOOK

American Federation of Television and Radio Artists
260 Madison Avenue
New York, NY 10016
212/532-0800

National Association of Broadcasting
1771 N Street NW
Washington, DC 20036
202/429-5300

National Association of Broadcast Employees and Technicians
7101 Wisconsin Avenue
Bethesda, MD 20814
301/657-8420

RADIO PRODUCER—TALK SHOW

The producer of a sports radio talk show acts as the quarterback of the show. The individual is responsible for booking the guests who are to appear on the show, as well as deciding which callers will get on the air.

The radio producer's main job is to dictate the flow of the show. This is accomplished by screening all calls. By properly screening all calls, the producer ensures that intelligent people with good opinions get on the air. If a record station plays a few bad songs in a row, the listener will have a tendency to change the station. The same is true of a call-in radio show. Several boring callers in succession will result in a listener not being entertained or informed. That listener will probably go elsewhere on the dial.

A producer screening calls is expected to perform a pre-interview. He or she will ascertain from the caller the subject to be discussed and the particular point or question to be explored. Once the decision is made that the caller meets the criteria for the broadcast, the producer will determine the order in which callers get on the air.

It is vital that the producer and the host maintain a good working relationship. By becoming acquainted with the host's strong points and weaknesses, the producer will ensure that the host is never embarrassed or compromised while on the air.

THE JOB FREQUENCY

Individuals interested in a career in radio production can find employment opportunities all around the country. Anywhere there's a radio station, there will be jobs available. Obviously, the greatest number of opportunities will be in large metropolitan cities with numerous stations. But the easiest way to land a job is by applying to small-market stations with a healthy turnover. The smaller stations act as a training ground for lower level employees, who eventually go on to more prestigious positions within the station or relocate to a lateral job at a larger market.

TUNE IN AT SCHOOL

As a rule, jobs in radio have various educational requirements depending upon the size and location of the station. Some small stations do not require anything more than a high school diploma and a proven track record. Other stations prefer experience in vocational schools.

Most quality stations, however, expect job applicants to have a college degree in radio, broadcasting, or journalism. Experience working for a radio station is mandatory in order to become a producer. Most people begin acquiring skills while working at a college radio station.

Internships are the most valuable experience you can have. One of the best internship opportunities is the College Conference and Summer Fellowship program, run by the International Radio and Television Society Foundation. The nine-week summer program begins with lectures and training seminars conducted by industry professionals. The students are then given actual supervised working assignments in their field of interest.

MOVING UP THE DIAL

The majority of producers working today started in the field as desk assistants. This entry-level position is also called tape editor. As the title implies, individuals in this job are expected to have experience editing audiotape.

Working in the studio, the desk assistant will record the audio of a game in progress and edit the taped highlights for use by the sports news reporter. In addition, the desk assistant will receive taped interviews from reporters who are on assignment. As the tapes are fed into the studio, the desk assistant is required to edit the tape into sound bites.

Since the majority of sporting events occur at night and on weekends, the desk assistant is a job with unpleasant working hours. To further test one's dedication and perseverance, the pay is horrid. On average, a tape editor can expect to earn no more than $18,000 a year. For this reason, experienced radio professionals recommend that entry-level candidates work at a station close to home. The message is clear: if you live with your parents, you won't starve.

A tape editor may be promoted to an entry-level producer and earn an annual salary of about $20,000 to $30,000, depending on experience. A successful producer can hope to become an executive producer, and earn approximately $30,000 to $40,000 per year. With the additional responsiblities come additional monies.

The executive producer will supervise the production staff and assign reporters for game coverage. Other duties handled by the executive producer may include acting as liaison with the advertising sales department; making certain that ad copy is current and voice-overs are updated; overseeing personnel schedules; and supervising the maintenance and upkeep of the Basys computer sytem, which has replaced the teletype machine in modern newsrooms.

The next step up the ladder is assistant program director. This position requires an extensive amount of paperwork. The individual in this job will supervise the newsroom operations. He or she may expect to earn an annual salary in the range of $40,000 to $50,000. The assistant program director coordinates the weekly assignment schedules for all personnel. This involves deciding who works on what days, and choosing which reporters will cover what events. Another important duty performed by the assistant program director is determining a budget for freelance staff.

TIPSHEET

ⓘ Gaining hands-on experience should be your first priority. High school students should volunteer at a local radio station to work part-time in any capacity. College students should be heavily involved with the campus radio station.

ⓘ Make it your business to locate an internship. The International Radio and Television Society Foundation runs an internship program called the College Conference and Summer Fellowship program. Look into it.

ⓘ Establishing contacts is vital. Attend seminars and network with people already working in the field. Trade magazines are helpful sources of information.

REAL-LIFE ADVICE

Eric Spitz,
assistant program director, WFAN Radio

Eric Spitz joined WFAN Radio as a producer in 1987, two months after graduating from SUNY Binghamton with a bachelor of arts in political science. While in college, Spitz gained valuable experience at NBC Radio, first as an intern, then as a studio producer for NFL and college football bowl games. At WFAN, his initial duties in-

personality sketch

Love of radio; detail-oriented; organization and communication skills; ability to make decisions; can juggle many projects simultaneously.

cluded scheduling guests for sports talk programs, and producing all broadcasts for the station's flagship team, the New York Mets.

In 1990 he was promoted to executive producer, supervising the producers, anchors, and off-air staff, as well as assigning reporters for game coverage. Spitz became assistant program director in 1992. His current responsibilities include supervising newsroom operations and staff; overseeing all aspects of station programming, including sports talk shows, sports news reports, and play-by-play broadcasts of the Mets, Jets, Knicks, and Rangers; and coordinating the weekly schedule assignments for all on- and off-air staff. He is also in charge of the station's internship program.

A tireless worker, Spitz has willingly sacrificed his annual three-week vacation to work for NBC Radio and Westwood One as an executive producer and producer for the Summer Olympics Games in Seoul, South Korea (1988), Barcelona, Spain (1992), and Atlanta, Georgia (1996).

"The key to where I am today is the college internship. In the radio business, an internship is the equivalent of law school or medical school. While radio isn't brain surgery or law, if you don't have internships and establish contacts at an early age, you're in trouble.

"I was fortunate to get an internship after my freshman year of college. But I knew I wanted a radio career, unlike most college-age kids who decide during their junior or senior year what they want. I interned in a newsroom, and that gave me the bug. Then I continued as a part-timer in the studio. I was producing network sportscasts while still in college. My internship not only gave me the knowledge of actually working in the field but, equally important, the opportunity to make contacts.

"People I knew at NBC Radio knew people who were starting WFAN in July 1987. Through a combination of knowledge, timing, and luck, I was able to get an entry-level job at WFAN. The station was a start-up operation. On the one hand, that's dangerous because there's no stablility. Most people would shy away from a start-up operation; they'd rather go work at some place established.

"My advice to anybody fresh out of school is to get involved in a start-up operation because you're more apt to move up quickly. That's what happened in my situation at WFAN. People got fired, or they got cold feet and jumped ship. So even though I had limited experience, I was able to move up. People were willing to give me a chance because I was there.

"In my role coordinating the internship program, I look for candidates with radio experience. Too many people love sports, and that's not enough to get you noticed. When you're dealing with the large number of resumes we get, you're forced to look for reasons to cut the number of applicants down to a managable number. So you need to have some radio production skills. You need to know how to edit audio tape, and how to transfer information from reel-to-reel onto cart. If you don't have those skills, don't apply. This is experience that can be gained at the college radio station, or with internships at smaller-level stations. Everybody who gets an interview knows how to edit tape.

"I tell college graduates who want to be on the air not to come to a big market station. They end up taking a behind-the-scenes job to get a foot in the door. You won't ever get better on the air by watching other people. You'll get better only by doing it. So if it's your goal to be on the air, go someplace and be on the air. Go to a small station and hone that craft.

"There's many small stations surrounding any large metropolitan area that will give you on-air experience. Yes, you're on a smaller station, yet you're still in a major market. You'll still surround yourself with the people who are covering the games for the larger stations. The idea is to network, to establish contacts in the market you wish to work, and keep those contacts."

SUCCESS STORY

Henry Henderson,
executive producer, WSCR

As executive producer of WSCR, sportsradio 820-AM, Henderson oversees 13 producers and 13 interns, which is the largest production staff in the Chicago area. He is responsible for the programming of guests for the station and serves as the primary contact with the Cubs, White Sox, Bears, Bulls, and Blackhawks. He is also the executive producer of WSCR's NFL game day coverage, as well as the co-host of the Sunday afternoon sports talk show during football season.

Henderson's long career in Chicago radio includes having worked as a producer for WJLS Talkradio and as an account executive for WPNT Radio. He was also the sports and overnight producer for WCRX Radio, the Columbia College station in Chicago, where he received his bachelor's degree in broadcast journalism.

ADDRESS BOOK

International Radio and Television Society Foundation
420 Lexington Avenue
New York, NY 10170
212/867-6650

National Association of Broadcasters
1771 N Street, N.W.
Washington, D.C. 20036
202/429-5498

Radio and Television News Directors Association
1000 Connecticut Avenue N.W.
Washington, DC 20036
202/659-6510

MAJOR ALL-SPORTS RADIO STATIONS

WFAN Radio
34-12 36th Street
Astoria, NY 11106
718/706-7690

XTRA
4891 Pacific Highway
San Diego, CA 92110
619/291-9191

WEEI
116 Huntington Avenue
Boston, MA 02116
617/375-8000

WIP
441 North Fifth Street
Philadelphia, PA 19123
215/922-5000

KFNS
7711 Carondelet Street
St. Louis, MO 63105
314/727-2160

WKNR
9446 Broadview Road
Cleveland, OH 44147
216/838-1220

KJR
190 Queen Anne
Avenue North
Seattle, WA 98109
206/285-2295

WFNS
7201 East Hillsborough
Avenue
Tampa, FL 33610
813/620-9100

SPORTSWRITER

A sportswriter is responsible for covering games and the people who play them. The writer may work for a local daily newspaper, a national weekly magazine, or a regional monthly publication such as a newsletter or other periodical. He or she will be assigned to write game stories and feature articles that profile athletes.

Additional duties performed by a sportswriter vary depending on the size of the publication. At a small newspaper the writer may be required to research, fact-check, and copy edit his or her own text. At a large magazine the writer will have support staff to help gather information and collect quotes.

Some established sportswriters report only on a specific sport. For those just breaking into the business, however, it's not unusual that they be required to cover a variety of events. For this reason, it's imperative that young sportswriters have an excellent knowledge of all sports.

A writer must be a gifted storyteller, able to unfurl facts in ways dramatic, entertaining, and informative. The ability to write clear, concise copy is only half the battle. Experience is also imperative to a journalist's sixth sense: what makes a story THE story. A good reporter not only spots the interesting news, but develops it by use of a creative or unique angle.

MEET THE PRESS

In cities that host professional sports franchises, newspapers assign a writer to cover the daily activities of the team. This individual, called a beat writer, travels with the club and is expected to report all the news that pertains to the team. Duties include writing game stories, gathering quotes from players and coaches, writing follow-ups, and developing feature stories.

The sportswriter covering a game sits in the press box, a special section for working members of the media. The press box is equipped with telephone lines that allow the writer to send in his story via computer modem. The press box is also where the writer obtains the press notes and media guides that are made available by the team's media relations department. These press kits—which contain player biographies, statistics, and historical background on the team—are valuable sources in aiding the writer to present the most factual information possible.

All articles must be written on deadline. For the beat writer this often means fashioning creative and vivid prose under intense pressure. An individual usually will write the text of game action as it happens, leaving space for quotes and a lead paragraph to be filled in later.

Once the game is over, the writer really goes to work. He or she will attend press conferences or enter the locker room to speak with players and coaches in order to collect insightful quotes from the game's key participants. If a night game ends at 11 p.m. and the newspaper's deadline is midnight, the writer has precious little time to formulate a well-crafted piece.

THE WRITE STUFF

The explosion of the sports industry has created excellent employment opportunities for sportswriters, whether full-time, part-time, or on a freelance basis. Every major newspaper in the country has an entire sports department, and smaller papers have at least one writer devoted to reporting the sports news.

While it's true that the daily newspaper is dwindling in number, the speciality sports publications and sports trade magazines are increasing in kind. Individuals often enter the field by working for a sports-specific publication, an industry trade periodical, a pro team's newsletter, or college team's game-day program.

Sportswriters who begin as a beat writer may advance their career by going to a more prestigious publication or by becoming a magazine feature writer. Sportswriters at large metropolitan papers can become columnists, and columnists can augment their earnings through the syndication process and by writing books. (Syndication is a process by which a writer collects a royalty whenever his or her material is reprinted.) Writers who command a national following often find the door open in radio and television commentary.

National magazines—because of their longer lead time and devotion to accuracy—provide an excellent training ground for aspiring sportswriters. A magazine like *Sports Illustrated* employs as many as 25 reporters on the editorial staff who basically serve as researchers and fact-checkers. Although reporters seldom write, they do gain invaluable exposure to good journalism and learn the art of their craft from competent editors.

Salaries for sportswriters can range from $15,000 to upwards of $150,000 a year. This earnings discrepancy is based on several variables, not the least of which is the writer's experience and name-recognition factor. The amount one can earn is also dependent on the size, location, and prestige of the publication the individual is working for.

The priviledged few who are able to command salaries over $150,000 do so because they deserve to. Their bylines attract readership, which increases circulation, in turn maximizing advertising revenue, ultimately generating more profits for the publisher.

BOLD TYPES

To be a writer, as Red Smith once observed, all one needs do is sit down at a desk and open a vein.

Unlike yesteryear, when interested youngsters started their newspaper career as a copyboy, the scribes of today are an educated lot. The majority of publications require a degree in journalism, English literature, or communications. Even a liberal arts background is preferable to no education at all.

A skillful command of the language is a necessity for this job. It's often said that writers write. An impressive degree is useless without suitable examples of one's writing style. Individuals interested in the field of journalism should work on the college newspaper and create a portfolio. All job applicants are required to provide clips—published examples of his or her writing style.

For people who can only imagine rubbing elbows with their heroes, the role of sportswriter is a dream job. A sportswriter is paid to attend events and talk to famous people in the sports world. But the job requires frequent travel and little allowance for a social life.

A sportswriter, remember, is working while others recreate. The majority of games are played at night and on weekends. Despite the nomadic lifestyle, sportswriters love what they do and most remain in the profession for decades. They find their work rewarding and, whether it be a newspaper or a magazine, enjoy the satisfaction of holding in their hands a tangible product of their labor.

TIPSHEET

① High school students should contact their local newspaper and volunteer to cover their high school sports teams; college students should work on the college newspaper.

① Get a part-time position or an internship at any kind of publication in any department. Don't worry if it's not sports; the experience is what's important.

① Make a portfolio of your best clips and begin sending copies to editors. Include a cover letter suggesting story ideas and offer to write the articles on speculation. This means you submit the story with no obligation. You get paid only if the story is accepted.

REAL-LIFE ADVICE

Frank Deford,
columnist, *Newsweek*

The author of eleven books, Frank Deford is a columnist for *Newsweek,* a sports commentator for National Public Radio, and correspondent on the HBO television show, *RealSport.*

After graduating from Princeton University in 1962, he joined *Sports Illustrated,* where he quickly rose from reporter to

personality sketch

Skillful writer; knowledge of sports; keen observer with a nose for news; ability to meet deadlines; good communications skills.

senior writer. During his 27 years at *SI*, Deford was the most celebrated writer in the magazine's history. Among his many honors, he was six times voted Sports-writer of the Year by his peers at the National Association of Sportscasters and Sports-writers. *The American Journalism Review* has cited him as the nation's best sportswriter, and twice he was honored as magazine writer of the year by the *Washington Journalism Re-view*. In broadcast, he has won both an Emmy and a Cable Ace award.

Deford, 57, left *SI* to serve as editor-in-chief of the *National Sports Daily* during its brief but celebrated existence, and he later wrote for *Vanity Fair*. Two of his books—*Alex: The Life of a Child* and *Everybody's All-American*—have been adapted for the screen.

"The only way you improve writing is by writing. I don't know any shortcuts. People want to think that somehow there's an easier way to do it; there isn't. The only way you can write better is to write.

"The same is true of interviewing; you get better by doing it more and more. Try to get alone with a person and try to make it more a conversation than an interview. Don't go in with a set group of questions. You will do much better if you pick up on what people are saying. Ask them to explain themselves as opposed to going down a laundry list. Never ask questions, particularly of important people, that you can find the answers to ahead of time. It's just wasting their time. So try to ask questions that are different. You can't ask bizarre questions. Think ahead of time about the information you hope to learn, and then be flexible enough to follow the person's lead, rather than ask a set list of questions.

"Most young sports writers make the mistake of thinking that sports writing is statistics, knowing more earned run averages than the next guy. That's simply not true. That stuff is easy. Sportswriting is writing, as opposed to bald statistics. Be very careful about how much you use statistics. You can only give people a small dose of that; use it for illustration. If you're writing about a team's defense, then you can use a statistic to exhibit defense. Those illustrations are important but you've got to use them sparingly or it becomes too technical a read. The more you keep the human element in there, the better. The same way with quotations. Don't just drop it out like a transcript. Look for the best quotes; look for the quotes that illustrate.

"If you're writing about something where television is involved, it's even more incumbent on you to find a different angle. If all you do is report what people see on television you're providing no service whatsoever. It's as simple as that. That's no good. When you're writing about a game, I think one thing you can do is try to focus on one or two people. Look at it from their point of view. You've got to look at a cant, at an angle; if you look at it head-on that's where everybody else is looking. Now the trick, of course, is that you can't go so far afield that you lose the forest for the trees. You can't be so unique that you miss the major point. And that's just instinct, to know how far you can go without being too far out.

"It's so hard to get into sportswriting now. It's so much more competitive than it ever was when I came in. You really have to grasp whatever job you can and hope for the best. You try to set yourself apart by creating your own style. You look for a voice. A writer's voice is projected by selection. What you choose to write about tells a lot about who you are.

"I was always interested in writing about people and where they came from. Much of my writing is marked by that. History interests me. What kind of town did they grown up in? What kind of family? We're not created out of whole cloth. What made this person? Other people aren't intrigued by that and sometimes you can't draw straight lines. You can't explain why Michael Jordan is a genius, for example, just because he came from x, y, and z. It doesn't matter what it is that distinguishes you. Be yourself. That's an old, old cliche going back to Polonius and beyond. Be yourself; don't try to ape somebody else."

REAL-LIFE ADVICE

Dave Anderson,
sports columnist, *New York Times*

Dave Anderson has been a sports columnist at *The New York Times* since November 1971, after having been a general assignment sports reporter since joining the newspaper in 1966. He won a Pulitzer Prize in 1981 for distinguished commentary.

Prior to joining the *Times,* Anderson was a member of the sports staff of the now defunct *New York Journal-American* for 11 years. Before that, he was a sportswriter with the *Brooklyn Eagle,* which folded in 1955.

Anderson received a bachelor of arts degree in English literature from Holy Cross College in 1951. The author of 21 books and more than 350 magazine articles, Anderson's "Sports of the Times" column is published three times a week. He was inducted into the National Sports Writers and Sportscasters Hall of Fame in 1990.

"When I was in college you couldn't get a journalism degree and I don't think you need journalism in college. I think you're better off with an English lit background. You should be knowledgable in as many areas as you can, not just sports.

"In May of 1953, Harold C. Burr—who was an elderly baseball writer and a great man—fell in the lobby of a hotel in Cincinnati and broke his hip. So now, suddenly, the *Eagle* has no baseball writer covering the Dodgers. So they gave me the Dodgers beat. As it turned out, including Henry Chadwick, who was the original American baseball writer, the *Eagle* had had roughly a half-dozen guys whose beat was the Dodgers. I was maybe the seventh guy.

"I covered the Dodgers for two seasons. Then in February 1955 my wife and I were literally packed to go to spring training—I mean the clothes were in the bag—when the *Eagle* went on strike.

"Later that year the *Journal-American* had an opening in their sports department and I covered Rangers hockey and the football Titans, who changed their name to the Jets, and boxing. I covered Joe Namath's first training camp, and around that time Muhammad Ali defeated Sonny Liston for the heavyweight championship.

"When the *Journal-American* folded I joined the *Times* in 1966. I worked as everybody's swing man. I was the second man on pro football, I was doing sidebars at the fights. In 1968 I covered the Jets and boxing, which was incredible because Namath and Ali were the two biggest names of that era.

"Then on November 1, 1971—I'll never forget the date—I became a columnist. I've always said a column should be about big issues, big games, or big names. There are a few different types of columns. There's the point-of-view column where you come out and say something about an issue. There's the personality column, as long as you have a point-of-view with it, a reason for writing it. Then there's the entertaining column, what you would call a good read. It can be humorous. You can't save the world every day.

"A good columnist is a fly on the wall, being somewhere the reader would love to be. You try to recreate the conversation, so that your reader feels like they're eavesdropping. And you need variety so your reader doesn't know what to expect that day. As a kid in Bay Ridge, Brooklyn, every morning I read the *Times,* the *Tribune,* and the *Sun* because I wanted to read Red Smith, Jimmy Cannon, and Arthur Daley. They were the great columnists.

"They made me want to be a sportswriter. The whole trick to being a writer, to me, is being a reader. If you never read, how would you know how to write anything? If you want to be a writer, read. By reading you see what type of writing you like, the styles that impress you, the ones you may eventually emulate. I don't mean you copy someone else's style. I have my own style, but it's an amalgamation of many styles."

SPOTLIGHT

Jim Murray,
sports columnist, *Los Angeles Times*

If you are an avid newspaper reader, you can't escape Jim Murray's syndicated sports column. Since 1961, a column penned by Murray for the *Los Angeles Times* has been good for a few belly-laughs. In the world according to Murray, a fighter doesn't just get beaten up, he becomes "sort of a complicated blood clot." And a golfer is not an athlete, he's an "outdoor pool shark."

Back in '61, before the age of computers, writers on the road would type hard copy, and Western Union would wire it to the home papers. The reports they received from Murray were unlike any others. He described Elgin Baylor as being "as unstoppable as a woman's tears." His poetic wit gained many admirers, and he became nearly as famous as his subjects.

After graduating from Trinity College in Hartford, Murray worked a city-side stint at the *New Haven Register*. When he was classified 4-F at the start of World War II—as a youth he'd had rheumatic fever—he hopped a train for Los Angeles, where Murray talked his way into a job as a reporter and eventually became a rewrite man for the Hearst-owned *Examiner*.

In 1950, *Time* magazine offered Murray $7,000 a year to be the magazine's Hollywood reporter. Over the next three years he worked on a dozen cover stories on such subjects as Mario Lanza, John Wayne, Betty Hutton, and Marlon Brando. Whenever a sports assignment in Los Angeles came up at *Time,* Murray got the call.

When *Time's* founder Henry Luce decided in 1953 to launch a sports magazine, Murray was asked to help start it. He did, and the next year *Sports Illustrated* published its premier edition. Murray eventually became *SI*'s West Coast correspondent. In 1961 he jumped to the *L.A. Times.* In one of his early installments Murray commented, "Writing a column is like riding a tiger. You don't want to stay on, but you don't want to get off either."

It's certainly been a wild ride. Murray roasts sports figures with no mercy. Here is Murray on Woody Hayes, the gruff Ohio State football coach: "Woody was consistent. Graceless in victory and graceless in defeat."

Covering a St. Louis Cardinals football game, Murray was no less evocative. He described how the team's former offensive guard, Conrad Dobler, stretched the limits of the rules: "To say Dobler 'plays' football is like saying the Gestapo 'played' 20 Questions."

A zinger? Most certainly. Murray has bent many a nose out of joint. But even so, if you have at least half his affection for the sports world, Murray makes you care about the games and the people who play them.

He has long championed the cause for racial equality. It was Murray's needling of the Masters that helped that tournament change it's no-blacks stance: "It would be nice to have a black American at Augusta in something other than a coverall." And he was utterly flabbergasted by the incessant stalling until Satchel Paige was inducted into baseball's Hall of Fame: "Either let him in the front of the Hall—or move the damn thing to Mississippi."

Now 77, Murray still writes three columns a week for the *Times*. In 1990, he won the Pulitzer Prize for distinguished commentary. During one stretch of 16 years he won the National Sportswriter of the Year award 14 times, including 12 years in a row. His column is carried by more than 80 newspapers today and at one time was in more than 150.

ADDRESS BOOK

National Sportscasters and Sportswriters Association
Box 559
Salisbury, NC 28144
703/633-4275

Writers Guild of America
555 West 57th Street
New York, NY 10019
212/245-6180

PHOTOGRAPHER

The photographer at a sporting event is expected to document the game through the eye of the camera lens. The individual must be a graphic storyteller, deciding which players and what game action should be captured on camera at each moment.

The photographer is responsible for capturing on film what words cannot express. Sports evoke a wide range of emotions, from the elation and jubilation of victory to the despair and disappointment of defeat. The successful photographer can relate the feelings and atmosphere behind that instant of winning or losing, and do so with a timeless quality.

Photographers may have varied responsiblities, depending on the specific assignment. Some may be required to shoot live game action only, while others may be asked to shoot more aesthetically for feature stories or essays. No matter what the assignment, the photographer is expected to compose and frame images.

Developing a plan of camera angles is essential to success in this field. As part of the job, the individual is required to determine the type of equipment needed, such as the number of cameras and lenses. The goal is to attain the most effective camera shots possible. To accomplish this, the individual must be sure that the lighting, focus, and angles are correct.

Photographing a live sporting event is a pressure-packed, yet ultimately rewarding job. Since there is no eraser on a camera, the photographer has only one chance to create a proper picture. Creatively talented, innovative photographers can put their signature on a heart-stopping, theatrical moment and turn it into a transcendent image.

DARKROOM DYNAMO

For over three decades with *Sports Illustrated,* the images of Walter Iooss Jr. have defined sports photography. Iooss' career began with *SI* in the 1960s, when the magazine was published in black and white and photographers used single-shot cameras, and flourished during the 1980s, when full-color, double-truck photos and motor-drives had become commonplace.

Iooss (pronounced "yoce") has captured some of the most memorable moments in sports: the game-winning reception by the Pittsburgh Steelers' John Stallworth in the 1980 Super Bowl, and "The Catch" by San Francisco's Dwight Clark in the 1982 playoffs against Dallas are two of his classic images now frozen in memory.

A DEVELOPING FIELD

The greatest number of employment opportunities will be at major newspapers and magazines that staff a large photo department. Individuals may work on contract or free-lance. Shutterbugs working for a large publication may receive help from one or more assistants. The assistants can do simple maintenance on camera equipment, set up flashes in arenas, and caption film.

Smaller print organizations offer more hands-on opportunities for those entering the field. At smaller publications, the photographer may have to develop his or her own film as well as perform basic darkroom duties.

Earnings for photographers vary greatly, but can range from approximately $15,000 to $150,000. Variables include the experience, expertise, and reputation of the photographer. Earnings are also dependent on the prestige and size of the newspaper or magazine. Photographers just starting out in a small market will earn less than their counterparts at large newspapers and magazines in major cities.

Individuals can supplement their earnings through picture syndication. This is a process by which a photographer collects a royalty whenever his or her picture is reprinted. Another source of revenue available to the successful photographer is a contract to produce a coffee-table type book.

There are a number of paths for career advancement for photographers. Some individuals learn their craft by first working as an assistant for an established photographer. Here they can glean from a master the techniques of lighting, lens selection, and camera angles. Others begin their career as a photographer for a small town newspaper. These individuals can advance their careers by working for more prestigious papers in larger cities.

Most in this field aspire to shoot the championship sporting events. Iooss, 53, has covered all 30 Super Bowls. In January 1994, his cover picture of Dallas Cowboy running back Emmitt Smith was his 11th *Sports Illustrated* Super Bowl cover. Though he had not shot another football game that season, Iooss got the cover shot ahead of a dozen other *SI* photographers at the game.

POINT, SHOOT, AND CLICK

Applicants for photo positions will be required to show their portfolio. A portfolio is the photographer's calling card. While some employers require photographers to earn at least a bachelor's degree in photography, for the most part, there is no formal educational requirements for this job.

Individuals who pursue a college education do so because they wish to learn photo history and theories of picture taking. The college newspaper also provides a training ground for aspiring photographers, as well as the proper darkroom equipment to experiment with new techniques.

Those who do not pursue college often obtain training by participating in internships, apprenticeships, or jobs as photo assistants or darkroom technicians. Common to all in this field is a love of images.

As a boy growing up in East Orange, New Jersey, Iooss had wallpapered his entire bedroom with pictures from sports magazines. Images ruled his life, and he watched tons of television. "It was a Dumont TV with a screen about five inches across," says Iooss. "I think watching that little box was the beginning of my visual sensibility."

When Iooss was 15, he and his father went to a New York Giants football game. Walter's dad had brought along a camera. From his grandstand seat Walter peered through the 300-millimeter lens, and his world changed forever.

"I discovered life through a telephoto lens looks pretty good because you can eliminate everything you don't want to see," he told *Sports Illustrated's* Bruce Newman in 1994. The young Iooss then began to practice his new hobby by photographing his friends as they played stickball. He even charged his classmates $5 for each print.

At 16, Iooss telephoned the *SI* picture department in New York and convinced an assistant editor to take a look at his portfolio. A few months later, the magazine bought one of his pictures of a Princeton game for the opening spread of the 1960 college football preview issue. And the rest is history. Iooss has been with *SI* for 36 of the magazine's 42 years, and his pictures have graced the cover a record 176 times and counting.

ZEN PHOTOGRAPHY

During the continuous procession of movement coming into the lens, the great shooter is invariably able to press the button at just the right time. Photographers who become successful are renowned for having the uncanny ability of being able to stand in a pack of 20 photographers all competing for the same shot and yet be the only one to get the defining moment.

In the championship game between the Cowboys and the Packers at Green Bay's Lambeau Field in 1967, Newman writes, Iooss left himself little room for error. The temperature at game time was minus 16 degrees. The intense cold made the photographer's job particularly difficult. "You'd put film in, and it would snap," Iooss recalls. "Try to wind it—snap."

When Green Bay took over possession of the ball for its final drive, Iooss decided he could not load another roll of film. He was standing in the end zone with four frames left, and there were four downs to play. He had one shot per down. Then came Bart Starr's famous touchdown sneak with 13 seconds left. Iooss snapped off his final frame in perfect focus and got the picture that ran in the magazine—the only picture that mattered.

ANGLING FOR POSITION

Experience is essential in this job in order to develop an eye for timing. Iooss's principal asset is his ability to somehow see and feel things not apparent to the rest of us. "The angle I shoot from is the best angle," Iooss says. "There are no other angles."

On September 4, 1994 Iooss covered his first regular-season football game in five years when the New England Patriots opened in Miami, at Joe Robbie Stadium. A rain storm had turned the field into a quagmire. Late in the fourth quarter, the majority of photographers had packed up and called it a day.

With the press areas now clear, Iooss was free to roam the sidelines. He inexplicably told his assistant they needed to move to the other end of the field because something was about to happen. On the very next play Miami receiver Irving Fryar caught a 35-yard pass from quarterback Dan Marino to win the game. Iooss had a three-frame sequence and the cover shot in the magazine the following week.

STRANGE BUT TRUE

While some photographers carry so much equipment that they look like tourists on holiday, Iooss travels light, using fewer cameras than most. This allows him access to places others had not gone before.

Iooss at work looks like a loner because, at most events, he sets himself physically apart from the pack. "I started out shooting from the stands," he says. "I found all these other angles that were quite beautiful to shoot from. If you're with everyone else, your pictures are going to look like everyone else's."

His fellow photographers soon began to follow his every move; wherever Iooss went, the other shutterbugs were sure to go. Mike Ehret, who for over 12 years has worked as Iooss's assistant, swears that unknowing photographers follow Iooss into stadium bathrooms!

IMAGE CONTROL

While shooting diver Greg Louganis for a book about the 1984 Summer Olympics, Iooss experienced something he describes as the "transcendent moment" of his career.

"It was like God jumped in your camera for one picture and said 'O.K., this is it.'" he says. "I was moving the camera so quickly that it was taking the red of the sky and swirling it. It looked like flames of hell coming out of the pool.

"I was very excited about this shot, so when Louganis finally looked at it, I was just waiting to get stroked. But he takes one look at it, hands the picture back to me and says, 'I'm bent.' I said, 'Excuse me?' He says, 'I'm bent. Look at me. I'm crooked.' And he walks out.

"At first, I couldn't believe it," Iooss continues. "But then I realized that we each see something different in a photograph. To me that was as good an action picture as I'll ever take. What really establishes a great photographer is when he creates an image that has his signature.

"This is what we all want, to make an image that we control: backgrounds, setups, lighting, composition. Controlling a picture is what the art of photography is about, because most of our lives are out of control. If you can put a person in position where you want him, with the light just right, it's yours, it's no one else's."

Reprinted courtesy of *Sports Illustrated* November 14, 1994. Copyright © 1994, Time Inc. All rights reserved.

SPOTLIGHT

Bruce Bennett,
principal, Bruce Bennett Studios

In March 1974, Bennett, an accounting student at C.W. Post, was looking for a way to earn extra money to help pay his tuition. A photography and sports buff, he snuck into the photo area at Nassau Coliseum during a New York Islanders hockey game. Shooting in black and white, he subsequently sold a roll of film to *The Hockey News* for three dollars a photo.

More than 20 years later, Bennett is still taking photos at hockey games. And his company, Bruce Bennett Studios, has grown into the world's leading provider of hockey photographs. Bennett and his staff of 14, based in Hicksville, Long Island, account for an annual placement of some 5,000 hockey images in editorial and licensed products. Bennett photos have appeared in such major publications as *Sports Illustrated, Life, Time, People, Us, The Sporting News,* and *Newsweek.*

"Before you go on an interview, you should gain a passing knowledge of every phase of photography so as not to appear to be in over your head. I didn't pick up a camera until my first year of college, in 1973, when I started taking scenic photos for fun.

"All my photography was self-taught. I went to the library and took out every photography book, one at a time, to learn about the craft and different techniques. I took classes in college for the easy credits after I was already working in the field.

"After graduating college in 1978 [with a bachelor of science in accounting from C.W. Post], I worked for Long Island Magazine for two years as photographer and photo editor. I shot everything and edited everything myself. There I got the experience I needed to do things other than hockey. You don't live in this business by being a specialist. You have to be able to shoot interiors, exteriors, portraits, and products for corporate work.

"My big break was *The Hockey News* buying my pictures. Not so much because of the three-dollar price tag, but because they'd give me an occasional media pass to a game. Right away I noticed that all the photographers were sitting in a corner of the press room eating together. On the other side of the room were all the writers. I'd find an open seat and sit with the writers. I'd start off a discussion, to show them I was educated. That led to many breaks. As these writers would work on projects for books or magazines, I would be the first person they would call for photography.

"I always had a good basic knowledge of hockey, and that helped, but there's no substitute for experience. Instinct and anticipation is a function of experience. The more games I shot, the better I got at anticipating the play.

"When I got started and needed experience, I went to the local hockey rink a couple of nights a week. I'd photograph adult leagues, industrial leagues, pee wee leagues, then come back with contact sheets. For $5 a print people would order them like crazy. The following week I'd come back with 8x10 prints and collect a ton of money. Most of that money I reinvested back into the business."

Bennett now shoots about 140 games per year, and often works seven days a week during hockey season. He has shot the Stanley Cup playoff series for the last 19 years, and the NHL All-Star Game for the last 15. Through his lens, he has captured some of hockey's most historic moments—such as Bobby Nystrom's overtime goal that won the Islanders the Stanley Cup in 1981 —and Bennett's images are viewed by a worldwide audience.

"Probably my most recognized picture is of Wayne Gretzky scoring his 77th goal [during the 1981-92 season] to break Phil Esposito's [single-season] record. I was in Buffalo on assignment for *Time* magazine. Funny, it's not a shot I would say is a great hockey photo, but it is THE moment with the puck crossing the goal line. That shot has been sold almost 20 times.

"You never know what you've shot until the roll is developed. You might think you have it and when you process it you've got a referee blocking half the frame. Even if it's 1/250th of a second, that shutter is closed at the split second it's taking the picture, so you can't really see what you've got. You might have a good inkling, but someone might be blocking your view or you might be out of focus.

"We mostly shoot the games at F4 with longer lenses so a decent amount of stuff won't be sharp. Most of the work we do is with strobe lights, and we're held up by the recycle time of the strobe unit, which is anywhere from two to five seconds. So if you shoot too early, the guy could score a goal, celebrate, and be back on the bench by the time you're ready to shoot again."

ADDRESS BOOK

American Society of Media Photographers
14 Washington Road
Princeton Junction, NJ 08550
609/799-8300

National Press Club
529 14th Street N.W.
Washington, D.C. 20045
202/662-7500

National Press Photographers Association
3200 Croasdaile Drive
Durham, NC 27705
919/383-7246

Sports Illustrated
1271 Avenue of the Americas
New York, NY 10020
212/522-1212

Bruce Bennett Studios
329 West John Street
Hicksville, NY 11801
516/681-2850

PICTURE EDITOR

The picture editor is responsible for acquiring a selection of photographs that are appropriate for a particular story or project. Picture editors may work for any type of publication. Duties may vary depending on the kind of company the individual works for, as well as the particular assignment being worked on.

Photo editors will be expected to acquire pictures in one of two ways. The individual may either order images from stock agencies or coordinate photo shoots. The scope of these tasks is as different as filming a movie is to renting one.

When ordering existing photos from a stock agency, the editor is required to negotiate the best possible rate for use of those photos. The individual will also make sure that the licensing agreement for which the images are being granted is adhered to. When color transparancies arrive from the agency, he or she then functions in the role of a traffic manager. The images must be logged in and tracked as they make their way from the photo department to the art director, to the printing plant, and back to the agency.

The picture editor may also be involved at the initial stage of conception. This is usually an editorial meeting, where discussion centers on an upcoming issue. If the decision is made to create an image for a particular asssignment, the picture editor will select a photographer to perform the assignment, based on the criteria for the particular project.

In making the assignment, the editor will be required to explain in full detail what is expected of the photographer. The editor must negotiate the photographer's day rate as well as inform the photographer as to the company's copyright policy. Once the photographer accepts the assignment, the editor must handle all the logistics of credentials, equipment, airfare, and lodging. The editor will also instruct the photographer as to how the film should be prepared for processing and the means of transporting it to a darkroom.

Once the developed film is in the editor's possession, he or she must edit the images, making selections to present to the editorial staff for final approval. The editor will then work with the art department's layout artists and graphic designers to ensure the image's proper camera-ready treatment. The image should then be filed appropriately and available for future use.

HAVE LOUPE, WILL TRAVEL

Photo editors are needed wherever pictures are published and in companies that house images. Employment opportunities can be found at newspapers and magazines all across the country, at news agencies with picture collections, and at stock photo agencies that do business by renting out their warehouse of pictures. The large sports stock agencies are Allsport, Duomo, Focus on Sports, and SportsChrome.

In the four major professional sports, an arm of the enterprises or properties divison is devoted to photography. Jobs are available in the areas of operations and team photography, licensing, imaging, library, and administration and traffic.

The department of operations and team photography is responsible for setting up photographers' schedules, handling the logistics of credentials, equipment, and airfares, as well as processing film and performing the initial editing of film. The licensing division is responsible for selling images to the league's business partners, which may include trading card companies, poster companies, as well as sponsorship and marketing groups. This area also generates revenue by syndicating photos.

The imaging department electronically scans photographs and stores the images in a digital server. This department also performs the conventional duping of pictures for the majority of clients that still require conventional film in order to reproduce images.

Members of the library staff function as cataloguers or archivists, protecting original transparencies and ensuring their accessibility to clients and staff. The adminstration and traffic division is responsible for the financial dealings of the photo department, trafficking its physical inventory of film as it moves between client and office.

AUTO-ADVANCE

Aspiring candidates to any one of these positions should have a full understanding of photography. Individuals need to know what makes a vivid image: composition, lighting, framing, focus. The best exposure to photography is picture taking. Once you've mastered the technical and physical aspects of photography, the aesthetics will be easier to absorb and appreciate.

The educational requirements among picture editors currently working in the field vary from person to person. You can't earn a degree in picture editing, but the majority of individuals in this position have a college degree in photography, visual arts, film, fine arts, graphic design, or a related liberal arts background. Experience and a proven track record are your best entry into this profession.

Nobody ever got rich as a picture editor. Salaries range from $18,000 at an entry-level position in a picture collection to $45,000 as a picture editor on staff with a magazine's photo department. A photo editor running the division for a major magazine may command a salary as high as $75,000, but the individual will have years of experience and a reputation of respect within the industry. Individuals who ascend the corporate ladder may hold jobs as darkroom technician, picture researcher, assistant picture editor, picture editor, photo editor, deputy photo editor, and director of photography.

CAPTURE THE MOMENT

Picture editors working in the sports industry also need to have a comprehension of the game. The editor is ultimately responsible for determining the subjects and events in each picture. A portrait of an individual, of course, presents little or no problem. But in a football game, for instance, if a key third-down play proves to be the big play—that's the shot every photo editor wants in print. The picture editor will be expected to anticipate this photo request and present the photographer's resulting image.

A responsible photographer can greatly assist the picture editor by accurately captioning the film and returning it with a team roster included. (Other captioning methods frequently used by photographers are written notations on the processing bag; separating certain significant rolls of film and then numbering those rolls; and preparing a caption sheet.) But the editor's best defense is a good offense. An editor who watches the game live or on videotape will be aware of what transpired during the game. A prepared editor can better determine the correct image for the correct moment.

A story making the rounds at *Sports Illustrated* describes a harried picture editor who was responsible for selecting images to illustrate a winning streak put together by the Boston Celtics. Unfortunately, an oversight by the editor had caused a reject picture to mistakenly be placed in the slide projector. When the offending image appeared on the screen, an irate managing editor demanded to know the identity of the player wearing jersey number 33. "Why I am looking at a picture that's out-of-focus?" he snapped. The embarrassed photo editor calmly replied, "Because he's Larry Blurred."

TIPSHEET

- Go to the library and look at as many picture books as possible. This will give you an understanding of the many photography techniques that are available to you.

- Purchase some camera equipment and begin taking pictures. Assess the quality of your work; you needn't improve your picture-taking ability so much as learn what makes a good image.

- Picture editors are made, not born. You need to gain experience by working at a photography studio, a darkroom facility, or a local newspaper. Hang around photographers and pick their brains.

ⓘ Start out working in a stock agency. You need to learn how to handle color transparencies and comprehend the systems of picture administration before you can tackle the task of making assignments and editing photos.

REAL-LIFE ADVICE

Carmin Romanelli,
director, NBA Photos

Carmin Romanelli brings 15 years of photographic management experience to his position as director of NBA Photos. His responsibilities include generating, archiving, and distributing all photography used by the NBA, its business partners, and over 300 media clients around the world. Romanelli and his staff of twenty oversee nearly one-million unique images in the league archives, and expect to add 75,000 more each year.

personality sketch

Excellent visual skills; knowledge of sports and photography; organized; ability to communicate your vision to photographers; detail-oriented.

A 1976 graduate of the Germain School of Photography (now part of the visual arts program at the Media Arts Center in New York), Romanelli held various darkroom positions and then for three years ran his own photo studio. He returned to school at New York University to pursue a degree in film and cinematography. While attending NYU, he worked part-time beginning in 1983 for the Time Life color lab. In 1985 he was named manager of the color lab, a post he held for five years.

In April 1990, he joined *The National Sports Daily* as director of photography, with overall responsiblity for photo department budgeting and meeting the newspaper's daily deadlines for pictures. When *The National* folded the following year he joined *AdWeek* as the trade magazine's first photo editor. There he worked with the art director to redesign the magazine's aesthetic appeal. Eighteen months later he was recruited by the NBA.

"You don't go to college to become a photo editor; there's no courses that I know of that teach you how to edit photos. Photo editors are trained. The best thing you can do is to expose yourself to as many different aspects of photography as possible. Work as a shooter, a picture editor, and in a darkroom. Get a sense of what each field is all about before gravitating to the position that's ideal for you.

"Working as an intern for a publication will give you experience and a full understanding of the different skills that you'll need in each area. After you've gotten a little taste of what the different areas are all about, then make a decision as to whether you want to be a photographer or a picture editor. If you're going into the picture editor side, you should take some business classes to help broaden your skills with negotiations and budgets.

"At NBA Photos, we've lately been hiring part-timers that work on a temporary basis over a period of six months to a year. During this time we evaluate the person as to whether or not they have the right tools to work within our department. We call for a unique mixture of photography knowledge and basketball knowledge. You have to know the game, and hopefully, you have some background in photography and understand a little about the way the business works. At that point, if we have openings on the staff we generally hire from among those part-timers into an entry-level position of an assistant photo position. The pay starts at around $25,000.

"The work is very production oriented, and it tends to be mundane. The temps need to demonstrate that they can work consistently, accurately, and maintain a good level of production. They need to demonstrate a good understanding of basketball and then continue to expand their knowledge of players and teams. They should become familiar with our library so they'll know how to file and access material.

"They also need to become familiar with the way we handle requests and the types of material we select for the various clients that we handle requests for. With that, we then expect them to fit nicely into our group because teamwork is very important here. And we look for people who are willing to work hard and stay focused on whatever projects they have until they are completed successfully."

SPOTLIGHT

Steven E. Sutton,
principal, Duomo Photography, Inc.

Back in the early 1970's, in order for newspapers to meet picture deadlines, the photographers were forced to leave an event around 10 o'clock at night. At track meets, the field events, such as the pole vault and high jump, often stretch past midnight. If a world record was set, the newspaper would never have a picture.

Steve Sutton was determined to use this void to his advantage. But first he needed to get inside. "I snuck into the old Madison Square Garden when the guard wasn't looking. I'd get thrown out once in a while, but sneaking in is still the way to [break in to the business] now. You have to be creative."

During a track meet late one night in 1972, the elusive Sutton was squatting in the Garden's photo area, when Sweden's Kjell Isaksson set a world pole vault record. Sutton captured the dynamic moment, and *The New York Times* published his first picture of note. "I got five-dollars for it," says Sutton. "That's how you begin to establish a reputation and develop communications with writers, editors, and photo editors."

More than twenty-five years later, Sutton is still taking photos at track-and-field events. And his company, Duomo Photography, has become an international stock and assignment photo agency. Sutton and a staff of 15, based in New York, specialize in the creation of authentic released sports photography and worldwide coverage of sporting events and personalities. Duomo's bold, vivid images have appeared in international advertising and promotional campaigns, and been featured on magazine covers and in brochures, posters, annual reports, and books.

Sutton and his brother, Paul, incorporated Duomo Photography in 1977. Both have degrees in architecture from Pratt Institute in Brooklyn, New York. Steve, who is older by four years, graduated in 1971; Paul in 1975. The brothers must have a close relationship. "We've always worked together," laughs Steve, "there's a difference." Steve studied architecture in Italy for a semester, and that's where the company name originates from. The Duomo is the main cathedral in Florence.

"We started covering amateur sports initially when everybody was doing professional sports, and no one understood why," says Steve. "I ran track and field in high school, and I started taking pictures of the team. That's the origin of how I got started. Taking pictures with a little box camera my father had given me."

The brothers decided to create a company image as opposed to becoming free-lance photographers. "Back then," says Steve, "and probably still now, free-lance photographer was a dirty word. So we established ourselves as a business, not only to get assignments, but to sell stock photography." The brothers shot pictures and, if a magazine requested an image of a personality, Duomo would have it. "Stock photography wasa business that didn't exist in the 1970's," adds Steve. "Now it's more prolific."

To distinguish Duomo as unique in this competitive industry, the Sutton brothers forged more than a photo agency. They hired an all-purpose team of researchers, editors, marketers, librarians, and administrators to handle billing and traffic, as well as a technical staff with vast and diverse experience. The brothers demand that photographers do more than snap pictures. As stated in the brochure, photographers "should shape concepts, develop longstanding relationships with athletes and sports leaders, and understand the connection between corporate campaigns and the athletic motif."

What does that mean? "Covering a track meet," says Steve, "the basic picture of everybody crossing the finish line that you see all over the place, that doesn't intrigue us. During the heats, I'll never be at the finish line. I went to the Track & Field World Championships in Rome in 1987. I wasn't at the finish line for five days. When I got to the finish line for the 100-meter final, the other photographers asked, 'Where have you been?' I was in the building.

"The secret is looking for the places where everybody else isn't. I usually get to the stadium a day ahead of time. I walk around the stadium, looking for certain light and different background. You have to learn the sport. Some sports have limitations on where you can go, and as a photographer, you have creative constraints. You just hope for things to happen, but you also have to be experienced enough to trust your instincts.

"The sport I still enjoy the most is track and field because it's 15 sports in one. The key point is to get there a day ahead of time. You walk through the building, so that you know how to get from Point A to Point B in the quickest fashion. It's a war game in essence, because the events are continuously going on. You may be at the hurdles now, but in fifteen minutes you need to be at the javelin, so you can't arbitrarily roam through the stadium. You have a plan in place before the day's competition begins."

Duomo Photography covers the most popular events in pro sports like the Super Bowl, of course, but the company is most recognized for its international exposure. Duomo regularly covers track and field, swimming, gymnastics, skiing, and figure skating, as well as the Summer and Winter Olympic Games (images date back to the Munich Summer Games of 1972). Clients have access to almost every major sports star of the past generation.

All images are at Duomo's fingertips. "We very tightly edit what we have," says Sutton, "it's the best of the best. The rest of it is thrown away. But that group of pictures could probably make another library for somebody else."

SUCCESS STORY

Maureen Grise,
picture editor, *Sports Illustrated*

Talk about being on the fast track: Maureen Grise graduated from college on a Saturday, interviewed at *Sports Illustrated* on the following Friday, and was hired on Sunday.

Grise, 25, has known that photojournalism was her calling since the age of 10. It was then that she and two friends founded *The Northwood Times,* a 25-cent monthly chronicling the events of Northwood Lane, the street on which Grise grew up in Stamford, Connecticut. In high school, she was picture editor for the high school newspaper and yearbook, a double-play she repeated in college.

During her undergraduate days at Syracuse University, she was a staff photographer at the *Daily Orange.* She worked as a summer intern at the *Stamford Advocate,* shooting various local assignments such as community meetings and Little League games. While earning her degree in photojournalism from Syracuse, Grise obtained a part-time, paying job as a lab technician for the *Syracuse Post Standard and Herald Journal.*

A massive letter-writing campaign during her senior year paid off when *Sports Illustrated* granted her an interview, to take place immediately after her graduation. In the spring of 1993, *SI* hired her for a temporary project that turned into a permanent position. Now Grise oversees all of the magazine's baseball photography. She spends long hours editing slides (more than 10,000 weekly) and securing photo credentials. In May of 1997, she expects to graduate from Columbia University's master's in journalism program.

ADDRESS BOOK

Allsport
320 Wilshire Boulevard
Santa Monica, CA 90401
310/395-2955

Duomo
133 West 19th Street
New York, NY 10011
212/243-1150

Focus on Sports
222 East 46th Street
New York, NY 10017
212/661-6860

SportsChrome
236 B Grant Avenue
Cliffside Park, NJ 07010
201/568-1412

Careers in Sports Medicine

R obert Jackson was 32 years old in 1964 when he traveled to Tokyo for the Summer Games as a physician for the Canadian Olympic team. At that time, an athlete with torn knee cartilage would require career-threating surgery. Athletes who did return to action required at least a year of rehabilation. More often than not, the long zipper scar was a fearful reminder of the hobbling arthritic condition to come.

While in Tokyo, Dr. Jackson became aware of a revolutionary procedure called arthroscopic surgery. Other contemporary doctors made a lengthy incision to expose the entire knee joint. But Dr. Jackson learned how to poke a tube with a telescopic lens through a quarter-inch opening, and clean out the damaged cartilage with little trauma to the knee. "It was amazing," says Jackson, who is now the chief of orthopedic surgery at Baylor University Medical Center in Dallas, Texas. "There was no guesswork."

Jackson returned home to his new position as team doctor for the Toronto Argonauts of the Canadian Football League. In 1967 he performed the first arthroscopic surgery on an Argonaut. Still, his colleagues were slow to accept the new procedure. "We could only teach it one-on-one," says Jackson. "There were no visual aids, no videos, nothing."

It wasn't until famous athletes like Bobby Orr and Willis Reed underwent arthroscopic surgery, and then quickly returned to action, that the procedure gained attention. "Slowly it began to snowball," says Jackson. "We'd start to get a few athletes, athletes with smart business managers or athletes who'd already been cut and not gotten better."

During the 1970s, fiber optics made arthroscopy easier to perform and by the 1980s the surgery had become maintstream. When marathon runner Joan Benoit qualified for the 1984 Olympics, and subsequently won the gold medal, just 17 days after her knee surgery, the miracle of arthroscopy was hailed throughout the country. Now the procedure is so commonly reported that it's difficult to term it revolutionary.

There was a time when the field of sports medicine consisted only of a bottle of rubbing alcohol and some adhesive tape. Athletes slapped dirt on an injury and continued to play for fear of losing their jobs. Today, some of the most prominent orthopedic surgeons in the country serve as team doctors—for example, Stephen O'Brien, an orthopedic surgeon at the Hospital for Special Surgery in New York, is the orthopedic specialist for the New York Giants, and Michael Dillingham, the associate director of Stanford University's Sports Medicine department, handles the San Francisco 49ers.

The income that doctors receive from teams is relatively insignificant, but they derive significant benefits from their association with the clubs. In San Francisco, for instance, Dr. Dillingham is connected in the public mind to the 49ers, giving him a kind of visibility that other orthopedic surgeons can only dream about. It seems undeniable that a doctor's medical practice can profit from an association with a team. Wouldn't you trust the doctor who operated on Steve Young to perform your procedure?

The late Dr. Robert Kerlan was a prominent orthopedic surgeon who became a pioneer in sports medicine. During his career, he served as team physician for the three main Los Angeles sports teams: Lakers, Rams, and Dodgers.

A native of Aiken, Minnesota, Kerlan moved to Los Angeles to play basketball for UCLA, then transferred to Southern California. A graduate of USC and its School of Medicine, he began volunteering as a team physician with schools and colleges in the Los Angeles area in the early 1950s.

He joined the medical staff of the Dodgers when they moved from Brooklyn to Los Angeles in 1958. He was joined in 1965 by Dr. Frank Jobe, and their thriving sports medicine practice drew athletes from around the country.

Dr. Kerlan was a founding member of the American Orthopedic Society for Sports Medicine, a clinical professor in the Department of Orthopedic Surgery at the USC School of Medcine and a past president of both the National Basketball Association Team Physicians and the National Football League Physicians Society.

One wonders what Kerlan, who died of pneumonia in 1996 at age 74, would say about the central conundrum faced today by every team doctor who is placed in the position of having to answer to two different masters: player and team. To whom does the doctor owe his allegiance? Is it the player, who is his patient? Or is it the team, which pays the doctor, makes the decision about whether to retain him as team physician and, more often than not, wants the injured player back on the field as quickly as possible?

Professional clubs have recently begun to put the team doctor role up for bid, and this is an ominous trend. It used to be that teams paid the doctors who treated their players. Now the doctors are beginning to pay the teams. The practice became public in early 1995 when ABC News reported that the NFL expansion franchise Jacksonville Jaguars had let it be known that medical groups interested in providing care for the team's players would be expected to purchase luxury suites and pay for advertise-ments in the game-day programs, in exchange for the right to be called the team's "official health-care provider." The Jacksonville medical group that won the contract is said to have indirectly paid around $1 million for the privilege.

When the Orlando Magic entered the NBA in 1989, the physicians from the Jewett Orthopaedic Group became a team sponsor and even purchased arena signage reading "Jewett Orthopaedic Clinic/Your Team Physicians." In today's competitive health-care market, even hopsitals want the world to know who takes care of the hometown team. Hospitals used to disdain advertising. But all this talk of health-care reform has led to an increase in the number of ads.

"If we can keep the New York Jets running, just think what we can do for you," reads Lenox Hill Hospital's recent print ad, completed before the season started. Unfortunately for Lenox Hill, the highly-injured Jets fin-ished the 1996 season with an anemic record of 1-15.

Even if you don't plan on becoming a physician, there are career oppor-tunities available to those of you interested in the field of sports medicine. Employment prospects can be explored in the areas of athletic training, strength and conditioning, nutrition, psychology, and performance enhancement (not to be confused with personal trainers and aerobics instructors from your local gym).

The American College of Sports Medicine is the world's largest organization in sports medicine and exercise science. Despite its name, the college is not an educational institution; it's a professional society that runs certification programs for certain occupations. It's open to graduate and undergraduate students in fields related to health, physical education, exercise science, and biology. It also publishes a monthly *Career Services Bulletin,* which prints announcements for job and internship programs.

ADDRESS BOOK

The American College of
Sports Medicine
P.O. Box 1440
Indianapolis, IN 46206
317/637-9200

ATHLETIC TRAINER

A sports team's athletic trainer is a highly educated and skilled allied health-care professional. The individual works in cooperation with the team physician to insure that a uniform program of player medical care of the highest standards is maintained throughout the organization.

The trainer must provide immediate treatment and rehabilitation of injuries caused during practice or in game situations. In evaluating injuries, the trainer must also determine whether a specialist is needed for further consultation.

While athletic trainers are specialists in dealing with the health-care problems of athletes, to be sure, the prevention of injury is one of the trainer's primary goals. To this end, the individual is expected to set up an injury prevention program. In this role, the trainer can help athletes avoid unnecessary medical treatment that causes the athlete to miss valuable playing time.

In preparation for a game or practice session, the trainer will tape, bandage, wrap, and brace an athlete's ankles and knees. Other jobs performed by the athletic trainer include:

   Ordering medical supplies within the team budget and monitoring the use of these supplies.

- Establishing training room rules and policies.

- Maintaining medical files.

- Coordinating off-season rehabilitation programs for players and keeping in contact with those players.

- Planning and administering physicals and drug testing.

Athletic trainers must develop a trusting relationship with each athlete to better determine when and how an injured player can return to practice and competition. Athletes are motivated patients; they desperately want to get back in the game at any cost. To this end, the trainer may also serve as counselor or advisor to the injured athlete.

TRAINING THE TRAINER

Stringent educational requirements have been in place since 1990, when the American Medical Association recognized certified athletic training as an allied health profession.

An interested individual must earn, at the very least, a bachelor's degree in athletic training, health and physical education, or exercise science. Nearly 100 educational institutions offer athletic training curriculum programs. Entry-level subjects include human anatomy, physiology, biomechanics, kinesiology, injury evaluation, emergency first aid, and rehabilitation procedures.

Further requirements stipulate that all candidates combine classroom instruction with clinical experience. Individuals must graduate from an accredited program in no less than two years, while completing a minimum of 800 hours of supervised experience. Students can accomplish this by working for head trainers at college.

After graduation, candidates wishing to obtain certification must pass a three-part examination: a multiple-choice section to measure broad knowledge; an oral portion that evaluates particular skill levels in all areas; and a written simulated test designed to approximate real-life decision making. This last portion of the test evaluates an individual's ability to resolve cases similar to those he or she might encounter in actual field work.

HEALTHY JOB OUTLOOK

Individuals interested in athletic training may find employment in high schools, colleges, sports medicine clinics, hospitals, corporate health programs, health clubs, and in professional sports.

It's interesting to note that less than 5 percent of all trainers are employed in the pro leagues. The steadiest job growth in the field is at the secondary school level, as high schools have begun mandating that a trainer attend every sports contest. Sports medicine clinics are also a fast growing segment of the industry.

High schools, universities and hospital/clinics are the biggest employers of the nation's roughly 19,000 certified athletic trainers. Of the 427 entry-level positions tracked in 1992 by the National Athletic Trainers' Association (NATA), 234 were in the hospital/clinic setting, 135 with colleges/universities, and 58 at high schools, according to Crayton L. Moss, director of the Athletic Training Program at Bowling Green State University in Ohio.

NATA offers a comprehensive athletic trainers' job referral service. This service lists job openings in all athletic training settings in the United States.

LADIES WELCOME

Although athletic training was once considered a male-dominated pro-fession, today over 40 percent of all NATA members are female. Thisis an amazing number, particularly since NATA didn't accept its first woman until 1966. According to NATA published reports, more than half of the certified trainers during this decade have been women.

PAY SCALE

Athletic trainers without certification represent the minimum level of entry into the field and will be limited in employment opportunities. Salaries for high school athletic trainers with no certification start at about $23,000.

College trainers are usually required to possess a license, so earnings will improve commensurately. The head athletic trainer at a university will earn a salary in the range of $25,000 to $80,000. The amount you make will depend upon your degree of education and experience, as well as the size of the school. The assistant college trainer will make between $15,000 and $40,000.

Professional sports trainers who have several advanced academic degrees can earn between $40,000 and $90,000 a year. Assistants in the pros earn from $35,000 to $70,000 depending on their level of experience.

TIPSHEET

☺ Scholarships and opportunity grants are available through the NATA Research and Education Foundation.

☺ Athletic trainers may have to meet individual state licensing and regulation requirements. To determine if this applies to you, check with the state where you wish to practice.

REAL-LIFE ADVICE

Ronnie Barnes,
head trainer, New York Giants

At 28, Ronnie Barnes was one of the youngest head trainers ever in the National Football League. A graduate of East Carolina University, he was that school's first graduate of the sports medicine program. He received a master's degree from Michigan State University in administrative services and also served as trainer. He initially joined the Giants in 1976 as a student intern and assumed his full-time capacity with the club in 1980.

> ## personality sketch
>
> *Compassionate; empathetic; loyal; trustworthy; organized; able to communicate in layman's terms.*

"I think it's important for someone who wants to go into athletic training to make that decision in their freshman year of college, or just prior to going to college.

"You need to be a good science student and gain an advanced understanding of how the body works and how it reacts to different stresses. That requires a strong background in anatomy, physiology, and mechanisms of injury. To go back and take those courses after having spent two or three years in college is almost impossible, although it can be done.

"If one can decide early on, in high school, that this is the profession for them, then it would be helpful to volunteer at a physical therapy clinic or a college athletic training program.

"I started as a student intern. I knew John McVay, (the Giants head coach from 1976-78), who was a Michigan Stater. He suggested that the

Giants might take me on for the summer. Three years later I became the head trainer. It was very rewarding for me.

"Obviously, I believe internships are important. Internships are available for undergraduate college students, but only a few are given to graduate students or people who have already graduated.

"Those attracted to the profession of health care are generally interested in helping people. You should have an interest in medicine, but you should also enjoy being in a service business.

"Athletic trainers are paid well, but income shouldn't be the single most important motivating factor. Salaries are good at major colleges, private clinics, hospitals, and in the pros. But trainers are needed at all levels. Even high school programs have trainers. But no matter where you are, you'll work long hours. During the football season I work 12-hour days, from 7 a.m. to 7 p.m.

"Athletic trainers are responsible for preventing and treating injuries, developing protocols for rehabilitation, and rendering first aid. It's a thankless job in some respects. Your picture is never going to be on the front page of the newspaper unless you're helping take a player off the field who happens to be famous.

"But there's also a great reward you get from working with an injured athlete. You watch them go from not being able to do what they love to do, which is play sports, and you're able to keep them in shape and recondition them so they can get back to play. When those athletes return, that's the ultimate gratification."

SUCCESS STORY

Ted Arzonico,
head trainer, New Jersey Nets

Ted Arzonico, 35, has served as head athletic trainer of the NBA's New Jersey Nets for five years. He completed his undergraduate work at Central Connecticut State University in 1984, where he received a bachelor of science in physical education. He went on to earn a master's degree in sports medicine from Springfield (Mass.) College in 1986. The New Jersey native was the head trainer for West Essex (N.J.) High School for one year, then spent two years as head trainer for St. Thomas Aquinas College in Sparkhill, New York before coming to the Nets. He served as an assistant trainer with the Nets for three seasons before taking over the top spot.

ADDRESS BOOK

National Athletic Trainers'
Association
2952 Stemmons Freeway
Dallas, TX 75247
214/637-6282

NUTRITIONIST

A sports nutritionist is like a food coach, advising athletes on how to eat sensibly—not only for their own health, but also for the sake of the game. It is important to all athletes to be physically fit and healthy. No player ever said, "I owe my success to the fat-free dill sauce." But studies reveal that proper diet, combined with conditioning, will lead to improved performance.

The main function of the sports nutritionist is to determine what foods will go on the training table. The responsibilites differ depending on the goals to be attained, and the nutritionist may work with an individual athlete or with a team. In the latter case, efforts will be coordinated with the head trainer and the strength and conditioning coach.

The nutritionist may be expected to help some athletes gain weight, while helping others to shed excess pounds. Taking into account the athlete's body type, i.e., height, weight, and metabolic levels, the nutritionist can develop a program suited to each player's needs. The nutritionist may also be called upon to talk to the players individually about specific dietary needs and show them the connection between performance and diet.

"I worry that we spend so much time talking about fats, proteins, and carbohydrates, that we forget to talk about the quality of the food," says Heidi Skolnik, nutrition consultant for the New York Giants and Mets. "It doesn't matter that a food is low-fat if it's not a high-quality food."

In other words, an athlete eating an entire box of fat-free cookies is still eating cookies. That's why it's vital that the nutritionist first determine the person's dietary quirks, habits, eating schedules, and routines. A dietary program will only work if the athlete can live with it.

For football players averaging 250 pounds, meals are serious business. The challenge for the sports nutritionist is to devise healthy menus to be gobbled up by hungry athletes who, by nature, have a fast-food mentality.

Besides developing daily menus, the nutritionist delivers presentations on such topics as the hidden dangers of drive-through cheeseburgers.

"McDonald's and Burger King is part of our culture; it's unrealistic to think athletes won't eat it," says Skolnik. "An informed player can eat fast food but make a more conscious choice. You can order grilled chicken with a baked potato, or chili and the salad bar. There are ways to eat fast food and still maintain a smart sports nutrition diet."

While the area of sports nutrition is growing, the majority of people working in the field do so on a part-time or voluntary basis. Primary employment for nutritionists is usually a teaching position or conducting research at a university. Other avenues of employment are working in cardiac rehabilitation in a hospital, consulting within a private practice, working in a health club, or working for a corporate fitness center.

The well-qualified individual will be knowledgable in sports nutrition, have experience working with athletes, and possess the ability to communicate effectively with athletes and coaches.

HERE'S THE DISH

There is no specific training one can take to become a sports nutritionist, but several options exist to become qualified in the area. The best strategy depends on how many degrees you wish to obtain. If you are interested in a doctorate, then you should select a college with a strong human nutrition department.

If you are interested in a bachelor's or master's degree, you may want to consider becoming a registered dietician. This is accomplished by earning a bachelor of science degree in food and nutrition at a school that meets the requirements set forth by the American Dietetic Association.

Appropriate areas of study include nutrition or a related field such as education, psychology, exercise physiology, or health. Many people choose to combine nutrition courses with those in exercise science to broaden their educational base.

Students become eligible to take the registration examination by completing a postgraduate, accredited internship. An internship typically lasts from six months to two years. Longer internships usually offer a master's degree in conjunction with the experience.

It's important to remember that education must go beyond the printed textbook. Aspiring sports nutritionists should be knowledgable about the most common dietary concerns athletes face, and be familiar with nutritional myths held by athletes.

Experience with physically active people is essential. This experience can be gained by volunteering nutritional services to high school or college sports teams, a local health club, or even little league. With an advanced college degree, you may also become involved with athletes through research. While most amateur athletes and teams cannot afford to hire a sports nutritionist, corporate wellness programs and health club facilities may provide a means of employment.

FUELED FOR ACTION

A dietician who possesses the educational background to qualify as a sports nutritionist should contact trainers and coaches of local teams. Volunteer to talk to their athletes as a group or individually. Get to know the coach's philosophy and the nutritional information, if any, given to the athletes.

John Wooden, UCLA's basketball coach from 1949–75, was an early proponent of sports nutrition. He regularly served his players a training meal four hours before tipoff. The favored menu: a 10- to 12-ounce steak (cooked medium), small baked potato, green vegetable, three stalks of celery, four small slices of melba toast, honey, hot tea, and fruit cocktail. Wooden was indeed ahead of his time in many ways. The Wizard of Westwood led his Bruins to 10 NCAA championships in 12 years between 1964 and 1975.

All competent nutritionists are staunch believers in making only subtle changes to existing eating habits rather than revolutionary ones. A responsible nutritionist should not recommend a wacky diet supplement. This is particularly true when working with world-class athletes.

"The hottest new dietary trend is no trend at all," says Ann Grandjean, the director of the International Center for Sports Nutrition. "Olympic athletes tend not to do trends; it's one of the things that separate them from other athletes. Their diets generally contain adequate carbohydrates and calories and are fairly well balanced."

Dr. Dan Benardo of Georgia State University is the U.S. women's gymnastics team nutritionist. He says that the growth rate and overall health of the team is monitored closely, and that the American women gymnasts are older and larger in stature than their chief international competitors.

"Some of the other teams look cadaverous compared to us," he says. "Our girls look like normal kids." To drive home his point, Dr. Benardo says that Shannon Miller grew six inches and gained 35 pounds between the 1992 Olympics and the 1996 Summer Games.

EAT LIKE A COW; DRINK LIKE A FISH

Dr. Benardo incorporated a "two-and-a-half-hour rule" for the gymnasts, stipulating that all members of the team should eat a snack every two-and-a-half-hours, from morning till night. The only no-nos for gymnasts are fried foods, processed meats such as bologna and salami, and fats like margarine, butter, and oil if they aren't already cooked into foods.

Consuming small quantities of food throughout the day, often called "grazing," helps the athletes keep up their energy level. It also tends to boost their metabolic rates so that they can eat more, and thus take in more vitamins, minerals, and fiber, while maintaining the same low level of body fat.

Another big challenge faced by nutritionists is keeping their athletes hydrated. Members of the U.S. Olympic women's soccer and field hockey teams aren't considered dressed for practice unless they have a full water bottle in hand. Kris Clark, a nutritional consultant to these squads, has instructed the team members to drink 64 ounces of water daily, at least 32 ounces before noon and 32 before turning in for the night.

"Sixty-four ounces is a goal that they can remember," says Clark, "and it forces them to carry water with them to sip on all day long."

Clark also noticed that some athletes had too many carbohydrates and not enough protein in their diets. She says that several of the athletes were taking the high-carb message to extremes and getting 70 percent or more of their calories from pasta, breads, and other starches. As a result, they were falling below the recommended daily allowance for protein.

"Meat and other protein foods are not only good sources of iron," says Clark, "but also providers of B-complex vitamins, manganese, and zinc."

The most important benefit of these vitamins and minerals is improved energy metabolism. According to Clark, protein is essential to the building and repair of muscle tissue, while research suggests a link in zinc-deficiency with an increased risk of injury.

FEEDING MIND AND BODY

In the high stakes world of the National Football League, teams are always on the look-out for a competitive edge. The New York Giants know that eating right can provide that edge.

Now in her fifth season as the Giants' nutritionist, Heidi Skolnik is happy to feed the team's hunger for dietary information. One day each week, from the beginning of training camp throughout the season, Skolnik visits the Giants players and talks turkey. She finds most of them receptive to her ideas.

"These players are well educated," says Skolnik, who earned a master's degree in exercise physiology from Ithaca College. "They come from colleges that stress performance. They're ready to learn and willing to adapt to seek out what's best going to improve their performance."

A look at the Giants' training table personifies Skolnik's influence. A typical dinner offering might include mixed green salad, chili soup, chicken, venison, shrimp, spaghetti with marinara sauce, potatoes, mixed vegetables, fruits, and chocolate cake.

The multitude of choices is for a good reason. The key to success, as preached by Skolnik, is diversifaction of caloric intake. Every player is given a pamphlet that offers advice on healthful eating strategies.

"Portions make the difference," says Skolnik, who is the founder of Nutrition Conditioning, Inc., in New York City. "Instead of eating a 24-ounce steak, eat a 12-ounce steak with two baked potatoes, broccoli, a side salad, and soup. Now you're building around the traditional diet."

A food-friendly philosopher, Skolnik warns her athletes against skipping meals. Players who work out intensely require calories in order to have fuel to burn. It's the composition of the calories that determine whether the meal is a healthy one.

Skolnik is the first to admit that the Giants' dedication to nutrition is complemented by the weight training program that accompanies her work. She knows the heavy lifting is the easy part.

"Weight lifting is a structured workout," she says. "With food, you eat on your own. It's social, it's emotional. People have to understand they feel better when they eat better. They see the difference in their performance."

TIPSHEET

- If you're looking for colleges that offer degrees in nutrition, the first step is to contact the admissions office at the universities within your geographical area.

- Writing and public speaking are two important skills for the sports nutritionist. Polish your speaking skills by volunteering to talk at related community events. You'll not only hone your speaking skills, but you'll gain exposure as well. Contact local organizations who publish newsletters. They may be interested in printing a nutrition column.

- Since it's difficult to gain direct experience with athletes from each sport, it's absolutely essential to stay on top of current issues in the sports world by reading. It's important to read not only scientific literature, but also popular sports magazines and newsletters to better learn specifics of the sport, understand demands of training, and appreciate the stress of competition.

REAL-LIFE ADVICE

Heidi Skolnik,
founder, Nutrition Conditioning, Inc.

As the sports nutrition consultant for the New York Mets, Giants, and New Jersey Nets, Heidi Skolnik focuses on the correlation between food and performance.

After graduating as an exercise physiologist from Ithaca College in 1983, she worked at Morgan Stanley brokerage house for four years. There she developed a company-wide health promotion

> ## personality sketch
> *Interest in exercise and fitness; an understanding of athletes; compassionate and nonjudgmental; ability to communicate ideas.*

policy and directed the corporate fitness program. She then spent four years directing corporate programs at the Sports Training Institute with a client list that included General Motors and Johnson & Johnson.

Skolnik served as president of The Competitive Edge for one year before becoming vice president, director of nutrition for Plus One Fitness Clinics. In 1996 she founded her own compnay, Nutrition Conditioning, Inc. She also serves on the executive committee for the American College of Sports Medicine.

"When I started the field was very limited. At that time, I don't even think colleges offered a sports nutrition major. But now entire programs are devoted to it. Clearly, the educational path you choose now can be much more direct than the one I took. The sports sciences will always remain important, but the programs that exist now are only going to get stronger and more streamlined and more direct. Finding these programs is the first place to start.

"When I speak to college students my big message is create your own path. I tell them: Trust yourself, know yourself. Don't be afraid to take a different route. Some people are planners; they know what they want and figure out how they're going to get there. But that's not me.

"I wasn't the traditional exercise science major. I came from a nutrition and dance-exercise background. Instead of hiring two people, I told potential employers, just hire me. So use your uniqueness as your strength. Don't see your differences as being a limitation. Figure out how to market those differences; use them to distinguish yourself from the crowd.

"Get involved in the field. Read as much as you can, and go to continuing education conferences. There you'll learn the answers, and you'll network. It's also a great training ground to practice the things you're not good at. And go to lectures as much as you can. I do lots of free lectures. Every time I lecture it leads to my getting three additional jobs.

"Wherever you are, there's always connections. And you never know. If you're working in a fitness center, or the local high school, or at a sports medicine clinic, your clientele is your network. Those are the people that are out there and will think of you when they hear about a great job opportunity. So don't necessarily go for the glory; do your job, be overprepared, and be nice. The rest will take care of itself.

"That's how I got the job with the Giants. Somebody I had indirectly worked with told the team about me. I'm not sure they made the job available to the public, meaning I didn't read about the opening in the newspaper. I had to submit my resume and be interviewed, but I never would have had the opportunity to compete for the job had I not been recommended. Of course, once I got the Giants job it does become self-perpetuating."

ADDRESS BOOK

International Center for
Sports Nutrition
502 South 44 Street
Omaha, NE 68105
402/559-5505

STRENGTH AND CONDITIONING COACH

The strength and conditioning coach is responsible for all weightlifting activities. It used to be that only professional and college football teams employed a strength and conditioning coach. Today, athletes in all sports rely on weight training to build strength and increase flexibility.

The individual works in conjunction with the team doctor and head trainer to establish a rehabilitation program for injured players. Other job duties include:

- ① Establishing a safe and effective strength and conditioning program for athletes.

- ① Monitoring and supervising that program.

- ① Developing and maintaining a strength and conditioning manual.

- ① Maintaining weight room equipment and supervising weight room activity.

BRAIN AND BRAWN

To become a certified strength and conditioning specialist, candidates must pass a two-part examination consisting of scientific foundations and practical/applied sections.

The scientific foundations section consists of 100 multiple choice questions that are designed to assess candidates' knowledge in human anatomy, exercise physiology, biomechanics, and nutrition. The practical/applied section consists of 90 multiple choice questions, 30 of which involve viewing a videotape and answering questions associated with the exercises shown, as well as the muscles and joints shown. The other questions in this section assess the candidates' knowledge in the areas of program design, exercise technique, organization and administration, and testing and evaluation.

BULK UP YOUR WALLET

The National Strength and Conditioning Association, which was formed in 1978, has about 12,000 members. A survey conducted in 1993 reveals that a college strength and conditioning coach can earn between $25,000 and $45,000 a year. Earnings at the professional level increase to a range of $60,000 to $80,000, depending on the individual's reputation and longevity in the league.

REAL-LIFE ADVICE

Dana LeDuc,
strength and conditioning coach, Seattle
Seahawks

LeDuc was an All-America and NCAA shot put champion at the University of Texas, where he earned a bachelor of science degree in education. After graduating, he was hired as the Longhorns' strength and conditioning coach, a position he held for 16 years. He then took his talents to the University of Miami under coach Dennis Erickson. In 1995, when Erickson became an NFL head coach with the Seattle Seahawks, LeDuc went with him.

"I'm responsible for the physical and cardiovascular development of the athletes. That encompasses their conditioning level and their body composition level, based on their position. We come up with an individual plan for each player based on his position group. The optimal body fat percent level for offensive and defensive linemen, for instance, is 18 to 19 percent; for running backs, 8 to 11 percent; for wideouts and defensive backs, 3 to 6 percent.

"In the off-season, players lift weights about four times a week. During the season, they lift less. I work 50 to 60 hours a week, seven days a week, for 11 months. Right after the season ends I get four weeks off.

"Weight training exercises should take the athlete through a range of motion to provide flexibility. Early on, when developing a base of training, I recommend higher repetitions with moderate weight because it's important to lubricate the joints, to prepare the body and tendons for the advancement of heavier weights.

"Most players come to me already motivated to work. The young players are especially hungry because they want to make it in this league; they continue to work and strive to get better. If a player is not motivated to lift regularly, I explain the importance of longevity in their career. The added strength will help them improve performance, at least from the standpoint of being able to take blows more efficiently. Increasing the density of muscle fibers is like adding armor.

"Communication with the trainer is important. I read the injury report and keep my own files on each player's workout. You want to get an injured player back in the mainstream, but you need to keep abreast of where the player is in rehab so as not to overdo anything.

"The conditioning area is for people who want to get into the prepatory part of coaching. You should get a master's degree in exercise physiology to understand how the human anatomy works. Start out at the collegiate level as a volunteer and work your way into a program. Then you could become a graduate assistant with a small scholarship to defray the cost.

"Volunteering is a first step to setting up a network of people who can help you find where the jobs are. Go to the national conventions in strength and conditioning, and subscribe to the magazines.

"I was very lucky to get the job at Texas. The football team had never trained with weights, to be honest. They did conditioning and running with vests on, and light dumb-bell work and lots of sit-ups. Then they bought Nautilus equipment and needed someone to supervise it. At the time, these programs were barely in existence around the country. I was training with free weights one day when coach [Darrell] Royal asked if I'd like the job. I said yes.

"An NFL weight room is not that big compared to college facilities. At the college level, there's 17 to 25 sports you'll train. Here in Seattle, I've got 1 sport with 53 players. But the workout is intense. We use a number of free weights, platforms to do Olympic lifting, machines to isolate various muscle groups, basic pressing styles, incline press, bench press, a full set of dumb-bells, traditional squat racks, abdominals, and lots of neck exercises. That's an area we want to protect."

SPOTLIGHT

Bill Foran,
strength and conditioning coach, Miami Heat

For many professional basketball players, the best way to avoid injury is by maintaining peak fitness and conditioning year-round. That's the job performed by Bill Foran, now in his eighth season with the NBA's Miami Heat.

Foran joined the organization after spending the previous four years at the University of Miami as its head strength and conditioning coach. There Foran helped keep U.M. football players in shape for the national championship years of 1987 and 1989. Prior to his tenure with the Hurricanes, he spent four years in a similar capacity at Washington State University.

A graduate of Central Michigan University, he earned a dual degree in physical education and health education in 1977. He went on to earn his master's degree in exercise physiology from Michigan State University in 1981. Foran is president and co-founder of the National Basketball Conditioning Coaches Association and a co-author of two published books: *Condition the NBA Way* and *Power Conditioning for Basketball.*

ADDRESS BOOK

*National Strength and
Conditioning Association*
530 Communications Circle
Colorado Springs, CO 80905
719/632-6722

*N.S.C.A. Certification
Commission*
P.O. Box 83469
Lincoln, NE 68501
402/476-6669

SPORTS PSYCHOLOGIST

The team psychologist works to help athletes overcome psychological problems that affect their performance. The outer game—competition itself—requires physical skills and is played against an external opponent. The inner game—far more mysterious—is played against such formidable opponents as self-doubt, anger, and nervousness.

The main duties performed by the team psychologist include counseling an athlete whose motivation has waned, or whose self-confidence is suddenly lost. The individual also tries to help when athletes are distracted by something in their personal life, or should the problem of substance abuse need to be addressed.

FREUD TO JUNG TO LOEHR

Jim Loehr was the first sports psychologist to be given public recognition. When his pupil, tennis player Gabriela Sabatini, defeated the heavily favored Steffi Graf in the finals to win the 1990 U.S. Open, his work with Sabatini was widely cited as a determining factor.

While he teaches the mental game just as systematically as a coach would drill an overhead, Loehr (pronounced "Lair") did not work on Sabatini's backhand or her serve. He improved her mind—specifically conditioning her mental toughness and allowing her to control negative thoughts and emotions.

The insight at the heart of Loehr's theories is that whatever goes on in the mind has a direct impact on the body. He says, "A thought is a physiological event. If you can take the pressure off yourself," he adds, "then winning will take care of itself."

What you think, he argues, determines how you feel, and those emotions have physical consequences. The anxiety prompted by a fear of losing will cause increased heart rate, shortness of breath, and tightening of muscles. All of these reactions make it impossible to play up to one's potential.

There are now dozens of sports psychologists working with top athletes across the country. What sets Loehr's work apart is that he has focused on an aspect of tennis that has been traditionally ignored: the nearly 70 percent of the time during a match when a player is between points rather than playing.

During practice sessions Loehr uses biomechanical feedback machines to monitor an athlete's level of tension in a specific muscle at any given time. Loehr's initial findings were convincing. "Athletes in an ideal performance state would always report that they felt a profound sense of muscle relaxation," he says.

The diagnosis was satisfying in yet another way. "Psychology has always suffered from the criticism that its results are not experimentally verifiable," says Loehr. "I love sports because it's such a dramatic arena in which to see whether the theories work. How athletes perform is a way of verifying that what you're saying isn't just mumbo-jumbo."

YOUR CAREER RORSCHACH TEST

All of the sports psychologists working today are college graduates with a bachelor of science degree in psychology, and the majority have gone on to earn an American Psychological Association–approved doctorate.

Despite the high level of education in classrooms, hospitals, and clinics, a psychologist who wished to pursue a career in sports can gain practical experience only by working in the field. This requires a broad-based approach and a taste for humble pie. No sports psychologist starts out working for a world-class athlete. The individual must scrape and claw for every morsel of opportunity in the client food-chain.

This is not to suggest that aspiring sports psychologists scour Little League playing fields in search of a slumping seven-year-old. Rather, a sports psychologist trying to make a name for himself (or herself) will be required to work with junior athletes, amateurs, and even semi-pro ballplayers. The possibility of asking for payment may not be realistic when working with athletes at these levels. But the opportunity to hone your craft and practice the art of behavior modification is invaluable to the up-and-coming shrink.

MIND GAMES

Increasingly, the difference between winning and losing can be fractions of a second. That's where the most successful athletes bring their mental edge into play. Members of virtually every U.S. Olympic team underwent some battery of mental tune-ups before competing in the Summer Games in Atlanta.

"For many elite athletes, sports psychology has become as important to optimal performance as good nutrition and proper medical care," says Sean McCann, Ph.D, the U.S. Olympic Committee's chief sports psychologist.

It's mind-blowing to watch the ever-expanding opportunities now available for sports psychologists. The field can accomodate a variety of practitioners, all with very different methods. Today's highly educated athletes crave any information that can put them over the top. And some may even pay very dearly for it. A psychologist, like any medical doctor, may charge by the hour ($50 to $250), by the procedure (a battery of exams to compile a mental profile can cost over a thousand dollars), or be paid on a retainer basis to be negotiated beforehand (including all travel expenses).

Many top athletes are using a process called mental imagery or visualization to help prepare themselves for competition. If you see yourself achieving a specific goal, according to this theory, you'll more likely be successful when called upon to perform it.

When combined with imagery, self-talk can also be a useful plan. Self-talk, or cue words, is internal reminders that instruct and motivate, and keep you focused. Self-talk takes positive thinking to its logical conclusion. On television you read the lips of athletes as they carry on an internal monologue. They exhort themselves to "Keep the elbow up" or "tuck the shoulder in."

Of course, psychological strategies amount to a hill of beans if the athlete is not levelheaded. For this reason, energy management is a cornerstone in the U.S.O.C.'s mental training program. Moderate levels of energy are preferable for some athletes, especially in sports that require subtle muscle control or complex decision-making. These athletes need to be intense without being tense.

THE TEAM SHRINK

Dr. Allan Lans has been available to the New York Mets on a year-round basis since 1988. It is his job to wander around baseball fields, watch workouts, and treat drug and other personal problems. For the most part, his busy schedule has forced him to give up his private practice.

When the Mets are home he can be found at Shea Stadium. When the team leaves town, he will sometimes accompany them, but more often he will visit one of the minor league teams, like the Tidewater (Va.) Tides or the Columbia (S.C.) Mets.

At first the club preferred not to advertise that a psychiatrist was in their midst. Said Al Harazin, who was then the club's executive vice-president and the man primarily responsible for bringing Lans on board, "We consider him the head of our employee-assistance program. We don't see him as the team shrink."

Lans gave lots of lectures when he joined the Mets on a part-time basis in 1984. But Lans, Harazin, and Frank Cashen, the former general manager, all believed that a player in trouble needs more than a lecture—he needs someone to talk to.

Lans started hanging around the ballpark on a regular basis and he went full-time in 1988. He knew it would be difficult for his bosses to evaluate his performance. "It sounds crazy," says Lans, "but I told them they would just have to trust me, that I would take care of the problems and tell them only what they needed to know."

Lans has been a psychiatrist since 1981. He came late to the profession. After getting an osteopathic degree from a small Iowa medical school, Lans, now 63, hung a shingle in 1959 and affiliated himself with Riverdell Hospital in Oradell, New Jersey.

Some twenty years later he decided to switch to psychiatry. After a residency at St. Luke's Roosevelt Hospital in Manhattan, he took a position as staff psychiatrist at the Smithers Alcoholism and Drug Abuse Center, which is where he was when the Mets called in 1984.

HEAD CASES

The case that garnered him the most publicity was related to drug abuse by the team's most famous star. Lans supervised Dwight Gooden's 28-day stay at Smithers in 1987, meeting with the pitcher two or three times a week.

"The trouble with my business," says Lans, "is there is no penicillin. The symptoms may be the same, but the causes are always different. I don't know of any player who at some point in his career hasn't endured a private hell."

In 1989, Darryl Strawberry posted in his locker a photo of Lans. Sportswriters approached Lans for an explanation. "Darryl," he said, "wants to be a Jewish psychiatrist when he grows up." All kidding aside, Lans saw more. Strawberry, he believed, was flashing a sign for help.

The following season Strawberry's wife accused him of threatening her with a loaded pistol. Lans flew to Los Angeles, spent three days with Strawberry at an airport motel and then enrolled him at Smithers to treat an addiction to alcohol.

Under Lans's supervision, Strawberry returned to the lineup, hit 37 home runs and drove in 108 runs. Then, as a free agent, he signed a $20 million contract with the Dodgers. Shortly after, the Dodgers announced the hiring of baseball's second full-time psychiatrist, Dr. Herndon Harding Jr., who would treat substance abuse and depression. The timing was hardly a coincidence.

Some teams employ part-time sports psychologists, like the Oakland Athletics' Harvey Dorfman and the Atlanta Braves' Jack Llewellyn. Unlike a psychiatrist, the psychologist doesn't have medical training and can't write prescriptions for drugs.

A psychologist will focus on performance shortcomings. Llewellyn worked wonders with pitcher John Smoltz. At the start of the 1991 season Smoltz's record was 2-11. But he was 12-2 in the second half after working with Llewellyn. By 1996, Smoltz was the most effective hurler in baseball and the recipient of the Cy Young Award, the highest honor bestowed on a pitcher.

FEELING NEGLECTED IN YOUR JOB?

The biggest challenge faced by a sports psychologist is gaining the players' trust. When Lans joined the Mets, nobody wanted to talk to him. The players were worried about their reputations. Whenever Lans walked into a room, conversation stopped. He understood.

"Nobody," Lans says, "likes talking to a psychiatrist." But Lans kept at it, talking to anyone who would talk back. "I didn't make believe I was a baseball player," Lans says. "I didn't hit fungoes or correct a hitch in a swing. I just was there."

In the practice of what he calls "baseball therapy," Lans practices without a couch or an office or patients who consider themselves patients. "What the ordinary psychiatrist counts on," he says, "is that if a guy wanders across his threshold, he's aware he has a problem. In the work I do, you can't count on that. Nobody walks across your threshold."

His office is a baseball diamond, or the locker room, or at the training table. And he constantly confronts the same issue. Is this a baseball problem or a personal problem, is it mechanical or mental?

Lans knows there will always be controversy about his job, but to him, the issue is clear. "If you would correct how a kid goes to his left," he says, "why not correct some problem in his life?"

REAL-LIFE ADVICE

Dr. Michael Simon,
sports psychology consultant

Dr. Simon develops, evaluates, and implements life-skills programs for Major League Baseball and the National Hockey League as part of their fan development initiative. As the president of The Sporting Mind he also works with the entire St. John's athletic program, U.S. Olympic women's judo team member Celita Schutz, and two Sunfish sailors who between them won three world championships in a three-year span.

Dr. Simon received his undergraduate psychology degree in 1985 from Washington University in St. Louis, and his master's degree in sports psychology from Ithaca College in 1988. He then attended Teachers College, Columbia University, where he earned another master's degree in 1990 and a doctorate in education in 1991.

While attending Washington University, Dr. Simon was a member of the baseball team and later played for one season with a non-affiliated minor league team in the Empire State League.

"If you want to work with athletes and provide performance enhancement service, you should get an American Psychological Association-approved doctorate. That means a degree in psychology with a specialization in sports.

"It's extraordinarily difficult, nearly impossible, to find a teaching job in the field. There's a major marketing problem in sports psychology. If five positions become available in any one given year—internationally— you're lucky. You have to resign yourself to being an entrepreneur. It takes a long time, you'll have to grind it out. But that's why, if you're having difficulty making it, you can always fall back on your degree in psychology.

"I got into sports psychology serendipitously. I played baseball at Washington University, and I'd gone back for an alumni baseball game. When I was sitting in my coach's office, on his shelf, I noticed a book on sports psychology. I didn't know you could put the two together.

"When I first got my doctorate I started working part-time for the U.S. Tennis Association at the National Tennis Center in Flushing Meadows. By working with these junior tennis players, I was able to gain solid work experience. But I was still struggling to make money. I always wanted to be involved with the mental and emotional aspects of baseball. I had a private practice, of course, but I didn't want to be a therapist. Since I wasn't commited to expanding the therapeutic practice, it became very difficult to make an income.

"My dream was to work with a major league ballclub as their sports psychology consultant. I always wanted to work with athletes on peak performance issues and try to help them overcome slumps or avoid choking. That didn't work. I tried and tried, but couldn't get a break. For two years I seriously considered getting out of the field. Then I created a life-skills program, which is another way of saying applied sports psychology.

"The program includes goal setting, team work, concentration, effective communication, conflict-resolution skills, anger management, stress and anxiety management, and building confidence and self-esteem. I called [the baseball and hockey offices] every single day for over a year. I finally got a meeting and I impressed the hell out of them. Why? Because I had a very powerful message: teach kids important skills through sports.

"I figured out what the major leagues wanted and needed. They already had youth programs as part of their fan development. They want to sell tickets in the future and get people to come to the ballpark, buy products, and watch games on television. That's what their business is all about. My pitch was to make it important; make it worthwhile for the kids. Tell them the significance of goal-setting, of respect, tolerance, and sportsmanship.

"I explained that by using my program's curriculum in a youth sports setting, important character-development skills and life skills can be taught through the kids' contact with sport. Now 85 percent of what I do is creating trained staff, implementing and evaluating youth sports programs that incorporate educational components. The other 15 percent of my time is spent on performance enhancement for individual athletes and teams."

SPOTLIGHT

Jim Loehr,
sports psychologist

The field of sports psychology barely existed in 1968 when Jim Loehr got his doctorate from a Jesuit college. He went to work in counseling and eventually became the director of a community mental-health center in southern Colorado. During that period, Loehr met the track-and-field coach at a local college. The coach convinced Loehr that in order to be a great coach, it was necessary to be a master psychologist.

Loehr, who was a good athlete growing up, was smitten by the idea of combining his two interests. In 1976 he quit his job and moved to Denver to set up a practice in sports psychology. Although there were a few university professors in the field, Loehr believes he was the first psychologist to try making a full-time living treating the performance problems of athletes.

For five years he barely eked out a living. Two professional teams and several world-class athletes consulted with him, but in each case he had promised not to mention their names publicly. For some reason people are concerned that seeing a psychologist somehow implies that they're nuts.

Loehr's breakthrough came in 1982, when a friend suggested to tennis star Tom Gullikson that he see Loehr. At the time, Gullikson was experiencing his worst year on the tour. Figuring he had nothing to lose, Gullikson agreed to come aboard. The deal was simple. Loehr would work with Gullikson at no cost. If his suggestions proved useful, Gullikson would have to say so publicly—to journalists, to coaches, and to other players. The deal was done.

Gullikson's performance turned around dramatically. He improved his ranking from around 100th in 1981 to the top 25 in the world by the following year. He reached the quarterfinals in singles at the U.S. Open and the semifinals in doubles with his twin brother, Tim.

The success with Gullikson gave Loehr name recognition. In 1982 he decided to move to Florida, drawn by the chance to work with the top young players in the game. By 1985 he had joined the Nick Bollettieri Tennis Academy in Bradenton. Loehr also serves as director of sports science for the United States Tennis Association.

ADDRESS BOOK

American Psychological Association
Sports Psychology Services
Division 47
750 First Street, N.E.
Washington, DC 20002
202/336-6013

The Sporting Mind
251 West 81st Street
Suite 2D
New York, NY 10024
212/877-4009

SPORTS PERFORMANCE MANAGEMENT SPECIALIST

A marathon runner who sees a psychologist can develop a great mental outlook, but still have a strained hamstring. A baseball player who works with a nutritionist can eat better, but still not be able to hit a fastball. A boxer who works with a personal trainer can lose 25 pounds, but may be too fatigued to fight.

A sports performance management specialist is an athletic trainer, psychologist, nutritionist, strength and conditioning coach, and personal trainer all rolled into one. Athletes seek out a performance manager to help them produce results on the field, and to increase the longevity of their career.

Despite being 5-feet, 8-inches tall and 140 pounds, Mackie Shilstone is a giant in the business of sports performance. From his home base at Kenner Regional Medical Center near New Orleans, Louisiana, he has given over 600 professional athletes the body, the drive, the stamina, and the performance they need to win.

But you don't have to be a pro athlete to employ a performance manager. Corporate executives who want more stamina on the job also benefit. "There's no difference between the heart rate of a baseball player batting with two on and two out and his team trailing by a run in the World Series, and an attorney in the court room defending a man for his life before a judge and 12 jurors," says Shilstone.

"There may be 20 million people watching the baseball player and 200 people watching the attorney, but they're both under the same stress level. Both must perform. If they don't, somebody loses."

THE PERFORMANCE GURU

Although many think of Shilstone as a fitness coach, that's not what he does. "My business is not fitness," he says. "My business is investment banking. I say that because each athlete is banking on the fact that his or her investment in my time will pay off at the bargaining table come contract time."

Today's player contracts are loaded with incentive clauses and bonuses based on reaching certain levels of performance. "That's why you have to do more than just get a client in shape," adds Shilstone. "I know a lot of people in pro sports who are really fit, but they can't perform. If you want to get fit, go to a health club. If you want to perform, come to a program like mine."

Since hanging out his shingle 15 years ago Shilstone seldom has lacked for work. And he's well paid for his services. The list of athletic clients who have employed his revolutionary training methods is impressive. Star pupils include baseball's Ozzie Smith, Brett Butler, and Will Clark; boxing's Michael Spinks and Riddick Bowe; and basketball's Manute Bol, just to name a few. Shilstone has become to the field of sports performance what Ballanchine was to ballet.

When Ozzie Smith came to Shilstone in 1985, the 5-10, 145-pound defensive wizard was an offensive weakling. The St. Louis Cardinal, who had managed to hit only .257 in 1984, wanted to get stronger with the bat while maintaining his quickness and range at shortstop.

Smith spent the winter with Shilstone and reported to spring training at 163 pounds with a lean body of just 7 percent fat. Smith's batting average jumped to .276 in 1985, then up to .280 in 1986, and the following year to a career high .303. That was nine years ago. The 41-year-old future Hall of Famer, who retired after the 1996 season, earned an average salary of $3 million a season since working with Shilstone.

When Will Clark began Shilstone's program in the winter of 1986, the first baseman weighed 203 pounds, with 17 percent body fat. He lost 10 pounds, reduced his body fat to under 11 percent, yet increased his strength. During the 1987 season Clark more than doubled his ratio of home runs to at-bats; from 11 homers in 408 at bats to 35 homers in 529 at bats. When Clark was rewarded by the Texas Rangers with a free-agent contract totaling $30 million, he had Shilstone to thank.

"I don't measure success by how much you can bench press or how fast you can run," says Shilstone, 45. "I measure success by a player's batting average or by how many games he can go without injury. I'm an applied exercise specialist; I'm interested in helping performance."

WORK WITH THE MASTER

Shilstone knows what he's talking about. He has master's degrees in nutrition and business administration, as well as college degrees in physical education and political science. He's a former instructor at Tulane University's Department of Exercise Sciences and has served as special advisor to the U.S. Olympic Committee on Sports Nutrition.

Internships to work with Shilstone have always been available, though understandably, the numbers are limited. But good news is on the horizon. Shilstone says he is planning to soon offer a sports performance management program at Louisiana State University. Students who are accepted to the program will have the opportunity to learn techniques from the master, earn certification, and acquire invaluable practical applications.

The core curriculum, as Shilstone invisions it, is a broad background of education in exercise science. Courses of study include biomechanics, cardiology, nutrition with an emphasis on metabolism, exercise physiology with an emphasis on energy management, components on strength to power, performance supplementation areas, and undergraduate work in psychology and business management.

According to Shilstone, these graduates will be an extremely attractive commodity in the job market. "You can approach a pro sports team, or a college, or a corporation that wants a fitness program for its executives, or a hospital or sports medicine clinic, and say, 'I can coordinate your nutrition program, your exercise science program, and your strength and conditioning program.' You create a management triangle," he adds, "and you can manage the triangle from any side."

PRESCRIPTION FOR GOING THE DISTANCE

Shilstone was first introduced to the public when boxer Michael Spinks, the light-heavyweight champion, moved up in weight to challenge unbeaten heavyweight champion Larry Holmes. At the time, veteran boxing trainers ridiculed Shilstone's methods. In a sport where jogging in combat boots is the preferred workout routine, Shilstone's regiment of isokinetic cord exercises and heart rate telemetry was deemed to be on the lunatic fringe.

Shilstone first began working with Spinks in 1982, when the fighter was preparing to defend his light-heavyweight title against Johnny Davis. Shilstone's role in camp was to help Spinks maintain 175 pounds. But when Spinks signed to fight Holmes, the objective was to add weight.

Shilstone developed a program with the theory that Spinks' conditioning should be specifically designed for boxing. He put Spinks through a series of sprint workouts so that the fighter's heart could experience the same variations it would during a bout. "I broke down the sport into what it was, 45 minutes of total work and 15 minutes of rest," says Shilstone. "That was when the bouts could go 15 rounds. We built an aerobic base and then did everything at three-minute intervals with a minute's rest."

Seven months before the Holmes fight, Spinks successfully defended his light-heavyweight crown against David Sears and weighed in at just shy of 171 pounds. When he reported to camp prior to the Holmes fight, he was 193 pounds with a body fat of 9 percent. By the time Spinks weighed in, he scaled 200 pounds with a body fat of 7.2 percent. Shilstone had effectively added seven pounds of muscle to Spinks' six-foot, two-inch frame.

"My job was to give him the body of a heavyweight and the movement of a light-heavyweight," says Shilstone. "You have to put on performance weight. As the weight increased, we conditioned it."

Shilstone's revolutionary training methods allowed Spinks to become the first reigning light-heavyweight champion to move up and capture the heavyweight crown. Shilstone proved that a fighter can benefit from lifting weights and sprinting, techniques long considered taboo in boxing.

A LESSON IN CIRCUIT TRAINING

A typical Shilstone workout includes a training circuit. This is an obstacle course of exercise stations that may feature stair machines, free weights, or calisthenics. At one station you may be doing push-ups. At the next you may be jogging in place. The key is to move quickly between stations to keep up your heart rate.

Trainers prefer circuits because clients get a high-intensity, full-body aerobic workout. And they don't get bored. Circuits are jam-packed sessions typically lasting no more than 40 minutes. Clients are able to maintain a strenuous pace because they're not using the same tired muscles repeatedly.

Each exercise station works different muscle groups. Shilstone's "super pro circuit" is based on a series of 15 exercises, which vary depending on the clent's fitness goals and medical history. The exercises emphasize core body areas, such as the stomach, lower back, hips, and buttocks. The key is alternating between upper- and lower-body exercises within the circuit.

"So while the upper body is resting, the lower body is working and vice versa," says Shilstone. "The blood is forced from the upper to the lower body, which creates a conditioning effect."

A circuit starts with an upper-body exercise such as push-ups or pull-ups for 30 seconds. The next station is aerboic exercise such as riding a stationary bike or jumping rope for 30 seconds. From there, it's on to a weight machine for 30 seconds of lower-body exercise like leg presses. Repeat the pattern of 30-second intervals of upper-body and lower-body exercises separated by 30 seconds of aerobic exercise for at least 30 minutes. Rest for no more than 15 seconds between exercises.

Shilstone asserts that by doing the circuit three days a week, every other day, after six weeks you'll notice a better body. After 12 weeks, he claims, you can lower body fat by 16 percent, increase endurance by 17 percent, and increase lower leg strength by 24 percent.

PRACTICAL APPLICATIONS

In addition to working with individuals, Shilstone is also under contract with professional sports franchises, including major league baseball's San Francisco Giants. As the nutritionist and conditioning consultant for the team, Shilstone has published a program manual that is followed throughout the organization. Each exercise is clearly illustrated and explained in language that is easily understood.

personality sketch

Health conscious; ability to motivate others; interested in body mechanics; organizational and supervisory; knowledge of workout equipment.

The program is also flexible to each individual player, depending on that player's training objectives. The set of exercises he prescribes to a pitcher will differ from those he gives to a position player. There are machines, which used in one way can help a hitter's hip turn, while used in another way can help a pitcher's leg drive.

"We learn more and more and update the program every year," says Shilstone. "This is like a cookbook, and we're constantly refining the recipe."

ADDRESS BOOK

Mackie Shilstone & Associates
4227 Canal Street
New Orleans, LA 70119